Health Care Social Work

Health Care Social Work

A Global Perspective

Edited by

REN WINNETT, RICH FURMAN,
DOUGLAS EPPS, AND GREG LAMPHEAR

UNIVERSITY PRESS

Oxford University Press is a department of the University of Oxford. It furthers the University's objective of excellence in research, scholarship, and education by publishing worldwide. Oxford is a registered trade mark of Oxford University Press in the UK and certain other countries.

Published in the United States of America by Oxford University Press
198 Madison Avenue, New York, NY 10016, United States of America.

CIP data is on file at the Library of Congress
ISBN 978-0-19-094216-8

1 3 5 7 9 8 6 4 2

Printed by Sheridan Books, Inc., United States of America

Contents

About the Editors

Ren Winnett, MSW, LICSW, is a licensed clinical social worker at Multicare Health System in Washington state and a lecturer at the University of Washington Tacoma. He earned his Bachelor of Arts (BA Hons.) at Queen's University in Canada and his Master of Social Work (MSW) at the University of Washington, Tacoma. His practice interests include psychiatric and medical social work. His research interests include intervention strategies for acute care patients; health, psychiatric, and substance use co-morbidity; and global trends in health care social work.

Rich Furman, MSW, PhD, is Professor of Social Work at the University of Washington Tacoma and is the 2012 recipient of the Council for Social Work Education's "Partners in International Education" award for his scholarship regarding transnational social work. He has published more than 120 scholarly articles and book chapters. He is author or editor of 17 books, including *Transnational Social Work Practice* (Columbia University Press, 2010) and *Social Work Practice with Latinos: Key Issues and Emerging Themes* (Oxford University Press, 2010), both of which he is coeditor. His main areas of research are men at risk and applied masculinities, with a special focus on transnational men. His practice background includes 10 years of experience in direct practice and administration.

Douglas Epps, MSW, is a doctoral student at the University of California, Berkeley, School of Social Welfare. He is coeditor of *The Immigrant Other: Lived Experiences in a Transnational World* (Columbia University Press, 2016) and *Detaining the Immigrant Other: Global and Transnational Issues* (Oxford University Press, 2016). His areas of research interest include globalization, social work, and immigration.

Greg Lamphear is coauthor of *Writing and Publishing in English: For Second Language and International Scholars,* (2014) and coeditor of *The Immigrant Other: Lived Experiences in a Transnational World* and *Detaining the Immigrant Other: Global and Transnational Issues.* He is also an award-winning radio news reporter who has worked with the Associated Press, National Public Radio, and the Canadian Broadcasting Corporation. He earned his Bachelor of Arts in Communications from California State University, Fullerton. Based in Asia, Lamphear works as a writer and editor. His work on this edited volume included content, developmental, and copy editing.

About the Contributors

Abdulaziz Albrithen, PhD, is the MSW Program Coordinator of United Arab Emirates University and has served as faculty at Umm Al-Qura University and King Saud University, Saudi Arabia. He is author of Arabic and English articles and book chapters on social work and translated *The Encyclopedia of Autism Spectrum Disorders* into Arabic.

Charlene Laurence Carbonatto, DPhil, MSW, MA(SW)(Medical), is a Senior Lecturer and MSW (Healthcare) Program Manager in the Department of Social Work & Criminology, University of Pretoria, South Africa. She is a social work health care specialist, teacher, and scholar. Her research foci include infertility; women's and reproductive health; HIV and AIDS; and geriatric, mental, and indigenous health care.

Helen M. Cleak is an Associate Professor in the School of Public Health and Social Work at Queensland University of Technology, Australia. She has an extensive practice and research background in health care and is currently working with health practitioners in Australia and India to develop a new health curriculum for Indian social workers.

Nemthianngai Guite is an Associate Professor at the Centre of Social Medicine and Community Health, Jawaharlal Nehru University (JNU). She earned her master discipline in social work from the University of Delhi and her MPhil and PhD in Social Medicine from JNU. The focus of her practice, teaching, and research is public health.

Govind Hariharan is a Professor of Economics at Kennesaw State University. His research focuses on health care, regulation, and investments. He has taught at universities throughout the world and has received numerous awards for his scholarship and teaching.

Sandy S. Kim, BA, is a health care advocate and leader in Tacoma. She specializes in culturally competent practice and mental health care.

Tomas Mainil is Senior Lecturer at Breda University of Applied Sciences, Academy of Tourism, the Netherlands. He specializes in sociology and research methodology, with a research focus on transnational health care and medical tourism.

Uzoma Odera Okoye is a Professor in the Department of Social Work, University of Nigeria, Nsukka, Enugu State, Nigeria. She obtained her doctorate in Social Work in 2002. She teaches research methods, social gerontology, and social work in health care settings at both undergraduate and postgraduate levels.

Malcolm Payne has professorial roles at Manchester Metropolitan University and Kingston University, London, and was Director of Psychosocial and Spiritual Care, St. Christopher's Hospice London. He is author of *Older Citizens and End-of-Life Care* (Routledge, 2017) and *Humanistic Social Work* (Lyceum, 2011), and he is coauthor of *Social Work in End-of-Life and Palliative Care* (Lyceum, 2009).

Dolly R. Sacristan, PhD, LCSW, is an Assistant Professor in the Social Sciences and Human Services Department at Ramapo College of New Jersey. In addition to teaching, she is a board-certified clinical social worker in private practice working with immigrant Latino families and children and adult survivors of trauma.

Tetyana Semigina, PhD and Dr. Hab., MSW, is a Vice-Rector for Research and a Professor in Social Work at the Academy of Labour, Social Relations and Tourism (Kiev, Ukraine). She also teaches at the School of Public Health, National University of Kyiv-Mohyla Academy. Selected publications are available at https://www.researchgate.net/profile/Tetyana_Semigina3

Manuela Sjöström, PhD, is a Senior Lecturer in the Department of Social Work, Gothenburg, Sweden, as well as a social worker with professional roots in Germany. He conducts research on and teaches about both the professionalization of social work in health care and cross-national comparative studies in social work.

Sabina Stan is a Lecturer in Anthropology and Sociology at Dublin City University, Ireland. Her more recent research and publications have explored cross-border patient mobility in the context of east–west intra-European migration and the uneven European health care space.

Peter P. Szto, PhD, is Professor of Social Work at the Grace Abbott School of Social Work, University of Nebraska at Omaha. His research area is social welfare development in China, with a special focus on health care. He has degrees from Calvin College, Michigan State University, Westminster Theological Seminary, and the University of Pennsylvania.

Tarik Tuncay, MSW, PhD, earned his doctorate in social work at Hacettepe University, Turkey, in 2000 and joined its faculty the same year. He studies the psychosocial aspects of mental and chronic illnesses among groups with low socioeconomic status, stigma reduction, and interventions to improve the functioning of underserved populations with serious mental or chronic illnesses.

1

An Introduction to Health Care Social Work

A Global Perspective

Ren Winnett, Sandy S. Kim, Rich Furman, Douglas Epps, and Greg Lamphear

Few things rival the transformative potential of health care. Whereas trauma, genetic vulnerability, communicable exposure, and environmental risk regularly precipitate a cascade of life-altering challenges, health care mitigates disease and injury with implications that are often far-reaching. From inexpensive malaria drugs that dramatically impact public health on a continent-wide scale to extraordinarily advanced reconstructive procedures tailored to the needs of specific patients, health care influences the quality and longevity of lives—often in ways that transcend national boundaries.

Given the enormous importance of health care, one might wonder why most people don't understand more about it—both regarding local health services and regarding global health trends. The same observation can also be made regarding our relatively narrow understanding of the complex roles fulfilled by the health care professionals providing this care—and particularly regarding the demanding and multifaceted responsibilities of health care social workers. Even social workers often understand "health care social work" through the limited lens of their own direct experience—a meaningful but restricted frame of reference whose assumptions may not generalize easily. Health care social workers' potential for impacting lives and influencing health care policy and services is considerable, but our appreciation of that potential is often constrained by history, politics, organizational barriers, and an absence of systemic knowledge about health care social work practice itself—especially outside of our immediate areas of expertise.

In considering whether social work health care education is as broad as it should be, and examining possible explanations if it is not, readers are encouraged to ponder the high perceived value of specificity in health care social work, as well as the relative disincentive of investing time and effort focusing on unfamiliar paradigms. For most social work practitioners, perceptions of health care social work inevitably relate to their own immediate environments because the rewards of mastering this essential information and achieving efficiency in local practice environments strongly encourage such a focus. The rewards of building complementary, but less immediately applicable, knowledge of other systems while working in settings characterized by severe time constraints and challenging caseloads are less evident. Health care laws, standards, services, resources, and protocols are sensitive to—and vary by—nation, state, county, and local catchment area. For this reason, social workers involved in direct health care practice are expected to be subject matter experts in their immediate practice settings, not necessarily someone else's setting (although mastery of a generalized body of knowledge for practice is certainly expected within geographic areas of licensure and certification).

For health care social workers, then, a great deal of energy and time are invested in becoming competent practitioners in the specific environments in which they work. Unfortunately, this expertise can sometimes create a degree of myopia when considering health care challenges and potential solutions. Such experiential bias can contribute to efficient decision-making (due to a reduction in the number of options being considered) but limit— and potentially discourage—interest in paradigm change and "thinking outside the box." Such a restriction in perspective is often challenging to overcome precisely because it can appear to be both advantageous and necessary to the practitioner. In fact, the more tightly a profession's clinical practices are regulated and expected to align with specific licensure expectations, well-defined practice requirements, and local needs, the less likely it is that approaches to practice in other places will appear worthy of consideration during decision-making. Social worker practitioners and students certainly consume research and writing from a variety of national and international sources, but it is human nature to prefer the familiar, particularly when systemic influences exist to reinforce practice along established patterns and ensure quality. This is certainly true for social workers, whose practice in health care settings is necessarily aligned with—and responsive to—the regulatory, organizational, and societal expectations of the host settings in which they work (Ashcroft & Van Katwyk, 2016). In such environments, there may sometimes be little immediate support for asking, "How do they do this elsewhere?"

This book is intended to offer the reader a complementary perspective on health care social work by considering the effects of transnationalism and globalism on direct professional practice. In doing so, the editors intend to encourage an expanded awareness of contemporary influences on social work practice in health care settings and provide meaningful commentary on the profession's considerable contributions to health care throughout the world. The goal of doing so is to support the profession's potential for influencing future health care services and addressing related social justice needs in meaningful ways by understanding global similarities and differences in practice.

In the United States, social, economic, and political circumstances continue to influence citizens' perceptions of their nation, society, social justice, and individual rights. Within this always evolving context, the topic of health care continues to invite fierce debate as affected parties struggle to define its purpose and structure within a rapidly changing country (Narain & Katz, 2016; Reckrey et al., 2014). Currently, the possibility of reaching a consensus about a preferred approach to health care appears especially remote, and the resulting uncertainty has created confusion as health insurers, health systems, health care professionals, and consumers struggle to define their roles and determine a way forward (Ambrose-Miller & Ashcroft, 2016; Craig, Betancourt, & Muskat, 2015; Lindsay, Tetrault, Desmaris, King, & Pierart, 2014; Rose, Hatzenbuehler, Gilbert, Bouchard, & McGill, 2016).

Uncertainty about the purpose and structure of the US health care system is not merely an issue of reimbursement; it is a bright-line testament to the reality that health care and the question of who has access to it, and how, have become contentious flashpoints in the debate regarding human rights, social justice, and the nation's obligation toward its citizens (Mitchell, 2015; Stipp, 2015). Accordingly, a need exists to clearly recognize social work contributions to health care and to consider the ways in which the profession can best assist in meeting the nation's future health care needs and honor its commitment to social justice and human diversity. This need exists concurrently with the one defined previously: the requirement that health care social work practice be adequately informed by a knowledge base that allows achievement of practice expertise specific to one's immediate environment and that supports broad awareness and understanding of health care social work on a global scale.

The social work profession has long possessed a distinguished history of contributions to the field of health care (Gehlert, 2012). From the earliest work of hospital almoners in 19th-century London to the subsequent emergence of hospital social workers in other British Commonwealth nations, the profession has developed a strong affiliation with hospitals that, although often initially contested by the larger medical community, has grown steadily over time (Allen & Spitzer, 2016). Social workers' emergence in early 20th-century American clinics and hospitals, often in the face of physician resistance, was also facilitated by forward-thinking doctors who recognized the importance of the environment in social medicine and public health and supported the emergence of social workers as an essential component of multidisciplinary teams tasked with better serving patients by understanding them within the context of their lives (Reisch, 2012). The growing influence of the profession in the American health care system, and resultant representation in later United Nation and World Health Organization developmental and supportive endeavors, also contributed to the transmission of professional knowledge to developing nations, some of which eventually instituted their own social work programs and developed professional legacies acknowledged, in part, in this text.

Although the profession of social work has undergone many changes in the past several decades, it remains unequivocally committed to the empowerment of the disenfranchised. A central and defining characteristic of the profession is its deep concern for social justice—an orientation that renders social work particularly well qualified to offer well-informed perspectives on the current glaring inadequacy of health care provision to many populations in the United States and other nations (Andrews, 2014; Wardian, Thaller, & Urbaeva, 2015) and to advocate for the prospect of better health care utilization and achievement of long overdue social justice and growth. In many ways, the United States and other nations have arrived at a series of critical junctures in the long process of defining themselves. The broad landscape of health care provides a context in which the social work profession can engage in this process with other participants and consider ways that our shared responsibility for achieving needed social change and providing effective care to individuals and families can be met. In the context of an increasingly globalized world community, the profession's potential for improving health care represents a significant—and critical—imperative.

Why This Book?

Given the pressing need for improvement in the health care systems of both the United States and other nations—and the daunting complexity of achieving any kind of consensus regarding how best to achieve this—it is not surprising that some might question the usefulness of conducting a broader analysis of health care social work from a global perspective. As previously suggested, readers may find themselves asking how a more global review of health care social workers' contributions can be helpful, given the pressures of providing care in uniquely localized environments. Such reservations are often driven by the understanding that nations necessarily enact health care systems that reflect their own governing philosophies, histories, and priorities—and that such contexts invariably change when one crosses borders. Such reservations accept that the social work profession must operate effectively within each of these environments and, to some extent, adapt to the prevailing needs and priorities of each nation. Given the sometimes stark differences between these environments, it is not surprising that readers may question the utility of studying health care social work in one place, especially a very dissimilar one, to practice more effectively in another one.

When considering the usefulness of examining health care social work from a global, rather than primarily a local or national, perspective, it may be beneficial to reflect upon our purpose for considering a broader view of the topic in the first place. As discussed previously, our often reactive resistance to expanding, rather than narrowing, our focus is often the byproduct of urgency and familiarity rather than any meaningful confirmation of a broader view, and it holds little value. When an issue demands immediate attention, the need to address it quickly is sharply felt and our commitment to examining fewer familiar approaches wanes. In the case of American health care, the need for systemic improvement is so acute that a kind of reactionary tunnel vision can occur. In this context, some readers may believe that the country's immediate health care needs are pronounced enough that limiting broader consideration of other health care systems (and dissimilar practice standards) seems both reasonable and responsible. Adherents of this perspective may argue that the health care debate is already contentious enough that consideration of even more alternatives will render things even less reconcilable, not more. To some, the benefits of considering the complex histories and organization of other nations' health care systems may seem unlikely to resolve the current crisis in American health care or do much to inform American health care social workers' efforts and advocacy within it.

We contend, however, that it is exactly because of the urgency and severity of the health care crisis in the United States (and elsewhere) that the need to consider sometimes markedly disparate alternatives is so important. This book is also predicated on the belief that the social work profession's potential for a continued role in addressing health care needs in America is growing and that understanding this expanding opportunity within the context of social work's global legacy ultimately enables social workers to better meet the nation's health care needs in creative and well-grounded ways.

The United States is a nation undergoing polarizing change, and the perspectives of many within it reflect these shifts in long-familiar patterns of ideological distillation. On many topics, the nation seems increasingly divided into clear bimodal, "either–or" stances, and the debate about the nation's health care system appears to be no different. "Everyone" is either a Democrat or a Republican. People "must" be either pro-immigration or anti-immigration. You "either" support efforts to dismantle the Affordable Care Act or approve of it. The resulting sense of crisis can harm our capacity for clear and thoughtful analysis about the nature of our challenges and interfere with consideration of potential solutions. In terms of health care, the debate regarding the Affordable Care Act and other proposed alternatives may appear to represent the full spectrum of our options, but it does not. Policy analysts, planners, and health care advocates—including social workers—understand that there are additional options for how health care in general, and health care social work in particular, is provided.

This book was conceived in the belief that the act of considering possibilities is always healthy and that doing so fuels insights that more habitual consideration of familiar choices cannot spark. We believe that this potential for new ideas and perspective change is one of the key reasons to explore social work practice in other countries. It is an investment in the unfamiliar and a professional vote of confidence in the capacity of social workers to make differences that transcend boundaries and serve people better—on a global scale.

In this book, readers will find chapters written by scholars and practitioners of health care social work from throughout the world, each providing valuable information on the performance of health care social work in unique historical, social, and political contexts. The chapters will assist readers in exploring health care social work in new and novel ways by considering largely unfamiliar details about the profession's development in different nations, contributory policy considerations influencing its activities, contemporary scope of practice, and implications for future practice and growth. In the process, readers will gain an opportunity to confirm the efficacy of certain assumptions and perspectives regarding the practice of health care social work and to meaningfully reflect upon the different experiences, histories, and conceptualizations of social workers elsewhere as a way of prompting useful problem-solving with new information.

Social work educators have increasingly observed that exploring social work practices in other cultural and national contexts helps students expand their thinking and perspectives. Faruque and Ahmmed (2013) note that

> as educators, we have a responsibility to help students grapple with the uncertainty of a rapidly changing world. The social work student should be ready to engage in contradictions, ambiguity, and discussions on the erosion of western lifestyle as we now understand it. This should not be construed as a negative consequence but an opportunity for dialogue and seeking creative action to unique global problems. Along with this is the need to value and promote differences of opinion, diverse ways of thinking about our planet, and unique ways of approaching social work practice. (p. 69)

The authors wish to challenge the assumption that significant social problems can adequately be understood through a purely national lens. The world has become an increasingly global place, and all social issues are made clearer through consideration of a global lens to assist us in fully contextualizing the nature of our problems and concerns.

Chapter Introductions

The chapters of *Health Care Social Work: A Global Perspective* are divided into two sections. In the first section, critical content regarding transnationalism, globalization, economic trends, and American health care social work practices is offered. The editors believe that this material affords social work students, practitioners, and scholars essential information with which to understand the concepts addressed in the second section of the book. Taken together, this foundation material supports a nuanced examination of the case studies comprising Section 2 and enables a largely unattempted exploration of global health care social work practices to occur. In support of this endeavor, the editors suggest that readers take the opportunity to review Section 1 before continuing on to subsequent chapters.

Foundation Chapters

The first of the three foundation chapters, "Health Care in a Global World" by Govind Hariharan, provides essential information for understanding the impact of economic influences on transnational health care. Hariharan examines the increasing influence of globalization on health systems and medical care throughout the world and discusses the ways in which this relatively new phenomenon has begun to impact health care despite the traditional insulating effects of stringent regulations on cross-border movement of medical goods, services, and health professionals. The impacts of advances in treatment, multilateral trade agreements, technological innovation, and increased movement of people are examined.

The second foundation chapter, "Transnational Health Care" by Tomas Mainil and Sabina Stan, is an important aid to understanding the global expanse of health care services in a consumer-driven world. Mainil and Stan explore the commodity of medical care in differing national domains and review motivating factors influencing medical tourism. The defining characteristics of transnationalism in health care, trends in movement across national borders to access health care services, the phenomenon of transnational health care as a transformative social and political force, and issues of social justice and equity in access are considered.

The third foundation chapter, "Health Care Social Work in the United States" by Ren Winnett, is structurally similar to the case study chapters in Section 2 and is included as a foundation chapter to allow readers an opportunity to immediately apply the transnational concepts introduced in Chapters 2 and 3 to the context of health care social work in America. In this way, readers are encouraged to consider a historically informed perspective on health care social work while adopting a broad view of the contemporary transnational influences that impact its role and potential.

Global Case Studies

The chapters in Section 2 support examination of health care social work from a transnational, global perspective. Each chapter provides a unique perspective on health care social work in a selected country. The editors are confident that this approach will assist readers in developing new insights about the ways social work practitioners provide services and contend with health care dilemmas throughout the world. Each chapter author provides an overview of their country's social work profession, a detailed history of the profession's involvement in that country's health care system, and an examination of the social and political context within which the nation's social work profession exists. Review of these items includes discussion of theories influencing the practice of social work in that country and invites comparison to, and analysis of, health care social work in other places.

The authors of chapters in Section 2 provide detailed descriptions regarding the nature of contemporary health care social work in their countries of focus. This analysis includes, among other stated foci, an exploration of current social work roles within health care and examination of the ways the profession has adapted to ongoing local, regional, and national policy considerations. Suggestions are made for social work practice advancements, and each author concludes with a review of emerging trends and potential future considerations for health care social worker practitioners.

An important organizational parameter of *Health Care Social Work: A Global Perspective* involves its preservation of psychiatric social work as a topic for scholarly review elsewhere. Limiting coverage of this critical subject was a difficult editorial decision because examining psychiatric care in health care settings is certainly congruent with a biopsychosocial perspective and recognizes the inherent interrelatedness of human functioning, strengths, and need. However, several important considerations supported exclusion of most mental health content from the book. First, many texts already address mental health care in social work practice, including health care social work practice. Second, the vast majority of mental health social work practice does not occur strictly within health care settings, and inclusion of services that do occur in them would necessitate provision of substantial information on corollary psychiatric services for health care-specific mental health programs to be understood in a useful context. Finally, to attend as fully as possible to the never before attempted examination of health care social work from a global, transnational perspective, inclusion of most mental health material was limited in response to space constraints. The result is a text that applies itself fully to overdue consideration of the effects of globalism and transnationalism on contemporary health care social work practice—and adds substantially to existing understanding of the profession's health care roots and contributions.

With these considerations in mind, readers are invited to examine the following organizational outline for the book. As noted previously, countries were selected to allow readers an opportunity to apply concepts identified in Chapters 2 and 3. Selected countries for case study include Australia, China, Cuba, England, India, Nigeria, Saudi Arabia, South Africa, Sweden, Turkey, and Ukraine.

Australia

In Chapter 5, "The Role of Social Work in Australian Health Care Settings," Helen M. Cleak examines the profession's presence in both hospitals and community health clinics. Cleak then discusses the development of social work as a specialized occupation in Australia and reviews the country's sociopolitical climate as an influence on this branch of social service. Several important issues relating to the Australian health care system are acknowledged, including the necessary emphasis on primary care and the emergence of new bioethical issues. The chapter concludes with insightful commentary regarding the future of Australian health care social work, as well as assessment of likely of challenges to come.

China

Revealing and informative, Peter Szto's chapter, "Health Care Social Work in China," addresses some of the opportunities and challenges faced by health care social workers in the world's second largest economy. A study of contrasts, Chinese health care involves a growing social work profession in the rapidly shifting balance between Western medicine and traditional Chinese medicine as the government grapples with reconciling competing free market and socialist economic principles. Szto discusses the sporadic role of social work within both the medical field and Chinese society, generally. He concludes with an examination of China's future health care social work needs and calls for dramatically increased preparation of social workers for practice.

Cuba

Despite its tumultuous political history and economic challenges, Cuba has developed an extensive health care system, one important component of which is partially administered by the country's health care social workers. Dolly Sacristan's research regarding social work practice in Cuba is detailed in Chapter 7, "The Role of the Social Worker in Health Care in Cuba," and includes interviews with practicing Cuban health care social workers. The chapter provides a revealing glimpse of a little known and rarely researched branch of the profession. In the process, the chapter's qualitative and exploratory data and macro research on Cuban health care provide compelling information on the history, development, status, contributions, and challenges of Cuban health care social work.

England

In Chapter 8, "Health Care Social Work in England," Malcolm Payne examines the social work profession and health care system of the United Kingdom's most populous country. He details the legal basis for the profession's practice in England and explains the role of the Health Care Professions Council, which functions as the profession's national regulatory body. Payne considers the critical work of medical social workers within England's government-provided health care system, the National Health Service, and advocates for improved integration of England's divided health and social care service systems.

India

Nemthianngai Guite's chapter, "Health Care Social Work in India," explores the role of medical social work amid India's disparate socioeconomic hierarchy and daunting public health disease burden. In the process, she provides a fascinating look at the historical context of health care and social work as a backdrop to considering the profession's status in India today. A detailed account of the many subfields of medical social work is included. Guite concludes the chapter with a glimpse of the many challenges currently facing health care social workers in India and advocates for increased preventive and integrative health care services as a critical investment.

Nigeria

Chapter 10, "Health Care Social Work in Nigeria" by Uzuma O. Okoye, considers the profession's contribution to health care within the unique and challenging context of Africa's most populous nation. Okoye provides a broad review of Nigerian social work, particularly in relation to health care, and discusses how missionaries, war, and other influences provided an evolving context into which the West African nation's new health care social work tradition eventually grew. The impact of political influences is also presented, and common roles for social workers in the Nigerian health care system are explained.

Saudi Arabia

In this informative examination of a young nation's emerging social work profession, Chapter 11, "Health Care Social Work in Saudi Arabia" by Abdulaziz Albrithen, describes a growing field within an often misunderstood country. Albrithen considers the history of social work in Saudi Arabia and details the profession's entry into health care in recent decades. The profession's evolution amid a rapidly growing population is examined, as is its unique application of values and ethics within the complex context of religious conservatism, gender segregation, political adaptation, and economic experimentation. Insights regarding the future of the country's health care system are offered.

South Africa

Charlene L. Carbonatto's chapter, "Social Work in Health Care in South Africa," provides a detailed portrayal of the triumphs and challenges of the profession within this post-apartheid nation. Carbonatto considers the development of social work in South Africa and examines barriers to achievement of social justice-informed health services in an era of continued social, political, and economic striation and mistrust. A review of the many daunting challenges facing the profession is undertaken, and recognition is given of the country's continued hard-fought health care evolution and social workers' potential for positively impacting this growth.

Sweden

Chapter 13, "Health Care Social Work in Sweden" by Manuela Sjöström, provides an overview of the evolving work of Swedish medical social workers. Sjöström offers an informative look at the historical development of the profession, the scope of its practice, and its jurisdiction within health care at this time. She also examines the nation's relevant social and political contexts and offers commentary on some of the challenges faced by the social work profession at its current "crossroads." Sjöström concludes with a discussion of the potential impact of these challenges on the future of Swedish medical social work.

Turkey

Chapter 14, "Health Care Social Work in Turkey" by Tarik Tuncay, is a comprehensive look at the field, from its historical roots in the Ottoman empire to its current role in the Republic of Turkey. Tuncay details the importance of the profession in light of the health care restructuring initiatives that commenced in the early 2000s. These addressed both private and public services and extended coverage to almost the entire population. Tuncay also considers the related systemic adaptations that followed these changes and identifies several potential areas for improvement, including the need for increased emphasis on evidence-based practice strategies for health care social workers.

Ukraine

Tetyana Semigina's chapter, "Health Care Social Work in Ukraine," provides a broad review of the many challenges Ukraine has faced in recent decades and examines the ways in which social and political upheaval have impacted the country's health care system and the developing field of medical social work. Semigina discusses contemporary health care and social work within this historical context and considers necessary steps for developing the robust social service and health care system needed by Ukrainians in an age of continued uncertainty and challenge. The chapter concludes with recommendations for advancing social work contributions to Ukrainian health care.

References

Allen, K. M., & Spitzer, W. J. (2016). The historical and contemporary context for healthcare social work practice. In K. M. Allen & W. J. Spitzer (Eds.), *Social work practice in healthcare: Advanced approaches and emerging trends* (pp. 7–29). Thousand Oaks, CA: Sage.

Ambrose-Miller, W., & Ashcroft, R. (2016, May). Challenges faced by social workers as members of interprofessional collaborative health care teams. *Health & Social Work, 41*(2), 101–109. doi:10.1093/hsw/hlw006

Andrews, C. (2014, August). Unintended consequences: Medicaid expansion and racial inequality in access to health insurance. *Health & Social Work, 39*(3), 131–133. doi:10.1093/hsw/hlu024

Ashcroft, R., & Van Katwyk, T. (2016). An examination of the biomedical paradigm: A view of social work. *Social Work in Public Health, 31*(3), 140–152. doi:10.1080/19371918.2015.1087918

Craig, S. L., Betancourt, I., & Muskat, B. (2015). Thinking big, supporting families and enabling coping: The value of social work in patient and family centered health care. *Social Work in Health Care, 54*(5), 422–443. doi:10.1080/00981389.2015.1017074

Faruque, C. J., & Ahmmed, F. (2013). Development of social work education and practice in an era of international collaboration and cooperation. *Journal of International Social Issues, 2*(1), 61–70.

Gehlert, S. (2012). Conceptual underpinnings of social work in health care. In S. Gehlert & T. Browne (Eds.), *Handbook of health social work* (2nd ed., pp. 3–19). Hoboken, NJ: Wiley.

Lindsay, S., Tetrault, S., Desmaris, C., King, G., & Pierart, G. (2014, May). Social workers as "cultural brokers" in providing culturally sensitive care to immigrant families raising a child with a physical disability. *Health & Social Work, 39*(2), e10–e20. doi:10.1093/hsw/hlu009

Mitchell, F. M. (2015, August). Racial and ethnic health disparities in an era of health care reform. *Health & Social Work, 40*(3), e66–e74. doi:10. 1093/hsw/hlv038

Narain, K. D., & Katz, M. L. (2016, November). Experiences with health insurance and health care in the context of welfare reform. *Health & Social Work, 41*(4), 244–252. doi:10.1093/hsw/hlw038

Reckrey, J. M., Gettenberg, G., Ross, H., Kopke, V., Soriano, T., & Ornstein, K. (2014). The critical role of social workers in home-based primary care. *Social Work in Health Care, 53*(4), 330–343. doi:10.1080/00981389.2014.884041

Reisch, M. (2012). The challenges of health care reform for hospital social work in the United States. *Social Work in Health Care, 51*(10), 873–893. doi:10.1080/00981389.2012.721492

Rose, S. M., Hatzenbuehler, S., Gilbert, E., Bouchard, M. P., & McGill, D. (2016, May). A population health approach to clinical social work with complex patients in primary care. *Health & Social Work, 41*(2), 93–100. doi:10.93/ hsw/hlw013

Stipp, K. F. (2015). A plain view of poor health in a land of plenty. *Social Work in Public Health, 30*(4), 360–372. doi:10.1080/19371918.2015.1024376

Wardian, J., Thaller, J., & Urbaeva, Z. (2015, January). The accumulation of multiple sources of psychosocial disadvantage and their correlation to reported overall health: Establishing a threshold. *Social Work, 60*(1), 45–54. doi:10.1093/sw/swu049

SECTION 1
FOUNDATION CHAPTERS

2

Health Care in a Global World

Govind Hariharan

Globalization is transforming not only trade, finance, science, the environment, crime, and terrorism, it is also influencing health and medical care. We cannot underestimate the effects of these changes on the health of populations and medical care. In addition to domestic problems, all national health systems must now deal with the international transfer of health risks and opportunities.

—Dr. Julio Frenk (2010)

Introduction

The incessant search for better economic conditions by workers and better and cheaper products and services by consumers, along with the drive to find newer markets to sell to and cheaper locations to produce in, has created a world far more integrated or globalized than at any other point in human history. The potential for higher wages in high-income countries provides the pull attracting labor from low-income countries, whereas large untapped markets or low wages in low-income countries provide the push for companies in high-income countries to seek out those markets or sources for low-cost production. Previous work, such as the conceptual framework of globalization as modeled in Huynen, Martens, and Hilderink (2005), provides a more holistic approach to framing the health impacts of globalization; this chapter focuses on the economic push and pull aspects.

As Dr. Frenk noted in the opening quotation of this chapter, health and medical care throughout the world are also beginning to be influenced by this new wave of globalization. Compared to many other traditional products and services, health care has been more insulated from the effects of globalization due to much more stringent regulations on cross-border movement of medical goods and services as well as health professionals.

However, during the past three decades, new discoveries in treatment, multilateral trade agreements, advances in technology, and increased movement of people have turned a trickle into a downpour. These flows have helped bring about greater availability and access to immunization and treatment, such as three-dose diphtheria–tetanus–pertussis (DTP3) immunization and treatment for HIV, but have also exacerbated the transmission of diseases across borders, such as the severe acute respiratory syndrome (SARS) virus and the recent Ebola epidemic.

The Economic Engines of Globalization

Globalization is multifaceted. Increases in the flow of goods and services and foreign direct investment brought about by lower transportation costs and the lowering of trade barriers are one engine of globalization that has increased access to new and better goods from the cheapest sources. International migration and easier movement of people are a second engine that has played a major role in not only providing income and employment opportunities but also enhancing the flow of ideas that integrate cultures and institutions. Last, innovation in information transmission has spread access to worldwide knowledge and production and distribution networks. These three engines of globalization are not distinct and can and do influence each other. For example, exposure to new goods and services brought about through movement of people or through the internet can and often does create new markets for goods and services.

Economic theory provides two distinct concepts in support of such trade. For example, if India can produce computers more cheaply compared to the United States while the United States can produce cars more cheaply compared to India, it would make sense for India to produce and sell cheap computers to the United States in exchange for cars bought cheaply by India from the United States. Thus, trade can make consumers in both countries better off because they are able to purchase cheap computers and cars, but what if the United States is better at producing both computers and cars? The theory of comparative advantage argues that even when the United States is better at both, if to produce one computer the United States has to give up production of three cars, while in India in order to produce one computer it has to cut back production of only two cars, both countries will benefit when India specializes in producing computers while the United

States produces only cars. In this example, India has the lower opportunity cost in producing computers (in terms of car production given up) and hence should use its scarce domestic resources exclusively on computers, whereas the United States has the lower opportunity cost in producing cars and hence should focus on that. Through trade, both countries will enjoy greater prosperity and the best use of their scarce labor and other resources.

Ortiz-Ospina, Beltekian, D., and Roser (2014) provide historical data which show that during the past three centuries, the world has gone through many periods of increased international trade. From the latter stages of the 19th century to the beginning of World War I, technological advances (lowering transport costs) and a lowering of trade barriers created the "first wave of globalization." A new wave of technological innovations and reduced trade barriers during the past three decades have resulted in trade volumes increasing to 50% of global production compared to just 10% at the end of the 19th century. This new wave of globalization is unique in the following ways: (1) The current wave of globalization is most pronounced between developing nations (South–South trade), whereas the previous wave at the turn of the 19th century was more pronounced within Europe and between developed nations (North–North trade); (2) the current wave is a result of a movement by countries and companies searching for efficiency in cost of production rather than colonialism; and (3) in the current wave of globalization, countries import car parts, for example, and export the finished product (intra-industry trade), whereas in the previous wave, countries exported different products from those they imported (inter-industry trade). The opening up of China to foreign trade in the late 1970s played a central role in this new wave of global trade. This new wave has resulted in global growth in incomes, which have increased rapidly; however, it has also sometimes been accompanied by worsening income disparities within countries.

Similar to global trade and at least partially due to the same driving forces of economic advantage, a wave of global migration occurred in the 19th century and a more pronounced new wave occurred in the 20th century that were distinctly different in origin, destination, and causes. McKeown (2004) notes that the major long-distance migration from 1846 to 1970 was from Europe to the Americas (55–58 million people), followed by migration from India and China to Southeast Asia and Indian Ocean and South Pacific islands (48–52 million people). The emergence of both steamships that reduced transportation times and costs and a global economy in European and North American countries and Japan were the sources of much of this migration. By the 1920s, much of this migration flow declined with restrictions and quotas in the United States and Italy, especially from non-Western countries. McKeown estimates that the 1990s level of migration for longer duration stays as a proportion of the world population was comparable to that of the early 20th century. However, if shorter duration migrants such as tourists and temporary workers are included, then the end of the 20th century experienced the larger wave of global mobility. According to the International Organization for Migration (2015), 2015 had the highest recorded number of migrants ever (244 million), and South–South migration (90.2 million) was larger than South–North migration (85.3 million). Note that 2015 also had the highest recorded level of forced displacement (15.1 million refugees by mid-2015). This recent spike in displacement and refugees, especially when accompanied by increasing protectionism in trade and risk of conflict, could portend a potentially greater impact on unmet demand for health services globally.

At the end of the 19th century and the beginning of the 20th century, technological innovations in energy, manufacturing, communications, and transportation brought about the Second Industrial Revolution. This resulted in a period of rapid economic growth, trade, and migration as people moved to cities and countries with higher paying jobs. The end of the 20th century and the beginning of the 21st century likewise experienced major transformations brought about by technological change, most significantly in information technology and communications, biotechnology, and medical technology. The resultant industrial revolution is still evolving and has been a driving force in the new wave of globalization, with rapid global economic growth, trade, and migration, but sometimes also rising disparities in income.

It is important to first understand some of the differences in the economic, demographic, and health system characteristics throughout the world that create the economic pull and push. This is discussed at the broad level of income and geographic regions in the next section.

Economics, Demography, and Health Systems Throughout the World

Economics of Nations

Economics as the study of the allocation of scarce resources across unlimited needs plays a significant role in health and well-being throughout the world. At an individual level, economic well-being has a significant direct effect on health status through an individual's ability to purchase or access medical care. Although health status may itself modify individuals' ability to work and improve their economic position, research has shown that even controlling for the direction of causality, income has a net positive effect on health (Chapman & Hariharan, 1994). Governments likewise are affected by the strength of their economies with regard to how much health care and health infrastructure they are able to provide for their citizens.

The World Bank and many other international organizations classify the economic position of countries as low income, lower middle income, upper middle income, and upper income based on their gross national income (GNI). GNI of a country measures the amount of income or value added generated by the people of that country, whereas gross domestic product (GDP) measures the value of final goods and services produced in a country. As shown in Table 2.1, there is wide variation in incomes per capita across the income groups and in different regions of the world. In 2015, the average country in the low-income group had an income per capita of $1,602 compared to $46,132 for the high-income group. Similarly, countries in the sub-Saharan Africa region had an average income per capita of $3,569 compared to $ 56,178 for countries in North America. This wide variation directly translates into how much these countries can spend on health care. In 2014, the annual health expenditure for countries in the low-income group was only $37 compared to $5,251 in high-income countries. Similarly, countries in South Asia spent an average of $69 per person per year on health care compared to $8,990 in countries in North America. Official intergovernmental aid plays a significant role in health care spending. In 2014, the sub-Saharan Africa region, for example, received net official aid per capita of $48, which helped pay for the critical health care needs in the region.

Although there is significant disparity across countries and regions, when compared across time, the disparity has narrowed during the new wave of globalization, with many countries in emerging economies growing at a much faster pace than those in developed economies. The two best examples of this are China and India. China, which plays a central role in this new wave of globalization, began the process of opening its economy to foreign trade in 1978. Through an emphasis on rapid economic growth and by capitalizing on its large number of low-cost workers, it soon became the manufacturing center of the world. The world's largest population mass

Table 2.1 Economy and Health Expenditure by Income Group and Region

Income Group	Gross National Income per Capita ($)	Health Expenditure per Capita ($)	Net Official Aid per Capita ($)	Regions	Gross National Income per Capita ($)	Health Expenditure per Capita ($)	Net Official Aid per Capita ($)
	2015	2014	2014		2015	2014	2014
Low income	1,602	37	56	East Asia and Pacific	16,128	643	4
Lower middle income	6,409	90	18	Europe and Central Asia	30,040	2,420	11
Upper middle income	15,665	518	6	Latin America and Caribbean	15,042	714	16
High income	46,132	5,251	0	Middle East and North Africa	18,847	433	78
				North America	56,178	8,990	0
World	15,655	1,061	22	South Asia	5,658	67	9
				Sub-Saharan Africa	3,569	98	48

Source: World Bank (2017).

during the past three decades with an economic growth rate averaging close to double digits rapidly moved from low income to upper middle income. China had a GDP per capita of $22,760 in 2015, and it is the second largest economy in the world behind the United States. During the 1980s and early 1990s, this growth was accompanied by reductions in income inequality, but income inequality began to worsen during the second half of the 1990s. This was particularly pronounced between remote farming communities and the coastal industrial centers. In the past decade, however, through active government intervention and social policies, poverty declined so much that China accounted for most of the global reduction in poverty during that time frame.

With the second largest population in the world, India entered a rapid phase of economic growth through market-oriented reforms in 1991. It now has a GDP per capita of $10,900 and is projected to become the third largest economy in the world in a few decades. India's economic progress was aided by the global technological revolution in the world and the availability of a large pool of low-cost information technology service workers. Unfortunately, this rapid growth, which has spawned a large upper middle class, has been accompanied by continued high income inequality, with large segments of the population left behind, especially in rural farming regions.

Demography

Demography—the study of the size, characteristics, and age distribution of a population—determines another large chunk of the demand for health care resources. The theory of demographic transition is based on more than two centuries of casual observation of a pattern in the relationship between economic strength, fertility, and death rates. According to this theory, during the preindustrial stage of an economy, death rates and birth rates are both high because poor levels of income and access to health care and sanitation drive high death rates, and birth rates are high to compensate for the high death rates (e.g., in sub-Saharan Africa). At the next stage, referred to as the developing stage, death rates begin to decline as improvements in health care and sanitation accompany an improving economy, but birth rates continue to remain high, resulting in a growth in population (e.g., in India). During the third stage often observed in developed economies, low death rates and low birth rates become the norm as better health and incomes help prolong life, and when accompanied by low birth rates, the result is a shrinking and often aging population (e.g., in China). Globalization and aid increase access to better medical care and may result in declining death rates, even among low-income countries. According to the "Global Monitoring Report 2015/2016" (World Bank 2016), although the global population living in poverty has decreased, an estimated 700 million people still live in poverty. In sub-Saharan Africa and South Asia, some countries still face extreme poverty and often have very young populations with high birth and death rates.

As shown in Table 2.1, East Asia and Pacific (EAP) and South Asia (SA) regions are home to most of the world's population, including the two countries with the largest populations in the world—China (EAP region) and India (SA region). Population size is largest in the lower middle income (which includes India) and upper middle income (which includes China) groups and is lowest in the low-income group of countries (many in sub-Saharan Africa). Table 2.2 provides additional relevant details for health care. The median age of the population is lowest in low-income countries, which also have the highest rates of population growth. High-income

Table 2.2 2013 Population Descriptors

Income Group	Population (in Thousands)	Population Median Age (Years)	Population Proportion Younger Than Age 15 Years (%)	Population Living on <$1 a Day (%)[a]	Population Proportion Older Than Age 60 Years (%)	Annual Population Growth Rate (%)
Low income	848,668	20.5	39.2	43.6	5.7	2.2
Lower middle income	2,554,925	25.2	31.2	22.7	7.9	1.5
Upper middle income	2,449,819	33.9	21.4	5.2	12.6	0.8
High income	1,272,686	39.8	17	<2.0	21.9	0.6
Global	7,126,098	30.2	26.2	14.6	11.7	1.2

[a]Purchasing power parity, international dollars.

Source: World Health Organization (2017a).

countries have a much higher percentage of the population older than age 60 years, thereby increasing these countries' need for young workers and immigrants. Coupled with the fact that in low-income countries, the percentage of the population living on less than $1 per day is close to 50%, the pull factor of global economic migration from low-income to high-income regions becomes most pronounced.

Health Systems Throughout the World

Health systems include health care finance, health care access, and the structure of health care, Tables 2.3 and 2.4 present some of the key statistics pertaining to health care finance in the regions of the world. As a group, high-income countries tend to have the highest share of total health expenditures (THE) as a percentage of their GDP. They also have the lowest share of out-of-pocket expenditure in THE. Low-income countries, on the other hand, tend to have a significant share of THE coming from external sources, such as international organizations and foreign governmental assistance. Even within income or geographic regions, there are differences in the share of out-of-pocket expenditures and in the role of government in health care provision. For example, whereas the United States relies quite

Table 2.3 Health Care Systems: Income

Income Group	Total Health Expenditure (% of GDP)	Public (% of Total)	Out of Pocket (% of total)	External Resources (% of total)
	2014	2014	2014	2014
Low income	5.7	42.4	37.2	33.2
Lower middle income	4.5	36.4	55.7	3.3
Upper middle income	6.2	55.2	32.2	0.3
High income	12.3	62.3	13.3	—
World	9.9	60.1	18.2	0.2

GDP, gross domestic product.
Source: World Health Organization (2017b).

Table 2.4 Health Care Systems: Geography

Regions	Total Health Expenditure (% of GDP)	Public (% of Total)	Out of Pocket (% of Total)	External Resources (% of Total)
	2014	2014	2014	2014
East Asia and Pacific	6.9	66.2	25.1	0.3
Europe and Central Asia	9.5	75.5	17	—
Latin America and Caribbean	7.2	51.2	31.7	0.5
Middle East and North Africa	5.3	60.7	31.1	0.8
North America	16.5	49.6	11.2	—
South Asia	4.4	31.2	61.5	2.3
Sub-Saharan Africa	5.5	42.6	34.5	11.2

GDP, gross domestic product.

Source: World Health Organization (2017b).

extensively on private health insurance, other high-income countries, such as Canada and United Kingdom, predominantly pay for health care through the government. In China, the private and public shares of THE are almost even at 44% and 56%, respectively, with most of the private expenditure on health being out of pocket. In India, on the other hand, only approximately one-fourth of THE is provided by the government, and the rest is almost completely accounted for by out-of-pocket expenditure.

There are also significant differences in availability or access to health care. Table 2.5 shows the levels of access across income or regions for some basic infrastructure drivers of health care. Access to an improved water source or sanitation facility has significantly improved in low- and lower middle-income regions since 1990, but it remains a stark reminder of the disparity throughout the world. As a result of the work of international organizations, rates of immunization for measles, DTP3, and tuberculosis have been equalized across regions. Access to qualified medical personnel, however, remains a significant source of disparity in medical care across both income and geographic regions.

Disparities in access to health and health expenditure would be expected to lead to disparities in health outcomes. As shown in Table 2.6, every

Table 2.5 Health Care Access

Income Group/ Regions	Access to Clean Water (% of Population)	Access to Sanitary Facilities (% of Population)	Child Immunization Rate		Tuberculosis		Physicians (per 1,000 People)	Nurses and Midwives (per 1,000 People)
			Measles (% of Children Aged 12–23 Months)	DTP3 (% of Children Aged 12–23 Months)	Treatment Success Rate (% of New Cases)	Cases Detection Rate (% of New Estimated Cases)		
	2015	2015	2015	2015	2014	2015	2008–2014	2008–2014
Low income	66	28	78	80	86	56	0.1	n.a.
Lower middle income	90	52	80	81	82	54	0.8	1.7
Upper middle income	95	80	94	93	84	78	2	3
High income	100	99	94	96	73	88	2.9	8.6
World	91	68	85	86	83	59	1.5	3.3
East Asia and Pacific	94	77	91	92	90	65	1.6	2.6
Europe and Central Asia	98	93	94	93	76	82	3.4	7.5
Latin America and Caribbean	95	83	94	90	75	81	2	4.2

(*continued*)

Table 2.5 Continued

Income Group/ Regions	Access to Clean Water (% of Population)	Access to Sanitary Facilities (% of Population)	Child Immunization Rate		Tuberculosis		Physicians (per 1,000 People)	Nurses and Midwives (per 1,000 People)
Middle East and North Africa	93	91	86	86	85	73	1.6	2.5
North America	99	100	92	95	84	87	2.4	9.8
South Asia	92	45	83	85	79	59	0.7	1.4
Sub-Saharan Africa	68	30	73	76	81	47	0.2	1.2

DTP3, three-dose diphtheria–tetanus–pertussis; n.a., not applicable.

Source: World Bank (2017).

Table 2.6 Health Outcomes

Income Group/ Regions	Life Expectancy at Birth (Years)	Neonatal Mortality per 1,000 Live Births	Infant Mortality per 1,000 Live Births	Male Younger Than Age 5 Years Mortality Rate per 1,000 Live Births	Female Younger Than Age 5 Years Mortality Rate per 1,000 Live Births	Adult Male Mortality Rate per 1,000	Adult Female Mortality Rate per 1,000
	2014	2015	2015	2015	2015	2009–2014	2009–2014
Low income	61	27	53	81	71	284	237
Lower middle income	67	26	40	54	51	223	155
Upper middle income	74	9	15	20	17	135	88
High income	81	3	5	6	5	107	60
World	71	19	32	44	41	185	130
East Asia and Pacific	75	9	14	19	15	131	88
Europe and Central Asia	77	6	10	12	10	148	72
Latin America and Caribbean	75	9	15	20	16	175	92

(continued)

Table 2.6 Continued

Income Group/ Regions	Life Expectancy at Birth (Years)	Neonatal Mortality per 1,000 Live Births	Infant Mortality per 1,000 Live Births	Male Younger Than Age 5 Years Mortality Rate per 1,000 Live Births	Female Younger Than Age 5 Years Mortality Rate per 1,000 Live Births	Adult Male Mortality Rate per 1,000	Adult Female Mortality Rate per 1,000
Middle East and North Africa	73	13	20	25	22	146	96
North America	79	4	5	7	6	131	78
South Asia	68	30	42	52	53	207	141
Sub-Saharan Africa	59	29	56	89	78	328	285

Source: World Bank (2017).

measure of health outcome, including life expectancy and infant mortality, is worst in low-income regions and improves significantly with income groups. Similarly, across geographic regions, poorer regions such as South Asia and sub-Saharan Africa perform much worse in these health outcomes compared to wealthier regions such as Europe and North America. Male–female disparities in health outcome also tend to be more pronounced in lower income regions compared to higher income regions.

Globalization of Health Care

As demonstrated previously, significant variations remain across broad income groups and regions with regard to economic strength, population, and health care systems. These variations create strong forces for trade and migration that, provided barriers to these flows are low, could make the new wave of globalization the great equalizing wave in health care. This section discusses the trade in medical goods and services and the migration of health professionals.

Trade Flows of Medical Goods and Services

Global trade in all goods and services increased from $6.5 trillion in 2000 to $16 trillion in 2015, as measured by the value of imports. Table 2.7 shows the trend in imports and exports for the world and for different regions. The difference between exports and imports measures the trade surplus. North Africa and sub-Saharan Africa and South Asia regions continue to remain small participants in the global trade flow, but their trade has tripled. Although trade flows from Asia Pacific, Europe, and North America doubled, they had the largest growth in trade deficits, which often leads to calls for greater protectionism in these countries. East Asia, which includes China, experienced the largest growth in trade surplus during this time.

Trade in medical goods includes a wide range of products from gauze to medical instruments, X-ray and other equipment, and pharmaceutical goods. During the new wave of globalization, growth in trade in medical goods has far exceeded growth in overall trade.

Exports of medical instruments (including veterinary) increased from $29.8 billion in 2001 to $103.3 billion in 2015. The United States, Germany,

Table 2.7 Merchandise Trade by Region (Million US $)

Region	Flow	2000	2007	2010	2015
World	Imports	6,517,591	14,038,778	15,157,516	16,437,144
	Exports	6,356,764	13,797,305	15,106,213	10,500,297
Asia Pacific	Imports	461,429	808,813	917,455	885,053
	Exports	567,030	883,403	1,014,394	846,699
Europe	Imports	2,533,380	5,596,213	5,353,780	5,261,330
	Exports	2,515,992	5,500,085	5,322,817	5,470,381
North America	Imports	1,499,277	2,403,320	2,363,824	2,742,898
	Exports	1,058,904	1,569,011	1,666,503	1,914,487
North Africa	Imports	46,956	112,469	161,273	186,267
	Exports	49,815	153,521	104,438	99,915
Sub-Saharan Africa	Imports	78,692	245,562	290,870	337,864
	Exports	93,394	279,469	341,385	349,061
Latin America	Imports	349,220	682,856	805,164	951,006
	Exports	344,523	735,051	839,766	877,651
East Asia	Imports	742,209	1,909,513	2,521,545	2,892,694
	Exports	748,292	2,185,425	2,717,456	2,568,653
South Asia	Imports	94,740	343,079	505,555	519,985
	Exports	91,012	271,120	373,614	397,551

Source: United Nations (2017).

and China were the top three exporting countries; the United States, Germany, and the Netherlands were the top three importing countries. Whereas higher income regions such as Europe and North America had a positive trade surplus, lower income regions such as sub-Saharan Africa and South Asia had trade deficits in medical instruments in 2015.

Exports of pharmaceutical products increased from $34.9 billion in 2001 to $186.8 billion in 2015. Pharmaceutical products are among the most traded commodities in the world, accounting for more than 1% of total world exports. Switzerland, Germany, and the United States were the top exporters in 2015; the United States, Germany, and Belgium were the top importers. In 2015, Europe had the largest surplus in pharmaceutical products, whereas Latin America and the Caribbean region had the largest

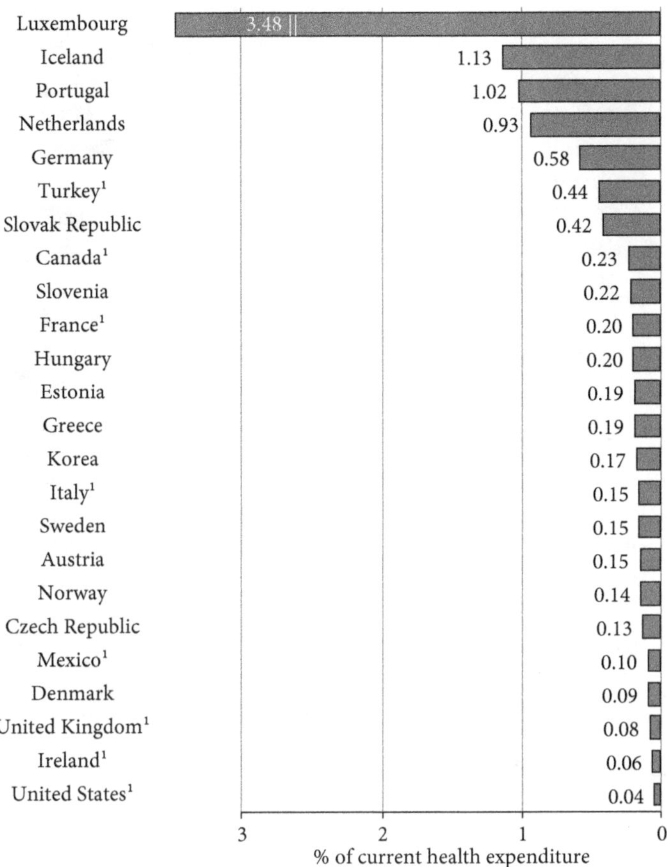

Figure 2.1 Imports of health services.
Source: OECD (2017).

trade deficit. China and Singapore are among the top exporters and India is among the top importers of pharmaceutical products.

The recent phenomenon of medical tourism refers to residents from one country seeking medical care in another country. Although data on this phenomenon are only beginning to be collected, an increasing number of residents of Organisation for Economic Co-operation and Development (OECD) countries are seeking care in other countries in which medical facilities are available and care is less expensive, such as India, Mexico, and Thailand. Figures 2.1 and 2.2 show the import and export of medical travel (services) as percentages of current or total health

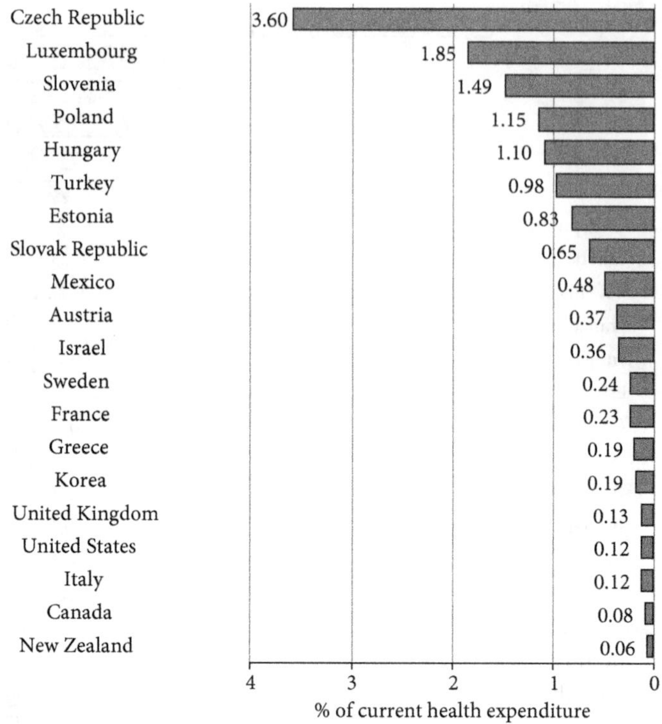

Figure 2.2 Exports of health services.
Source: OECD (2017).

expenditures for 2011 for OECD countries. Small countries within the OECD, such as Luxemburg and Iceland, tend to have higher levels of imports (residents traveling abroad for medical care), whereas former Soviet Bloc countries, such as the Czech Republic and Poland, tend to have high levels of exports (foreign residents traveling to other countries for medical care). Imports of health care travel services as a share of real health expenditures in the United States grew at an annual rate of 12.1% between 2006 and 2011. Exports of health care travel services for the United States grew as well at an annual rate of 4.4% during the same time frame. Although the phenomenon of medical tourism accounts for less than 1% of THE in most countries, its share is projected to increase rapidly as cost differentials create the push to seek less expensive care across borders.

Medical Labor Flows

Throughout this new wave of globalization, the world has been facing a growing shortage of skilled health care professionals. This problem is most acute in developed economies, which not only have a high demand for medical care due to their aging populations but also face a severe shortfall in available skilled workers, again due to their aging populations. In OECD countries, 5.9% of nurses are foreign trained, with New Zealand (24%) and Switzerland (19%) having the highest shares. Similarly, foreign-trained doctors account for 17% of all doctors in OECD countries, with Ireland (58%) and New Zealand (43%) having the highest shares of foreign-trained doctors. The United Kingdom and the United States have higher shares of foreign-trained medical professionals compared to the OECD average. Figures 2.3 and 2.4 show the main countries of origin for foreign-trained nurses in the United Kingdom and foreign-trained doctors in the United States as an example. As can be seen from the figures, foreign-trained nurses in the United Kingdom are predominantly from lower income Asian countries, including the Philippines and India, whereas doctors trained in India and Pakistan have the dominant shares. The share of foreign-trained doctors in the United States again is dominated by lower income countries from South Asia, such as India. The current wave of globalization has also

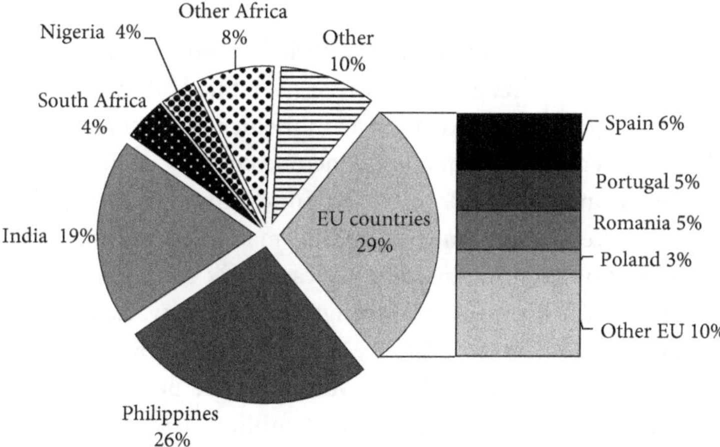

Figure 2.3 Foreign-trained nurses, United Kingdom, 2014.
Source: OECD (2015).

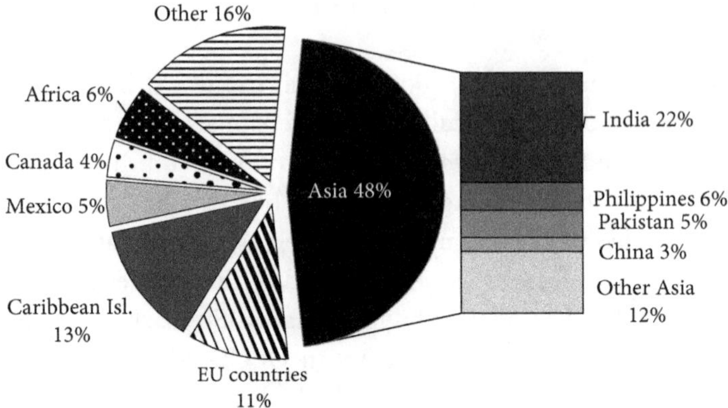

Figure 2.4 Foreign-trained doctors, United States, 2014.
Source: OECD (2015).

been witness to a reverse flow, with doctors in India and Thailand who were trained in Western medical schools returning to their home countries to cater to a higher income clientele in their own countries as well as medical tourists from higher income countries.

Technology in Medical Globalization

The role of both medical technology and information technology in the current wave of globalization cannot be overstated. Previously, I noted the exponential growth in global trade in medical instruments. A visit to a hospital or a health clinic in a high-income country such as the United States exposes one to a wide range of innovative medical technology, from magnetic resonance imaging (MRI) machines to robotic surgery. The availability of such technology varies widely throughout the world and is often tied to the economic strength of a country. According to the World Health Organization (WHO; 2014, 2017c), in many countries in Africa, less than 0.1 MRI machines were available per 1 million people in 2013 compared to more than 10 per 1 million people in many countries in Europe and North America. The world has also been transformed through information technology. The internet provides access to the best medical information and health care providers, even in rural areas and lower income regions. However, throughout the world, disparities exist in access to the internet and its cost. Table 2.8 indicates that in 2015,

Table 2.8 Access to Information and Communications Technology

Income Group/ Regions	Households with a Computer (%)	Individuals Using the Internet (% of Population)	Broadband Internet Subscription per 100 People	Broadband Internet Subscription Cost per Month ($)
	2015	2015	2015	2013
Low income	4.8	9.5	0.31	45
Lower middle income	19.3	28.6	1.86	16
Upper middle income	48.7	52.1	15.41	17
High income	83.2	81	30.97	27
World	44.9	44	11.34	22
East Asia and Pacific	47.7	49.8	15.76	22
Europe and Central Asia	76.3	71.7	24.71	20
Latin America and Caribbean	47	54.5	10.53	20
Middle East and North Africa	49.8	43.7	7.13	19
North America	87.1	75.9	32.02	39
South Asia	13.8	23.6	1.39	6
Sub-Saharan Africa	10	22.4	0.54	41

Source: World Bank (2017).

only 4.8% of the population in low-income countries had a computer compared to 83% in high-income countries. Similarly, less than 10% of the population used the internet in low-income countries compared to more than 80% in high-income countries. The cost of internet access was highest at $45 per month for low-income countries, whereas lower middle-income countries had the lowest cost at $16 per month. Across geographic regions, the same pattern emerges, with sub-Saharan Africa having the least access to the internet. The success of this wave of globalization in eradicating poverty and reducing disparities in health care throughout the world may well rest on access to the information technology revolution.

Conclusion

The economic facets of globalization are centered on the three engines of global trade in goods and services; global flow of people; and technological changes, especially in information technology. This chapter described some of the characteristics of the current or new wave of globalization that began in the last two decades of the 20th century and continues today. As noted by the International Monetary Fund (2002), what is unique about the current wave is the rapid emergence of countries such as China and some former Soviet Bloc countries, in addition to increasing interactions between developing economies. This chapter discussed some of the key trends and characteristics of this new wave of globalization, especially as it pertains to the provision of health care. Although this wave of globalization has improved the health and well-being of nations, more could be achieved in addressing disparities within countries.

References

Chapman, K. S., & Hariharan, G. (1994). Controlling for causality in the link from income to mortality. *Journal of Risk and Uncertainty, 8*(1), 85–94.

Frenk, J. (2010). Globalization of health and health services. *The Journal.* Winter 19–22.

Huynen, M. M., Martens, P., & Hilderink, H. B. (2005). The health impacts of globalization: A conceptual framework. *Globalization and Health, 1*(1), 14.

International Monetary Fund. (2002, March). *Globalization: A framework for IMF involvement.* IMF Issues Brief. Retrieved from https://www.imf.org/external/np/exr/ib/2002/031502.htm

International Organization for Migration, United Nations Migration Agency. (2015). *2015 Global migration trends factsheet.* Retrieved from https://publications.iom.int/system/files/global_migration_trends_2015_factsheet.pdf

McKeown, A. (2004). Global migration, 1846–1970. *Journal of World History, 15*(2), 155–189.

Organisation for Economic Co-operation and Development. (2015). *Health statistics*. Retrieved from http://www.oecd-ilibrary.org/social-issues-migration-health/data/oecd-health-statistics_health-data-en

Organisation for Economic Co-operation and Development. (2017). *Eurostat trade in services database*. Retrieved from https://data.oecd.org/trade/trade-in-goods-and-services.htm

Ortiz-Ospina, E., Beltekian, D., & Roser, M. (2014). Trade and Globalization. *Our World in Data, 1*(1), e21062. Retrieved from https://ourworldindata.org/international-trade

United Nations. (2017). *Comtrade*. Retrieved from https://comtrade.un.org/data

World Bank. (2016). *Development goals in an era of demographic change*. Global Monitoring Report 2015/2016. Washington, DC: Author.

World Bank. (2017). *World development indicators*. Retrieved from http://data.worldbank.org/indicator

World Health Organization. (2014). *Medical equipment: Magnetic resonance imaging (MRI) units per million population*. Retrieved from http://www.who.int/diagnostic_imaging/collaboration/mripermill_14.jpg

World Health Organization. (2017a). *Global health observatory data base*. Retrieved from http://apps.who.int/gho/athena/data/GHO/WHS9_86,WHS9_88,WHS9_89,WHS9_92,WHS9_96,WHS9_97,WHS9_90?filter=COUNTRY:-;WORLDBANKINCOMEGROUP:*&format=xml&profile=excel

World Health Organization. (2017b). *Global health expenditure database*. Retrieved from https://apps.who.int/nha

World Health Organization. (2017c). *Global health observatory data base*. Retrieved from http://apps.who.int/gho/athena/data/GHO/DEVICES08,DEVICES09,DEVICES10,DEVICES11,DEVICES12,DEVICES21,DEVICES22,DEVICES23?filter=COUNTRY:*;REGION:*&format=xml&profile=excel

3

Transnational Health Care

Tomas Mainil and Sabina Stan

What Is Transnationalism in Health Care

How can transnationalism in health care be defined? It is certain that in the contemporary world, many patients, medical professionals, organizations, and governments are looking beyond national borders to explore options to access health care services. As such, every movement across national borders seeking to provide or receive health care is transnational. When you are transcending the national health system and its borders, you are performing a transnational action. Ormond and Sulianti (2017) position international medical travel as a social force with transformative capacity. And indeed, transnational dynamics more generally change the lifeworld of patients and health workers who engage in cross-border health care.

If the health system of Romania is of lesser observed quality than its Hungarian counterpart, the resulting patient mobility (Kovacs, Szocska, & Knai, 2014) will change the lives of cross-border patients but also have a transformative impact on both health systems. This raises the question of equity of access: Not every Romanian patient is able to cross the border to receive better health services. Traveling for medical procedures also incorporates bio-value (Whittaker & Leng, 2016). When patients travel and improve their health, this raises the economic value of their bodies in their countries of residence. And transnational spaces and flows also challenge concepts of citizenship (Ong, 2006).

Transnationalism has been defined as sustained linkages between people, places, and institutions across the borders of nation states (Faist, 2010; Pordié, 2013). In transnational health care, these linkages are formed through the transnational flows of patients and health care providers, but also of technologies, information, and policies. Taking into consideration these flows does not mean discarding the nation state but, rather, considering new territorial assemblages regarding health issues and thus introducing what Bochaton (2013) calls a new transnational health care paradigm.

This paradigm covers not only medical tourists and migrant health care workers but also transnational families (Baldassar, 2007), where transnational care ties develop among migrants, aiding grandparents and their grandchildren overseas. According to Stan (2015), transnational health care practices can also lead to inequalities and marketization. This poses the issue of which governmental bodies should evaluate these processes within the transnational spaces. Even some analysts have viewed transnationalism as being "globalization from below" (Guarnizo & Smith, 1998); one can counter-argue that most of the dynamics in transnational health care are, in essence, informed not so much by grassroots and democratic logics as by contemporary neoliberal transformations.

In this chapter, we discuss transnational health on three levels. On the micro-level, we discuss the fact that patients are increasingly going abroad for health care. We also note that medical professionals are increasingly working abroad. On a meso-level, we trace the influence of transnational health organizations. On a macro-level, we highlight the role of governments in this global arena. Finally, we present a case study of the European Union (EU) as a transnational health care space.

Transnationalism and Patients

There is a vast diversity in the pathways followed by transnational patients and in their motivations to travel abroad for health care. At the core, patients need to be willing to travel abroad. This willingness has increased because of the changing landscape of international travel, availability of information, and marketing of health care services.

Medical travel contradicts the fact that health care is generally and originally marked by its high degree of localism (Exworthy & Peckham, 2015). Evidence of such movement, however, has become increasingly conspicuous during the past decade. For example, in Thailand, 104,830 medical tourists visited five private hospitals in 2010 (Noree, Hanefeld, & Smith, 2014). A recent UK study (Hanefeld & Horsfall, 2015) on bariatric surgery found out that transnational patients are more likely to be viewed as medical migrants rather than just tourists. Other authors are planning to study the ethics of medical tourism. Patients may be unaware of safety concerns, given their lack of familiarity with the destination health system and language or cultural barriers to adequate communication with health care workers (Penney, Snyder, Crooks, & Johnston, 2011). However, these patients may also sometimes benefit from more or less formal networks providing information and recommendations on specific providers (Hanefeld, Lunt, Smith, & Horsfall, 2015). This is confirmed by a Canadian qualitative study (Johnston, Crooks, & Snyder, 2012) in which the majority of participants sought advice from other medical tourists. The study also highlighted the importance of the reputation of the surgeon and the facility as opposed to the characteristics of the destination.

Transnationalism and Medical Professionals

The mobility of health professionals is part of a global agenda, following the World Health Organization's (WHO) 2010 code of conduct. In 2006, WHO estimated that 57 countries, 36 of which were in Africa, were facing severe shortages in trained health personnel. Health professionals' mobility impacts the performance of health systems by changing the composition of the health workforce in both sending and receiving countries (Glinos, 2014). According to Hardy, Shelley, Calveley, Kubisa, and Zahn (2016), financial incentives induce the migration of health workers not only from low- to high-income economies but also from weak to strong core economies and from weak to strong peripheral economies.

For source countries, health care worker migration entails financial costs related to the education and training of the health workforce, and it leads to gaps in service delivery and access. The phenomenon of brain drain can be regarded as an economic cost because emigrants usually take with them the value of their training sponsored by the country of origin (Kalipeni, Semu, & Asalele Mbilizi, 2012). In the Philippines, for example, a nursing degree became a popular option for many students due to the perceived high demand for nurses in many developed countries (Taguinod, 2013). After decades of Global South to Global North nurse migration, new sources of oil wealth in the Middle East have created new circuits of South to South health professional migration (Walton-Roberts, 2015). Of course, the receiving countries benefit from these professional migrations because they achieve important savings in training and education costs (Martineau, Decker, & Bundred, 2004).

Transnationalism and Organizations

Brown and Barnett (2004) note that

> the dynamics behind the growth of the corporate hospital sector in Australia are: increased access to international and domestic capital and shifts in investment, the emergence of corporate managerialism with the introduction of private sector management techniques and information systems; and changes to the mode of regulation and role of the state. (p. 332)

In our view, these dynamics are even stronger when they become transnational.

Hospitals worldwide have developed strategies to attract transnational patients. These strategies have been accompanied by the rising privatization of hospitals. Privatization often entails the development of corporate hospital chains. According to Connell (2015a), Asia hosts a number of private international hospital chains, such as Singapore-based Parkway Holdings. Also, Fortis Healthcare has 75 hospitals in 11 countries, and it has been linked with Parkway since 2010, when it purchased a stake in Parkway. Hospitals have also become more transnational due to Global North and Global South connections, as demonstrated by the Singapore and Dubai branches of the Johns Hopkins University hospital.

Sometimes hospitals are transformed into health "theme parks" (Lefebvre, 2008), with linkages to hotels. In Thailand, some private hospitals advertise a mix of medical procedures and recreational activities (Bochaton, 2013). According to Lunt, Horsfall, and Hanefeld (2016), some large international hospitals aim to integrate services by offering financing, travel, accommodations, full concierge, tours, translation services, and aftercare. This approach mimics the growth of supermarkets with expansion into additional retail and services.

Transnationalism and Governments

Some countries, such as the Philippines, have developed active policies to build a migration regime whereby health care professionals are trained mostly for export (Taguinod, 2013). Many others have developed national strategies to attract transnational patients. For example, Thailand, Malaysia, and South Africa have developed strategies to increase their services for transnational patients. Since 2003, the Thai government has attempted to make Thailand a global center for medical tourism by developing the Asia Initiative, a center of excellence in health care (Pachanee, C. A., & Wibulpolprasert, S., 2006). Malaysia is also among the most recognized international medical tourism destinations (Ormond, 2013). However, approximately 95% of patients in private hospitals aimed at medical tourists are national patients (Ormond and Sulianti, 2017). These results illustrate the myth and relative weight of the medical tourism industry.

South Africa is generally viewed as a medical tourism destination for cosmetic surgery (Crush, Chikanda, Sanders, & Maswikwa, 2015). However, the country is in fact much more active in attracting "medically disenfranchised" patients from neighboring countries who seek to access basic health care that is unavailable or inaccessible in their own countries. Between 2006 and 2012, an estimated 2.8 million individuals traveled to South Africa to obtain health care. Similar travel to countries such as Malaysia and Thailand also occurred, suggesting the importance of inter-regional medical tourism (Ormond & Sulianti, 2017). Countries such as Malaysia, Thailand, Singapore, South Korea, and Taiwan are investing in the development of medical tourism, and they view it as an economic engine for increasing national income (Ormond & Mainil, 2015). Finally, evidence of Libyan patient flows to Tunisia (Rouland, Fleuret, & Jarraya, 2016) shows the existence of transnational care networks and bottom-up globalization processes that are not driven by governmental policies.

Europe as a Transnational Health Care Space

Health care in Europe is viewed as traditionally being informed by the principle of universal access to services in particular national jurisdictions, which translates to the public and/or nonprofit delivery of services and strong involvement of national states in their regulation and funding (Maarse, 2006). Since the fall of the Berlin Wall in 1989, EU integration has both preserved and challenged the strong link between health care, public delivery, and nation states in Europe. Indeed, the principle of "subsidiarity" of past decades' EU treaties sought to keep health care policy under national rather than EU jurisdiction. However, during the same period, the increasingly economic, rather than social and political, nature of European integration (Greer, Jarman, & Baeten, 2016, p. 264) led to the extension of the common European market and the attendant transnational mobility of people, goods, services, and capital into new geographical, economic, and social spaces. Despite the Lisbon Treaty explicitly excluding health care from free movement stipulations (and thus, at least in theory, from the extension of the European common market to the sector), Europe has experienced the gradual convergence of rather diverse national health care systems toward health care services in which private actors and interests (including transnational ones) play an increasingly significant role (André & Hermann, 2009; European Foundation for the Improvement of Living and Working Conditions, 2011; Hassenteufel, Delaye, Pierru, Robelet, & Serré, 2000; Maarse, 2006; Pavolini & Guillen, 2013; Schmid, Cacace, Gotze, & Rothgang, 2010).

An important process that underlies the transnationalization of European health care—namely the diffusion, in Europe and worldwide, of a neoliberal health care governance model seeking to make health care services more market-like than public-sector-like—makes this articulation clear. In central and eastern Europe (CEE), the diffusion of the new model has been conducted through transnational policy-making networks with nodes situated in supranational actors such as the European Commission (EC), international financial organizations (e.g., the World Bank and the International Monetary Fund), or international nongovernmental organizations (e.g., Transparency International; Deacon & Stubbs, 2007; Stan, 2007). In EU-15 countries, the higher participation of native experts in the diffusion of the neoliberal governance model has also been reflected in their relatively greater importance in the transnational networks mobilized in the process (Stamati & Baeten, 2015). Finally, Marinsen and Vrangbaek (2008) note that "the EU has [had] an increasing impact on the organization and governance instruments of national health care" through a rising "Europeanized health care model" (p. 169). Rooted, especially since the 2008 financial crisis, in "the EU fiscal governance framework, [and] reinforced by the threat of central bank and market responses" (Greer et al., 2016, p. 278; see also Erne, 2015), the resulting European policy regime is "more about markets than about individual or aggregate health outcomes" (Greer & Jarman, 2012, p. 260) and has encoded budget austerity goals in EU laws and institutions (Legido-Quigley & Greer, 2016, p. 205).

In general, the involvement of the EU as "an extra, albeit thin, layer in organizing, financing and providing healthcare" has led to a "European healthcare union . . . in the making" (Vollaard, van de Bovenkamp, & Martinsen, 2016, p. 171). Indeed, health care is "produced, consumed, and provided across the internal borders of the EU," and member states (MS) can draw on common EU health care-related institutions, regulations, and financing (Vollaard et al., 2016, p. 171). In the area of cross-border care, examples are legislation on cross-border patient mobility and the recognition of professional qualifications, as well as recently developed institutional designs such as the network of national contact points for information on access and reimbursement for cross-border care in the EU (EC, 2015) or European Reference Networks for rare diseases.

The diffusion of a neoliberal health care governance model throughout Europe can be viewed as an instance of the transnationalization of health care policy. The process has been uneven because the model has been introduced at different moments, paces, and degrees, and it has involved different sets of elements in various national health care services. However, it has permitted the growth of a lucrative market for the corporate, for-profit provision of health care services (Lethbridge, 2013, p. 14).

Significantly, the process of marketization of health care has been accompanied by the rise in importance and consolidation of a number of European and non-European "health care multinationals" (André & Hermann, 2009; Lethbridge, 2013). Notable examples in the area of health care provision are Capio (based in Sweden and active in several EU countries), Medicover (a Swedish company active in CEE; Lethbridge, 2013, p. 16), and US-owned corporations such as Pacific Health Corporation (already present in 2009 with 56 hospitals in Germany) and Universal Health Services (already owned 14 hospitals in France in 2009) (Smith, Chanda, & Tangcharoensathien, 2009, p. 596).

Several companies active in health care belong to investment funds (Lethbridge, 2013, p. 25) because private equity investors have become increasingly attracted by "the historically high returns of the health-care market [in Europe]—many deals now fetching 10×" (British Private Equity and Venture Capital Association, 2013, p. 5). Another indication of the transnationalization of European health care provision is the rise in the international accreditation of health care organizations on the continent. Of the 329 international accreditations made by Joint Commission International (JCI) between 1999 and 2011, 67 (20%) were to hospitals or clinics located in the EU (Woodhead, 2013, p. 697). By 2016, the number of health care organizations accredited by JCI in the EU had increased to 142, which represents a 112% increase compared to 2011 (JCI, 2016).

In the past two decades, the increasing transnationalization of health care policy and provision has also been accompanied by a parallel internationalization (or transnationalization) of higher level health care professional training, especially in the field of medicine. An increasing number of higher level institutions throughout Europe have started offering medicine and nursing programs in non-national languages, most frequently English but also, albeit more rarely, French. In 2016, European University Central Application Support Services, which caters to students searching for cross-border higher level training in English in Europe, listed 160 health studies programs (16% of the total 988 programs offered by the platform) spread across 18 countries throughout the continent.

However, not only are health care policies, services, and students increasingly crossing borders in Europe but also health care workers have increasingly done so in the past decade. The transnationalization of the health care workforce has been most intense in EU-15 countries, although some CEE MS are also following suite (Maier et al., 2011). By the end of the first decade of this century, seven EU-15 countries registered very high (>20% of the total medical workforce: Ireland and the United Kingdom) and high (10–20%: Belgium, Portugal, Spain, Austria, and Sweden) reliance on foreign medical doctors (Maier et al., 2011, p. 26), with one EU-11 country registering very high reliance (23%: Slovenia; p. 27).

Whereas in some EU-15 countries (e.g., the United Kingdom and Spain), non-EU workers have been traditionally dominant among foreign health care workers, flows of EU health care workers, especially from the eastern areas of the continent, have started to grow in importance in the past few decades (Maier et al., 2011, pp. 35, 43). Mobility of doctors among neighboring MS has also increased in the past few years (Maier et al., 2011, pp. 35, 39). As a result, by 2010, a number of EU-15 countries (Austria, Belgium, France, Germany, and Italy) as well as Slovenia received their foreign health care professionals predominantly from the EU (Maier et al., 2011, pp. 37–38). Moreover, the share of medical doctors from other EU countries in the UK medical workforce rose from 6% in 1998 (Maier et al., 2011, p. 39) to 10.8% in 2016 (General Medical Council, 2016) following the intensification of inflows from the EU during the 2008 financial crisis (Hardy, Calveley, Shelley, & Zahn, 2012, p. 26).

In parallel with the rising transnationalization of health care in areas of policy, provision, training, and workforce during the past decade or so, intra-European cross-border patient mobility also increased. This followed more particularly the formulation of new citizenship rights and the development of new health care-related markets in the EU (Mainil, 2012). In addition, health insurers and providers in several EU MS have started to conclude bilateral arrangements on patient mobility (van Ginneken & Busse, 2011, pp. 317–318) and have also been increasingly drawn into cross-border collaborations in e-health and telemedicine (Footman, Knai, Baeten, Glonti, & McKee, 2014). According to the Special Eurobarometer 425 (EC, 2015, p. 4), the percentage of EU residents who received medical treatment in another MS increased from 4% of the total population in 2007 to 5% in 2014. The development of European legislation and bilateral agreements on cross-border care led to an intensification of frontier cross-border patient mobility (e.g., Benelux) but also to increasing flows of east–west and north–south citizenship-based cross-border mobilities (EC, 2015; Pacolet & de Wispelaere 2014a, 2014b).

At the same time, an already existent health and medical tourism industry expanded its infrastructure and geographical outreach, attracting private patients both to established high-class medical centers in western and northern Europe (Connell, 2015b) and also, increasingly, to a developing pool of internationally oriented medical facilities in southern, central, and eastern Europe (Issenberg, 2016). Finally, transnationally mobile Europeans working, studying, and living in another EU MS (and most notably in northern and western Europe, where intra-European migration is concentrated) have displayed strong preferences for recourse to health care services in their countries of origins (Favell, 2008; Migge & Gilmartin, 2011; Osipovic, 2013; Stan, 2015, 2016).

Conclusion

Several complementary, but not necessarily always opposing, processes drive the transnationalization of health care in Europe. The EU has developed legislation and initiatives that foster the transnationalization of health care based on citizenship rights and members states' commitment to the public/nonprofit provision of health care. Significantly, the rising marketization of health care has been triggered by the transnationalization of health care policy, by the extension of the single market to new sectors, and by the increasing cost pressures on health care policy following the 2008 financial crisis. In all these processes, the EU has played an important role, making the union an actor that fosters both citizenship and market-based health care transnationalization on the continent. However, although free movement of people is under significant pressure in the EU following the UK referendum on Brexit and the refugee crisis, the larger forces that drive the transnationalization of health care on the continent are here to stay. Although transnational forces are also present in other regions throughout the world, the EU can be perceived as an engine for the sustainable development of transnational health policiess.

References

André, C., & Hermann, C. (2009). Privatization and marketisation of health care systems in Europe. In M. Frangakis, C. Hermann, J. Huffschmid, & K. Lóránt (Eds.), *Privatization against the European social model: A critique of European policies and proposals for alternative* (pp. 129–144). London, UK: Palgrave Macmillan.

Baldassar, L. (2007). Transnational families and aged care: The mobility of care and the migrancy of ageing. *Journal of Ethnic and Migration Studies, 33*(2), 275–297.

Bochaton, A. (2013). The rise of a transnational healthcare paradigm: Thai hospitals at the crossroads of new patient flows. *European Journal of Transnational Studies, 5*(1), 54–80.

British Private Equity and Venture Capital Association. (2013). *Guide to investing in European healthcare.* Retrieved from https://www.bvca.co.uk/portals/0/library/documents/bvca%20guide%20to%20investing%20in%20european%20healthcare.pdf

Brown, L., & Barnett, J. R. (2004). Is the corporate transformation of hospitals creating a new hybrid health care space? A case study of the impact of co-location of public and private hospitals in Australia. *Social Science & Medicine, 58*, 427–444.

Connell, J. (2015a). From medical tourism to transnational health care? An epilogue for the future. *Social Science and Medicine, 124*, 398–401.

Connell, J. (2015b). Transnational health care: Global markets and local marginalization in medical tourism. In P. Parry, B. Greenhough, T. Brown, &

I. Dyck (Eds.), *Bodies across borders: The global circulation of body parts, medical tourists and professionals* (pp. 75–93). Farnham, UK: Ashgate.

Crush, J., Chikanda, A., Sanders, D., & Maswikwa, B. (2015). The rise of medical tourism to South Africa. In J. Hanefeld, D. Horsfall, & N. Lunt (Eds.), *Handbook on medical tourism and patient mobility* (pp. 323–331). Cheltenham, UK: Elgar.

Deacon, B., & Stubbs, P. (2007). *Social policy and international interventions in south east Europe.* Cheltenham, UK: Elgar.

Erne, R. (2015) A supranational regime that nationalizes social conflict: Explaining European trade unions' difficulties in politicizing European economic governance. *Labor History, 56*(3), 345–368.

European Commission. (2015). *Commission report on the operation of Directive 2011/24/EU on the application of patients' rights in cross-border healthcare.* Retrieved from https://ec.europa.eu/health/sites/health/files/cross_border_care/docs/2015_operation_report_dir201124eu_en.pdf

European Foundation for the Improvement of Living and Working Conditions. (2011). *Employment and industrial relations in the healthcare sector.* Retrieved from http://www.eurofound.europa.eu/eiro/studies/tn1008022s/tn1008022s.htm

European University Central Application Support Services. (2016). *Health sciences programs.* Retrieved from http://eunicas.ie/index.php/eunicas/search.html?discipline=82&ordering=&searchphrase=all&searchword=

Exworthy, M., & Peckham, S. (2015). Patients' willingness to travel. In J. Hanefeld, D. Horsfall, & N. Lunt (Eds.), *Handbook on medical tourism and patient mobility* (pp. 45–56). Cheltenham, UK: Elgar.

Faist, T. (2010). Towards transnational studies: World theories, transnationalization and changing institutions. *Journal of Ethnic and Migration Studies, 36*(10), 1665–1687.

Favell, A. (2008). *Eurostars and Eurocities: Free movement and mobility in an integrating Europe.* Oxford, UK: Blackwell.

Footman, K., Knai, C., Baeten, R., Glonti, K., & McKee, M. (2014). *Cross-border health care in Europe.* Geneva, Switzerland: World Health Organization, European Observatory on Health Systems and Policies.

General Medical Council. (2016). *List of registered medical practitioners—Statistics.* Retrieved from https://www.gmc-uk.org/doctors/register/search_stats.asp

Glinos, I. A. (2014). The possible effects of health professional mobility on access to care for patients. In R. Levaggi & M. Montefiori (Eds.), *Health care provision and patient mobility* (Developments in Health Economics and Public Policy No. 12). (pp. 67–80). New York, NY: Springer.

Greer, S., & Jarman, H. (2012). Managing risks in EU health services policy: Spot markets, legal certainty and bureaucratic resistance. *Journal of European Social Policy, 22*(3), 259–272.

Greer, S., Jarman, H., & Baeten, R. (2016). The new political economy of healthcare in the European Union: The impact of fiscal governance. *International Journal of Health Services, 46*(2), 262–282.

Guarnizo, E., & Smith, M. P. (1998). The locations of transnationalism. In M. P. Smith & E. Guarnizo (Eds.), *Transnationalism from below* (Comparative Urban and Community Research Vol. 6). (pp. 3–34). New Brunswick, NJ: Transaction Publishers.

Hanefeld, J., & Horsfall, D. (2015). Journey without end: Travelling overseas for bariatric surgery—A qualitative study of UK patients travelling for bariatric surgery. In J. Hanefeld, D. Horsfall, & N. Lunt (Eds.), *Handbook on medical tourism and patient mobility* (pp. 431–440). Cheltenham, UK: Elgar.

Hanefeld, J., Lunt, N., Smith, R., & Horsfall, D. (2015). Why do medical tourists travel to where they do? The role of networks in determining medical travel. *Social Science & Medicine, 124*, 356–363.

Hardy, J., Calveley, M., Shelley, S., & Zahn, R. (2012). *Opportunities and challenges related to cross border mobility and recruitment of the healthcare workforce.* European Public Services Union. Retrieved from http://www.epsu.org/sites/default/files/article/files/EPSU-Report-Migration-Health-Workers-Final-Version_Appendices-EN.pdf

Hardy, J., Shelley, S., Calveley, M., Kubisa, J., & Zahn, R. (2016). Scaling the mobility of health workers in an enlarged Europe: An open political–economy perspective. *European Urban and Regional Studies, 23*(4), 798–815.

Hassenteufel, P., Delaye, S., Pierru, F., Robelet, M., & Serré, M. (2000). La libéralisation des systèmes de protection maladie européens. Convergence, Européanisation et adaptations nationales. *Politique Européenne, 2*, 29–48.

Issenberg, S. (2016). *Outpatients: The astonishing new world of medical tourism.* New York, NY: Columbia Global Report.

Johnston, R., Crooks, V. A., & Snyder, J. (2012). "I didn't even know what I was looking for": A qualitative study of the decision-making processes of Canadian medical tourists. *Globalization and Health, 8*, 23.

Joint Commission International. (2016). *JCI-accredited organizations.* Retrieved from https://www.jointcommissioninternational.org

Kalipeni, E., Semu, L. L., & Asalele Mbilizi, M. (2012). The brain drain of health care professionals from sub-Saharan Africa: A geographic perspective. *Progress in Development Studies, 12*(2–3), 153–171.

Kovacs, E., Szocska, G., & Knai, C. (2014). International patients on operation vacation—Perspectives of patients travelling to Hungary for orthopaedic treatments. *International Journal of Health Policy and Management, 3,* 333–340. doi:10.15171/ijhpm.2014.113.

Lefebvre, B. (2008): The Indian corporate hospitals: Touching middle class lives. In C. Jaffrelot & P. van der Veer (Eds.), *Patterns of middle class consumption in India and China* (pp. 88–109). Thousand Oaks, CA: Sage.

Legido-Quigley, H., & Greer, S. (2016). Austerity, health and the Eurozone. *International Journal of Health Services, 46*(2), 203–207.

Lethbridge, J. (2013). *Expansion and consolidation? Major trends and eligibility for European Work Councils.* Greenwich, UK: European Federation of Public Service Unions, Public Services International Research Unit. Retrieved from http://www.psiru.org/reports/expansion-and-consolidation-major-trends-and-eligibility-european-works-councils.html

Lunt, N., Horsfall, D., & Hanefeld, J. (2016). Medical tourism: A snapshot of evidence on treatment abroad. *Maturitas, 88,* 37–44.

Maarse, H. (2006). The privatization of health care in Europe: An eight-country analysis. *Journal of Health Politics, Policy and Law, 31*(5), 981–1014.

Maier, C., Glinos, I., Wismar, M., Bremner, J., Dussault, G., & Figueras, J. (2011). Cross-country analysis of health professional mobility in Europe: The results. In M. Wismar, C. Maier, I. Glinos, G. Dussault, & J. Figueras (Eds.), *Health professional mobility and health systems: Evidence from 17 European countries.* (pp. 23–66). Copenhagen, Denmark: European Observatory on Health Systems and Policies.

Mainil, T. (2012). *Transnational healthcare and medical tourism: Understanding 21st century patient mobility—Towards a rationale of transnational health region development.* PhD thesis, NHTV Breda University of Applied Sciences, University of Antwerp, Belgium.

Marinsen, D. S., & Vrangbaek, K. (2008). The Europeanisation of health care governance: Implementing the market imperatives in Europe. *Public Administration, 86*(1), 169–184.

Martineau, T., Decker, K., & Bundred, P. (2004). "Brain drain" of health professionals: From rhetoric to responsible action. *Health Policy, 70,* 1–10.

Migge, B., & Gilmartin, M. (2011). Migrants and healthcare: Investigating patient mobility in Ireland. *Health and Place, 17*(5), 1144–1149.

Noree, T., Hanefeld, J., & Smith, R. (2014). UK medical tourists in Thailand: They are not who you think they are. *Global Health, 10*, 29. doi:10.1186/1744-8603-10-29.

Ong, A. (2006). *Neoliberalism as exception.* Durham, NC: Duke University Press.

Ormond, M. (2013). *Neoliberal governance and international medical travel in Malaysia.* London, UK: Routledge.

Ormond, M., & Mainil, T. (2015). Government and governance strategies in medical tourism. In J. Hanefeld, D. Horsfall, & N. Lunt (Eds.), *Handbook on medical tourism and patient mobility* (pp. 154–163). Cheltenham, UK: Elgar.

Ormond, M., & Sulianti, D. (2017). More than medical tourism: Lessons from Indonesia and Malaysia on South–South intra-regional medical travel. *Current Issues in Tourism, 20*(1), 94–110. http://dx.doi.org/10.1080/13683500.2014.937324

Osipovic, D. (2013). "If I get ill, it's onto the plane, and off to Poland": Use of health care services by Polish migrants in London. *Central and Eastern European Migration Review, 2*(2), 98–114.

Pachanee, C. A., & Wibulpolprasert, S. (2006). Incoherent policies on universal coverage of health insurance and promotion of international trade in health services in Thailand. *Health Policy & Planning, 21*(4), 310–318.

Pacolet, J., and de Wispelaere, F. (2014a). *Planned cross-border care: PD S2 questionnaire.* Brussels, Belgium: European Commission, Network Statistics FMSSFE.

Pacolet, J., & de Wispelaere, F. (2014b). *The European health insurance card: EHIC questionnaire.* Brussels, Belgium: European Commission, Network Statistics FMSSFE.

Pavolini, E., & Guillen, A. (2013). *Health care systems in Europe under austerity institutional reforms and performance.* London, UK: Palgrave Macmillan.

Penney, K., Snyder, J., Crooks, V. A., & Johnston, R. (2011). Risk communication and informed consent in the medical tourism industry: A thematic content analysis of Canadian broker websites. *BMC Medical Ethics, 12*, 17. doi:10.1186/1472-6939-12-17.

Pordié, L. (2013). Spaces of connectivity, shifting temporality: Enquiries in transnational health. *European Journal of Transnational Studies, 5*(1), 6–26.

Rouland, B., Fleuret, S., & Jarraya, M. (2016, June). *Emergence of a transnational care network: Private services and Libyan migrants in Sfax, Tunisia.* Paper presented at the academic conference IMTJ summit. Retrieved from

https://www.researchgate.net/profile/Sebastien_Fleuret/publication/
309770580_DU_TOURISME_MEDICAL_A_LA_MISE_EN_PLACE_
D'UN_ESPACE_DE_SOINS_TRANSNATIONAL_L'EXEMPLE_DES_
PATIENTS_LIBYENS_A_SFAX_TUNISIE/links/5822dd0f08aeb45b5886acfa/
DU-TOURISME-MEDICAL-A-LA-MISE-EN-PLACE-DUN-ESPACE-DE-
SOINS-TRANSNATIONAL-LEXEMPLE-DES-PATIENTS-LIBYENS-A-
SFAX-TUNISIE.pdf

Schmid, A., Cacace, M., Gotze, R., & Rothgang, H. (2010). Explaining health care system change: Problem pressure and the emergence of "hybrid" health care systems. *Journal of Health Politics, Policy and Law, 35*(4), 455–486.

Smith, R., Chanda, R., & Tangcharoensathien, V. (2009). Trade in health-related services. *Lancet, 373*(9663), 593–601.

Stamati, F., & Baeten, R. (2015). Varieties of healthcare reform: Understanding EU leverage. In N. Natali & B. Vanhercke (Eds.), *Social policy in the European Union: State of play 2015—Sixteenth annual report* (pp. 183–214). Brussels, Belgium: European Trade Union Institute, OSE.

Stan, S. (2007). Transparency: Seeing, counting and experiencing the system. *Anthropologica, 49*(2), 257–273.

Stan, S. (2015). Transnational healthcare practices of Romanian migrants in Ireland: Inequalities of access and the privatization of healthcare services in Europe. *Social Science and Medicine, 124*, 346–355.

Stan, S. (2016). *Transnational patient mobility and healthcare mobilities and governance processes in Europe: Towards a rising European healthcare system?* Paper presented at the IMTJ academic conference "Medical tourism: Time for a check-up?" Madrid, Spain, May 25–26.

Taguinod, F. (2013). *Licensed to care: Inhabiting the transnational economy of "global pinoy."* PhD thesis, Dublin Institute of Technology, Dublin, Ireland. Retrieved from http://arrow.dit.ie/appadoc/38

van Ginniken, E., & Busse, R. (2011). Cross-border health care data. In M. Wismar, W. Palm, J. FiguerasK. Ernst, & E. van Ginneken (Eds.), *Cross-border healthcare in the European Union: Mapping and analysing practices and policies* (pp. 287–344). Geneva, Switzerland: World Health Organization, European Observatory on Health Systems and Policies.

Vollaard, H., van de Bovenkamp, H., & Martinsen, D. (2016). The making of a European healthcare union: A federalist perspective. *Journal of European Public Policy, 23*(2), 157–176.

Walton-Roberts, M. (2015). International migration of health professionals and the marketization and privatization of health education in India: From push–pull to global political economy. *Social Science & Medicine, 124*, 374–382.

Whittaker, A., & Leng, C. H. (2016). Flexible bio-citizenship and international medical travel: Transnational mobilities for care in Asia. *International Sociology, 31*(3), 286–304. doi:10.1177/0268580916629623

Woodhead, A. (2013). Scoping medical tourism and international hospital accreditation growth. *International Journal of Health Care Quality Assurance, 26*(8), 688–702.

World Health Organization. (2006). *World health report 2006: Working together for health.* Geneva, Switzerland: Author.

World Health Organization. (2010). *WHO global code of practice on the international recruitment of health personnel* (63rd World Health Assembly, WHA63.16). Geneva, Switzerland: Author. Retrieved from https://www.who.int/hrh/migration/code/code_en.pdf?ua=1

4

Health Care Social Work in the United States

Ren Winnett

Introduction

The US health care system is a study in contrasts, conflict—and potential. Complicated and criticized, it has reached a crossroads whose most advantageous route is not yet charted. As the nation considers this evolving system, social workers' ethical beliefs, values, and perspectives strongly suggest a capacity to positively influence health care in the years to come.

Currently, US health care social workers find themselves adjusting to dramatically shifting political contexts—and the possibility of wholesale systemic change. Given these circumstances, it is reasonable to consider the profession's history, particularly within health care, as well as the social and political context in which US health care social work exists. A review of contemporary US health care social work practice and discussion of emerging trends and potential future issues are also warranted.

Social Work in the United States

America is a nation of impressive scale. The geographic footprint of its 50 states encompasses 3,531,905 square miles and contains approximately 323,127,513 people (US Census Bureau, n.d.).

Upon this broad landscape, Americans' perspectives regarding social welfare have evolved in complex ways. Although many efforts to recognize and address social, health, and economic needs have been made, opinions regarding how best to do so have varied widely. Ambrosino, Heffernan, Shuttlesworth, and Ambrosino (2001) note that public welfare in the United States has had a checkered past and faces an unpredictable future. With the ebb and flow of the economic cycle and the vacillation between liberal and conservative political stances, establishing a firmly embedded system of provisions for the needs of the poor, disenfranchised, people with physical and mental disabilities, and others at risk has historically been problematic. (p. 4)

During the nation's development, the influence of Elizabethan Poor Law, the Puritan work ethic, successive waves of immigration, and burgeoning urbanization all joined other phenomena in impacting perspectives regarding the nature and limits of social welfare (Ambrosino et al., 2001). Federal intervention during the Great Depression, as well as the civil rights movement, women's movement, and welfare rights movement, also affected (and reflected) evolving perceptions about social welfare and social justice and marked attempts to apply these new perspectives to pressing issues—often in the face of great resistance (Morales, Sheafor, & Scott, 2007). These events, and many others, also influenced social workers' perspectives regarding professional practice.

Today, the profession of social work is growing. From an estimated 649,300 social work jobs in 2014, the US Department of Labor (USDL) reports projected job growth through 2024 of 12%, or 74,800 new positions—a rate it terms "faster than average" (n.d.).

In the United States, social workers can be found in many places. Berg-Weger (2013) notes that these include schools, hospitals, psychiatric facilities, and programs for older adults and children—as well as corporations, the military, and law enforcement agencies. In such settings, social workers frequently conduct assessments, offer resources, provide case management services, determine client concerns and needs, provide counseling, supervise programs and people, participate in policy and program development and implementation, assist in community organizing, and participate in research (Berg-Weger, 2013).

Preparation for social work practice in the United States occurs in Council on Social Work Education (CSWE)-accredited academic programs. In a review of social work education, CSWE (2016) identified 503 accredited undergraduate programs and 242 accredited graduate programs, with total enrollments of 62,968 and 60,122 students, respectively. In the same report, a total of 77 practice and research-focused doctoral programs were identified as admitting 470 students during the 2014–2015 academic year. The total number of awarded US social work degrees during this period was 45,837, of which 42.8% were undergraduate, 56.5% were master's, and 0.8% were doctoral (CSWE, 2016).

Registration and licensing of social work practitioners are managed at the state level. Social workers can also pursue national accreditation through the Academy of Certified Social Workers (ACSW) and join numerous advocacy and interest groups to advance the work of the profession. The National Association of Social Workers (NASW) is the profession's largest organization and the publisher of its code of ethics (NASW, 2008).

The History of Health Care Social Work in the United States

Medical social work is recognized as the profession's first subspecialty. Its development in the United States was influenced by the public health and social reform movements of the late 1800s (Allen & Spitzer, 2016a). Its English predecessor, hospital almoning, addressed the nonmedical needs of patients and focused on reducing crowded hospital conditions (Gehlert, 2012). Early medical social work was similarly tasked (Reisch, 2012) but also emphasized "the importance [of] medical institutions [taking] into account both the individual and his or her environment" (Stuart, 2004, p. 17).

In the early 1900s, social workers in the United States were utilized to "help connect the client's environmental system with the hospital where care was rendered" (Dziegielewski, 2004, p. 50). The arrival of social workers in health care settings at this time is attributed to Massachusetts physician Richard Cabot, MD, who recognized the effect of psychosocial circumstances on the health of immigrant patients at his clinic and in 1905 hired Garnet Pelton and, soon after, Ida Maud Cannon to support his efforts to incorporate social medicine into patient care (Gehlert, 2012). Cannon's career subsequently spanned 39 years and greatly advanced the profession's growing role within health care.

Between 1905 and the late 1930s, social workers' presence in health care settings increased. By 1924, the total number of hospital social work departments in the United States had grown to 420—and by 1929, several university social work programs offered specialized curricula in medical social work to prepare students entering the field (Allen & Spitzer, 2016a).

By the late 1930s, hospital-based social work had grown exponentially to include more than 1,600 departments, and many university social work programs included medical social work training (Reisch, 2012).

During this period, additional developments influenced the role of US social workers in health care settings. The profession's identity and direction were both affected by the popularity of psychiatric social work (Cowles, 2003); increasing assignment of social workers to interdisciplinary, physician-led teams; and the growing use of group work (Reisch, 2012).

The growth of the profession was not painless. Among other challenges, Abraham Flexnor's 1915 assertion that social work was not a profession because it lacked a science-based body of knowledge and focused more on modification of client's environments, consultation, and the provision of referrals than on direct intervention created widespread distress among social workers (Cowles, 2003). However, Dziegielewski (2004) notes that Flexnor's comments ultimately "prompted social workers to try and clearly define what they did and the role they played among the helping professions" (p. 52).

In subsequent decades, important changes in American society and health care also influenced social work practice in medical environments. Reisch (2012) observes that "from the 1930s through the 1970s, the development of the U.S. welfare state played an important role in the evolution of hospital social work" (p. 878). Widespread construction of community hospitals under the Hill–Burton Act of 1940 and substantial expansion of access to medical care through Medicare and Medicaid in 1965 both significantly supported the profession's growth (Judd & Sheffield, 2010).

Reich (2012) states that by the mid-1970s, social workers were increasingly tasked with achieving productivity and outcome goals. As health care costs soared, this expectation intensified with the introduction of diagnosis-related groups (DRGs) in 1983 and continued pressure to contain costs (Judd & Sheffield, 2010).

In the 1990s, the increasing expense of health care continued to impact social workers as scores of US health systems underwent "reengineering" (Judd & Sheffield, 2010). Many systems eliminated social work departments entirely and assigned social workers to hospital units. This effectively reduced social work supervisory positions and minimized the profession's influence (Reich, 2012). The transdisciplinary approach that emerged during this period further diminished social workers' roles by increasing role competition with other disciplines at the same time an absence of evidence-based practice standards weakened the profession's authority (Reich, 2012).

Gehlert (2012) notes that throughout this period, health maintenance organizations (HMOs) restricted the social worker's ability to practice independently and DRGs limited the time available for intervention with patients. These imposed constraints on practice eventually encouraged the development of new techniques for intervention in time-restricted settings, such as task-centered work (Gehlert, 2012). Increased social work involvement with longer surviving, chronically ill patients also suggested new opportunities for service provision (Gehlert, 2012).

In 2010, the Patient Protection and Affordable Care Act (ACA) altered the context of health care social work provision in the United States. The ACA offered eligible individuals new health insurance protections, expanded eligibility, and altered the circumstances under which the nation's most vulnerable and disenfranchised could receive care. In addition, the ACA called for "collaboration across disciplines to meet patient-centered objectives" (Maramaldi et al., 2014, p. 534).

The Social and Political Context of Health Care Social Work in the United States

Perceptions regarding social welfare and health care have vacillated throughout American history and reveal important differences in the way individual autonomy and the role of government are viewed. To a large extent, these differences have remained unreconciled, leading Darnell and Lawlor (2012) to note that enactment of the ACA followed almost a century of political struggle and incremental social movement both toward and away from universal health care coverage. In years past, endorsements of such coverage were offered by Presidents Roosevelt, Truman, and Nixon, with later consideration also made by President Carter, Senator Mitchell, President Clinton, and President Obama. In each case, the concept of universal, publicly funded health services proved untenable for reasons involving political circumstance, special interest advocacy, and popular resistance (Darnell & Lawlor, 2012).

Darnell and Lawlor (2012) state that "the American approach to healthcare delivery is an especially complicated mixture of public, nonprofit, and for-profit entities" (p. 102) that collectively form a $2.5 trillion industry and politically oriented economy—and whose self-interests and advocacy broadly affect politics and decision-making. The absence of bipartisan agreement on the issue has ensured repeated political readjustment of funding, oversight, eligibility, and priorities.

The consequences of the US health care system's current structure are social inequity, treatment inefficiency, and mounting cost. Lynch, Greeno, Teich, and Delaney (2016) state that the United States spends 17.1% of its gross domestic product on health care—the highest level of any advanced country examined and 50% more than the next highest spending nation—yet achieves only middling results from this commitment, ranking below the mean on 15 of 25 health quality metrics. At the same time, Fairfax and Feit (2015) argue that the US health care industry is inherently racist and "promulgates health, while maintaining barriers to equalizing experiences, treatment, prevention, and relationships" (p. 411). Stipp (2015) observes that "there are deep inequities in health outcomes between the United States and its neighbor nations, and between U.S. groups" (p. 368).

Despite the previously mentioned challenges, progress has been made toward achieving a more equitable and effective health care system. In 2006, a bipartisan bill in Massachusetts launched a new state health care plan. The number of uninsured in the state subsequently dropped to 2.9% of the population, and the law became the model on which the ACA was based (Darnell & Lawlor, 2012).

When enacted, the ACA substantively altered the US health care system by requiring most individuals to possess insurance, protecting individuals with preexisting conditions, regulating rates, and controlling market practices (Darnell & Lawlor, 2012). The ACA placed emphasis on primary care as a means of addressing health care "costs, access, quality, and accountability problems" (Darnell & Lawlor, 2012, p. 113). It also created opportunities for the formation of accountable care organizations (ACOs) to serve the health care needs of specific groups in incentive-focused contracts. Since inception of the ACA, the total number of uninsured individuals in the United States has dropped dramatically from a peak of 50 million in 2013. Left unchanged, the law was projected to further reduce the number of uninsured individuals to 23 million by 2019 (Darnell & Lawlor, 2012). However, funding stabilization and market support efforts were also widely acknowledged as necessary to maintain the ACA's viability. In the years following President Obama's departure from office, debate about the future of the ACA has intensified.

Although the ACA did not create universal health care coverage nor end service inequities or access challenges, especially for disenfranchised populations (Mitchell, 2015), the law's emphasis on prevention and health promotion operationalized efforts to understand patients and their environments. This emphasis on understanding patients' psychosocial circumstances created new opportunities for social work leadership (Stanhope, Tennille, Bohrman, & Hamovitch, 2016). Such opportunities are particularly apparent regarding integrated primary health care clinics, where the ACA incentivized inclusion of substance abuse and behavioral health treatment in primary health care settings as a way of achieving less partitioned, more effective holistic care (Stanhope, Videka, Thorning, & McKay, 2015).

Today, American political discourse on health care remains partisan—and volatile. Recent changes in Medicare reimbursement guidelines have increased pressure on health systems and threatened their sustainability if performance targets are not met. These changes, when combined with continued political debate about the direction of health services, mean the nation's health care system will continue to evolve, perhaps radically. In the coming years, political, social, and economic circumstances will continue to drive review and revision of US health care in potentially far-reaching ways. Whether the nation turns more seriously toward consideration of a single-payer system or, instead, maintains its existing multi-payer system and either reduces services and protections or strengthens and stabilizes the ACA is not yet clear.

Health Care Social Work in the United States Today

In its recent "Occupational Employment Statistics" breakdown for health care social work, the USDL (2017) indicates that those employed in the position

> provide individuals, families, and groups with the psychosocial support needed to cope with chronic, acute, or terminal illnesses. Services include advising family care givers, providing patient education and counseling, and making referrals for other services . . . [health care social workers also] provide care and case management or interventions designed to promote health, prevent disease, and address barriers to access to healthcare.

In the same report, the USDL determined that approximately 159,310 individuals are employed as health care social workers nationally. Settings with the highest levels of employed health care social workers are identified as general medical and surgical hospitals (47,180), individual and family services (19,030), home health care services (18,930), nursing care facilities (15,530), and outpatient care centers (10,860).

In terms of distribution, social workers can be found in most segments of the US health care system. Allen and Ruffolo (2016) note the growing emphasis within health care on whole-person care, "including wellness and preventative counseling as well as acute and chronic care" (p. 69), and state that social workers' capacity for supporting the social and emotional needs of patients and families across the continuum of care is increasingly recognized. Specifically, they detail widespread "movement toward a system of health services that recognizes the importance of a whole-person perspective [and that] supports the manner in which social workers utilize multi-system, ecological, person-in-environment interventions" (p. 70).

Regarding social work-supported health care settings, Browne (2012) notes that direct services are commonly provided in public and private hospitals, clinics, health centers, physician practices, mobile care units, skilled nursing facilities, schools, military settings, correctional facilities, HMOs, centers for care of specific conditions (e.g., dialysis centers and HIV/AIDS centers), as well as other organizations addressing health issues. Social workers are also involved in many indirect health care-related services and organizations, including program and policy-planning teams at the local, state, and national levels; various community organizations; and government and research institutions (Browne, 2012).

Currently, US health care social work differs across practice settings. However, a number of useful descriptions of the profession's responsibilities exist. Allen and Spitzer (2016b, p. 120) identify the following "core characteristics and functions of healthcare social workers":

1. Preadmission assessments or high-risk screening upon admission

2. Patient/family psychosocial evaluation

3. Crisis intervention (emergency room, critical care, or other emergent situations)

4. Short-term supportive counseling for health condition/treatment adjustment

5. Longer range counseling (post-hospitalization; clinic or office-based)

6. Post-hospitalization care planning (case management)

7. Patient/family advocacy with other health team members/community agencies

8. Patient/family education regarding condition, adjustment issues, and care plan

9. Information/resource referral for immediate and post-hospitalization care needs

10. Collaboration/education with other health care providers regarding patient and family adjustment issues, home conditions affecting ongoing care, and available versus needed ongoing care resources

11. Research continuously enhancing practice and positive patient outcomes

When examining the allocation of time and energy afforded to different social work functions in US health care settings, the nature and purpose of the setting should be considered. Although many positions involve a relatively high commitment to psychosocial assessment and clinical intervention, other settings may assign priority to very different functions. In their study of contemporary social work roles in hospital settings in the aftermath of health care reengineering in the 1990s, Judd and Sheffield (2010) found relatively high emphasis on discharge planning; less emphasis on direct practice; and very low emphasis on bioethics, evidence-based practice, and income-generating projects.

Another useful description of health care social work roles was developed by considering the nature of the work rather than the specific tasks performed (Craig & Muskat, 2013). In this study, several descriptive themes were defined by interviewed social workers, including the roles of "bouncer" (controlling access when individuals act out), "janitor" (correcting errant situations and issues), "glue" (holding things together for patients, families, and teams), and "broker" (facilitating communication between stakeholders). Respondents also confirmed the roles of "firefighter" (crisis-responder), "juggler" (wearer of several hats, often simultaneously), and "challenger" (patient advocate).

An additional method of conceptualizing current US health care social work practice involves examining the relative duration of interventions with patients and families. Although this characteristic will also vary with setting and circumstance, it is common for health care social work to involve single-session practice. Gibbons and Plath (2006) note that despite the fact that this intervention format is widely utilized in fast-paced health care environments and "potentially encapsulate[s] social work at its highest level of skill" (p. 31), it is not well represented in the literature and is oddly minimized in terms of importance. Gibbons and Plath detail the potential of single-session intervention for reaching patients during a "window of opportunity" (p. 32) that might otherwise be lost.

Consideration of current US health care social work functions also necessitates awareness of social workers' increasing employment as patient navigators. Patient navigation is not a new role but, rather, an increasingly important position requiring both recognition of immediate patient needs and support of the patient's journey across a wide spectrum of experiences. Browne, Darnell, Savage, and Brown (2015) note that "the primary purpose of patient navigation is to eliminate the barriers that vulnerable patients encounter in the timely diagnosis and treatment of medical conditions" (p. 158). Desrosiers, Mallinger, and Bragg-Underwood (2016) similarly argue that although patient navigators do not necessarily have to be social workers, social workers utilize an ethical framework, practice competency, and an emphasis on social justice and diversity that clearly render them a strong fit for this work.

In terms of the practice perspective and conceptual framework that US health care social workers utilize, it is difficult to overstate the importance of the profession's use of the person-in-environment (PIE) perspective. Social workers' consideration of individual and environmental interrelationships and their effect on functioning affords other members of health care teams a valuable means of incorporating relevant information into medical treatment. It is the social workers' incorporation of the PIE perspective—and related use of biopsychosocial (and spiritual) assessment—that supports recognition of social workers' unique capacity to assist in telling the patient's story. Browne (2012) notes that the biopsychosocial model "addresses the biological, social, environment, psychological, and behavioral aspects of illness . . . [and] expands the traditional medical model of disease" (p. 20).

While utilizing biopsychosocial assessment to understand patient circumstances, health care social workers in the United States apply two types of theory to conceptualize human behavior as it relates to health. First, orienting theories are not specific to health issues or to social work practice but, rather, provide a way for practitioners of different disciplines to examine a broad range of human problems and devise interventions to assist clients (Gehlert & Bollinger, 2012). Examples of orienting theories include systems theory and psychodynamic theory. Second, theories of health behavior are specific to topics of health and are not limited to understanding problems but can also be applied toward understanding positive phenomena (Gehlert & Bollinger, 2012). The two types of theories of health behavior are those that assume behavior is based on rational choice and those based on the assumed influence of an individual's social networks.

In the process of utilizing PIE, biopsychosocial assessment, and orienting theories or theories of health behavior, US health care social workers apply many different tools to address patient needs. These often include solution-focused intervention, cognitive–behavioral intervention, and crisis intervention (Dziegielewski, 2004). Another common therapeutic tool is motivational interviewing, which Stanhope, Tennille, Bohrman, and Hamovitch (2016) define as an "evidence-based practice that provides structure for collaborative conversations related to health behavior change" (p. 476). Additional tools include harm reduction, task-oriented therapeutic intervention, and narrative therapy.

The influence of the ACA on current health care social work in the United States has been substantial. Through the perspective of systems theory, McCovery and Matusitz (2014) argue that the importance of cooperation and collaboration among different professions and organizations in public health has never been more critical to achieving positive community results—skills that social workers are particularly capable of demonstrating. Spitzer, Silverman, and Allen (2015) note the increasing emphasis on "achieving patient care goals while demonstrating an appreciation for the mission, priorities, and operational constraints of the provider organization" (p. 193), given the ACA's emphasis on integrated, collaborative care. They term such care "profession-in-environment" and note that its achievement "enhances the recognition of social work as a crucial patient care component" (p. 193).

The ACA has affected the social work profession in many other ways. It has increased pressure on social workers to consistently achieve timely discharges while decreasing readmission rates (Linton, Ing, Vento, & Nakagawa, 2015). It has also mandated the integration of care that considers health, mental health, and social conditions and, in doing so, empowered the profession's use of the biopsychosocial perspective and encouraged its assumption of leadership responsibility (Mann et al., 2016). In the process, the ACA has spurred new research and models for examining ways to meets its goals. Such work has examined social work involvement in patient-centered medical homes and ACOs to drive improved health outcomes and meet patients' needs (Gehlert, Collins, Golden, & Horn, 2015).

Looking Forward: Emerging Trends and Future Challenges

American health care continues to evolve. The emotional turmoil associated with this process is characteristic of the visceral political and social animus dividing the country on multiple issues. As the nation grapples with its concerns about the role of health care—and the right of individuals to it—the questions of years past continue to ring present. Should health care be accessible to everyone? Is it a right? How can it be made more effective, equitable, and affordable?

Regardless of the ACA's effects on future health care provision in the United States—or the defining characteristics of coverage that a replacement provides—several aspects regarding the needs of tomorrow's patients are already known. Social workers' obligations to future populations will remain unchanged—as will the profession's opportunity to advocate for social justice and to demonstrate leadership. As Spitzer (2016) notes, escalating health care costs, increased numbers of aging consumers with increased needs for care, potential changes in public financing of health care, increased patient decision-making expectations, potentially greater numbers of insured Americans accessing care, and technological advances expanding how and where care is provided will all act to influence opportunities for social work practice in the future.

Currently, increased demand for social workers is already occurring in ambulatory settings, in which concepts such as the medical home and integrated care model are creating opportunities. Increased need for social workers is also anticipated in programs for aging adults (Henning-Smith, 2017), and expected growth in services such as palliative care will also create opportunities (Jones et al., 2014). The need for continued social work advocacy to address problematic social influences on health will grow, especially regarding diverse populations (Davis et al., 2015). Increased emphasis on the biological aspects of biopsychosocial assessment is likely (Levesque, 2016), and scientific advances will continue to compel social work intervention in new areas of care, such as genomics (Werner-Lin, McCoyd, Doyle, & Gehlert, 2016). As research continues to support the influence of nonmedical factors on individual health, demand for social work intervention will continue (Rowe, Rizzo, Vail, Kang, & Golden, 2017).

Conclusion

The US health care system continues to reflect, in complicated ways, the competing demographics, beliefs, and perspectives of Americans. As the nation grapples with the challenge of achieving a health care model that best reflects the values and interests of those it serves—and struggles with the inevitability of change as political and economic circumstances shift—an obligation and opportunity exist for social workers to truly make a difference. In the current period of incivility and inequity, social workers can assist in demonstrating that a better health care system is possible when patients and their environments are truly considered and compassionate, respectful care is provided with the understanding that inclusive services, rather than costing more, benefit us all.

References

Allen, K. M., & Ruffolo, M. (2016). Knowledge and theoretical foundations of healthcare social work practice. In K. M. Allen & W. J. Spitzer (Eds.), *Social work practice in healthcare: Advanced approaches and emerging trends* (pp. 69–94). Thousand Oaks, CA: Sage.

Allen, K. M., & Spitzer, W. J. (2016a). The historical and contemporary context for healthcare social work practice. In K. M. Allen & W. J. Spitzer (Eds.), *Social work practice in healthcare: Advanced approaches and emerging trends* (pp. 7–29). Thousand Oaks, CA: Sage.

Allen, K. M., & Spitzer, W. J. (2016b). Healthcare social work practice skills and competencies. In K. M. Allen & W. J. Spitzer (Eds.), *Social work practice in healthcare: Advanced approaches and emerging trends* (pp. 95–125). Thousand Oaks, CA: Sage.

Ambrosino, R., Heffernan, J., Shuttlesworth, G., & Ambrosino, R. (2001). *Social work and social welfare: An introduction* (4th ed.). Belmont, CA: Brooks/Cole.

Berg-Weger, M. (2013). *Social work and social welfare: An invitation* (3rd ed.). New York, NY: Routledge.

Browne, T. (2012). Social work roles and health care settings. In S. Gehlert & T. Browne (Eds.), *Handbook of health social work* (2nd ed., pp. 20–40). Hoboken, NJ: Wiley.

Browne, T., Darnell, J., Savage, T. E., & Brown, A. (2015, September). Social workers as patient navigators: A review of the literature. *Social Work Research,* *39*(3), 158–166. doi:10.1093/swr/svv017

Council on Social Work Education. (2016). *Annual statistics on social work education in the United States: 2015.* Retrieved from https://www.cswe.org/getattachment/992f629c-57cf-4a74-8201-1db7a6fa4667/2015-Statistics-on-Social-Work-Education.aspx

Cowles, L. A. F. (2003). *Social work in the health field: A care perspective* (2nd ed.). Binghamton, NY: Haworth.

Craig, S. L., & Muskat, B. (2013, February). Bouncers, brokers, and glue: The self-described roles of social workers in urban hospitals. *Health & Social Work, 38*(1), 7–16. doi:10.1093/hsw/hls064

Darnell, J. S., & Lawlor, E. F. (2012). Health policy and social work. In S. Gehlert & T. Browne (Eds.), *Handbook of health social work* (2nd ed., pp. 100–124). Hoboken, NJ: Wiley.

Davis, T. S., Guada, J., Reno, R., Peck, A., Evans, S., Sigal, L. M., & Swenson, S. (2015). Integrated and culturally relevant care: A model to prepare social workers for primary care behavioral health practice. *Social Work in Health Care, 54*(10), 909–938. doi:10.1080/00981389.2015.1062456

Desrosiers, P. L., Mallinger, G., & Bragg-Underwood, T. (2016, Fall). Promoting socially just healthcare systems: Social work's contribution to patient navigation. *Advances in Social Work, 17*(2), 187–202. doi:10.18060/18609

Dziegielewski, S. F. (2004). *The changing face of health care social work: Professional practice in managed behavioral health care* (2nd ed.). New York, NY: Springer.

Fairfax, C. N., & Feit, M. D. (2015). How policy improves health. *Social Work in Public Health, 30*(5), 410–422. doi:10.1080/19371918.2015.1034002

Gehlert, S. (2012). Conceptual underpinnings of social work in health care. In S. Gehlert & T. Browne (Eds.), *Handbook of health social work* (2nd ed., pp. 3–19). Hoboken, NJ: Wiley.

Gehlert, S., & Bollinger, S. E. (2012). Theories of health behavior. In S. Gehlert & T. Browne (Eds.), *Handbook of health social work* (2nd ed., pp. 125–139). Hoboken, NJ: Wiley.

Gehlert, S., Collins, S., Golden, R., & Horn, P. (2015, November). Social work participation in accountable care organizations under the Patient Protection and Affordable Care Act. *Health & Social Work, 40*(4), e142–e147. doi:10.1093/hsw/hlv054

Gibbons, J., & Plath, D. (2006). "Everybody puts a lot into it!" Single session contacts in hospital social work. *Social Work in Health Care, 42*(1), 17–34. doi:10.1300/J010v42n0102

Henning-Smith, C. (2017). Gerontological social workers are key to a sustainable long-term services and supports system. *Journal of Gerontological Social Work, 60*(3), 178–183. doi:10.1080/01634372.2016.1272520

Jones, B., Phillips, F., Head, B. A., Hedlund, S., Kalisiak, A., Zebrack, B., . . . Otis-Green, S. (2014). Enhancing collaborative leadership in palliative social work in oncology. *Journal of Social Work in End-of-Life & Palliative Care, 10*(4), 309–321. doi:10.1080/15524256.2014.975319

Judd, R. G., & Sheffield, S. (2010). Hospital social work: Contemporary roles and professional activities. *Social Work in Health Care, 49*(9), 856–871. doi:10.1080/00981389.2010.499825

Levesque, A. (2016). Alzheimer's disease and social work practice: Implications of advances in neurosciences for social workers. *Journal of Gerontological Social Work, 59*(2), 75–76. doi:10.1080/01634372.2016.1151472

Linton, K. F., Ing, M. M., Vento, M. A., & Nakagawa, K. (2015). From discharge planner to "concierge": Recommendations for hospital social work by clients with intracerebral hemorrhage. *Social Work in Public Health, 30*(6), 486–495. doi:10.1080/19371918.2015.1058730

Lynch, S., Greeno, C., Teich, J., & Delany, P. (2016). Opportunities for social work under the Affordable Care Act: A call for action. *Social Work in Health Care, 55*(9), 651–674. doi:10.1080/00981389.2016.1221871

Mann, C. C., Golden, J. H., Cronk, N. J., Gale, J. K., Hogan, T., & Washington, K. T. (2016, August). Social workers as behavioral health consultants in the primary care clinic. *Health & Social Work, 41*(3), 196–200. doi:10.1093/hsw/hlw027

Maramaldi, P., Sobran, A., Scheck, L., Cusato, N., Lee, I., White, E., & Cadet, T. J. (2014). Interdisciplinary medical social work: A working taxonomy. *Social Work in Health Care, 53*(6), 532–551. doi:10.1080/00981389.2014.905817

McCovery, J., & Matusitz, J. (2014). Assessment of collaboration in U.S. health care delivery: A perspective from systems theory. *Social Work in Public Health, 29*(5), 451–461. doi:10.1080/19371918.2013.865109

Mitchell, F. M. (2015, August). Racial and ethnic health disparities in an era of health care reform. *Health & Social Work, 40*(3), e66–e74. doi:10.1093/hsw/hlv038

Morales, A. T., Sheafor, B. W., & Scott, M. E. (2007). *Social work: A profession of many faces* (11th ed.). Boston, MA: Pearson.

National Association of Social Workers. (2008). *Code of ethics.* Washington, DC: NASW Press.

Reisch, M. (2012). The challenges of health care reform for hospital social work in the United States. *Social Work in Health Care, 51*(10), 873–893. doi:10.1080/00981389.2012.721492

Rowe, J. M., Rizzo, V. M., Vail, M. R., Kang, S., & Golden, R. (2017). The role of social workers in addressing nonmedical needs in primary health care. *Social Work in Health Care, 56*(6), 435–449. doi:10.1080/00981389.2017.1318799

Spitzer, W., Silverman, E., & Allen, K. (2015). From organizational awareness to organizational competency in health care social work: The importance of formulating a "profession-in-environment" fit. *Social Work in Health Care, 54*(3), 193–211. doi:10.1080/00981389.2014.990131

Spitzer, W. J. (2016). The future of healthcare and social work practice. In K. M. Allen & W. J. Spitzer (Eds.), *Social work practice in healthcare: Advanced approaches and emerging trends* (pp. 439–464). Thousand Oaks, CA: Sage.

Stanhope, V., Tennille, J., Bohrman, C., & Hamovitch, E. (2016). Motivational interviewing: Creating a leadership role for social work in the era of healthcare reform. *Social Work in Public Health, 31*(6), 474–480. doi:10.1080/19371918.2016.1160338

Stanhope, V., Videka, L., Thorning, H., & McKay, M. (2015). Moving toward integrated health: An opportunity for social work. *Social Work in Health Care, 54*(5), 383–407. doi:10.1080/00981389.2015.1025122

Stipp, K. F. (2015). A plain view of poor health in a land of plenty. *Social Work in Public Health, 30*(4), 360–372. doi:10.1080/19371918.2015.1024376

Stuart, P. H. (2004). Individualization and prevention: Richard C. Cabot and early medical social work. In A. Metteri, T. Kroger, A. Pohjola, & P. Rauhala (Eds.), *Social work approaches in health and mental health from around the globe* (pp. 7–20). Binghamton, NY: Haworth.

US Census Bureau. (n.d.). *QuickFacts Selected: United States.* Retrieved June 22, 2017, from https://www.census.gov/quickfacts/fact/table/US/PST045216

US Department of Labor, Bureau of Labor Statistics. (2017, March 31). *Occupational employment statistics: Occupational employment and wages, May 2016: 21-1022 healthcare social workers.* Retrieved June 22, 2017, from https://www.bls.gov/oes/current/oes211022.htm

US Department of Labor, Bureau of Labor Statistics. (n.d.). *Occupational outlook handbook, 2016–17 edition, social workers.* Retrieved June 22, 2017, from https://www.bls.gov/ooh/community-and-social-service/social-workers.htm

Werner-Lin, A., McCoyd, J. L., Doyle, M. H., & Gehlert, S. J. (2016, August). Leadership, literacy, and translational expertise in genomics: Challenges and opportunities for social work. *Health & Social Work, 41*(3), e52–e58. doi:10.1093/hsw/hlw022

SECTION 2
GLOBAL CASE STUDIES

5

The Role of Social Work in Australian Health Care Settings

Helen M. Cleak

Introduction

This chapter provides an overview of health social work in Australia, particularly within the hospital and community health context. Social work within the evolution of health care services has always played a unique role in bringing a holistic and client-centered lens to patients and their families in a wide variety of acute, subacute, and community contexts. Even in the face of economic constraints, health social workers have been able to make an important contribution to the medical and nursing team in order to facilitate a patient's timely and appropriate discharge from the hospital. In the community sector, health social workers have made important contributions to brokering appropriate services and as advocates for better access to a range of other resources.

Brief Overview of Social Work in Australia

Social work in health care in Australia was one of the first established fields of social work practice and followed the British model of employing almoners in hospitals. In fact, the push for formal training of social workers came from the medical profession, which perceived the need to train hospital almoners (Alston & McKinnon, 2005). This training starting simultaneously in Sydney and Melbourne in 1929 and was a joint venture between hospitals and universities that addressed practical tasks such as arranging convalescent care, assessing ability to pay for drugs or appliances, and learning about "tolerance and acceptance of patients from a different social class" (Miller, 2015, p. 138).

Early Australian social workers were trained on the British model, which emphasized the social causes of poverty, rather than the American focus on psychology, and they played a key role in shifting the welfare sector from the old charitable distinction between the deserving and the undeserving poor. Through this model of intervention, social workers have continued to bring a contextual perspective focused first on assessing and supporting the patient's strengths and individual coping strategies and then on finding appropriate support from family and the community. By the 1970s, Australian social work education and practice had moved away from the earlier casework focus on addressing individual deficits to the development of new skills, emphasizing the promotion of social change (Mendes, 2005).

Health social work has continued to dominate the professional fields of practice within social work, with approximately 60% of qualified social workers employed in the health field in Australia, in acute and subacute hospitals as well as in community health settings (Browne, 2005). Their roles have broadened beyond the immediate medical concerns of patients and into the broader ecological context and its impacts on health outcomes. The "person-in-environment" focus guided the social work role toward assessment of the patient's social situation and its interrelationships with others, assisting patients with issues related to chronic disease and disability, drug and alcohol abuse, terminal conditions, and mental health issues. Social workers also took on the role of educating patients, assisting in navigating the health care setting, and providing the link between the hospital and community sectors.

In recent years, the incursion of economic rationalism, which proposes that all economic decisions should focus on productivity, profit, and efficiency, has resulted in hospital social work departments being decentralized into program areas or managed by larger allied health groupings.

In addition, like other health professionals, social workers have been required to account for their service delivery, through reporting to government funding bodies, and to show how they meet targets and standards for service provision (Giles, 2013). Although the roles of health social workers are usually secondary to medical and nursing activities, social workers are viewed as essential members of the caring team and are now employed in less traditional areas, such as in general medical practices, private hospitals, palliative care centers, and genetic counseling services.

The Social Policies and Political Context Within Which Health Care Social Work Currently Exists

Health care is a fundamental need in any society, and a country's health care system exists within a complex sociopolitical context that affects its services and delivery. Australia's health care system has its origins in the UK model and is shaped by philosophies of equality and equity. It is very different from the US system, which is based on market-driven principles (Willis, Reynolds, & Keleher, 2012).

The Australian health care system is a mixture of public and private health care provision. Much of the publically funded health system is called Medicare, which was introduced in 1984. Medicare is a compulsory, universal health insurance scheme that is based on equal access for all Australian citizens and is funded by a progressive taxation levy, which means that those who earn more, pay more (Willis et al., 2012). Medicare offers free treatment in public hospitals as well as direct payment to primary care services such as general practitioners, medical specialists, and some allied health professionals, including mental health social workers. The federal government also subsidizes pharmaceuticals so that people can access affordable prescribed medicines.

Health is the second largest spending category for the Commonwealth government, and it is the largest category for all the state governments (Daley, 2013); it is approximately 9.7% of the gross national product. Australia, like most countries, is facing steadily increasing costs providing health care, which relies on a highly skilled and labor-intensive workforce as well as an increasing use of technology-dependent services (Browne, 2005). Much of the growth in health expenditures can be attributed to nondemographic factors such as the development of new technologies, pharmaceuticals, and diagnostic and treatment techniques, as well as community expectations of the health system (Australian Institute of Health and Welfare [AIHW], 2014).

During the past two decades, government reforms have been driven by an underlying philosophy of neoliberalism which suggested that the best way to manage an economy is to put it in the hands of the private sector rather than the public or government sector. Economic rationalism emerges from this approach, which prioritizes the attainment of economic goals over social concerns.

Despite targeted funding arrangements, Indigenous Australians generally have poorer health prospects and outcomes compared with non-Indigenous Australians. For example, the life expectancy for Indigenous boys born between 2010 and 2012 was 10.6 years lower than that for non-Indigenous boys, and 81% of Indigenous deaths occurred before the age of 65 years compared with 35% for non-Indigenous Australians. Indigenous Australians developed end-stage kidney disease at more than six times the rate of non-Indigenous Australians (95 per 100,000 compared with 14 per 100, respectively). In 2013–2014, Aboriginal and Torres Strait Islander people were hospitalized at greater than twice the rate of other Australians (AIHW, 2014).

The latest "Closing the Gap" report published in February 2017 by the Australian government shows that although there has been some improvement in education and health outcomes for Indigenous Australians, many of the targets are not on track to be met. For example, the target to halve the gap in child mortality by 2018 is on track, with Indigenous child death rates declining by 33% between 1998 and 2014, and immunization rates for Indigenous children are high. However, although total Indigenous mortality rates have declined, particularly from circulatory diseases (e.g., heart disease and stroke), the gap in life expectancy is still significant (Department of the Prime Minister and Cabinet, 2016).

Despite this, Australia has much to celebrate. According to international standards, the country has one of the highest life expectancies in the world, good mortality and morbidity rates, and is able to keep health costs down while maintaining high access to services (Browne, 2005).

Health workforce shortages are a worldwide phenomenon, and it has been recognized that the major threat to the Australian health system is a failure to have a sustainable and appropriately trained workforce to keep up with the increased demand for health care. Within social work, most of the workforce is female, and 14% are older than age 55 years (AIHW, 2009, p. 48). The government responded by establishing Health Workforce Australia in 2011 to facilitate increased enrollment of students in a range of health-related tertiary courses, including social work, and funding innovative clinical training models in health and mental health settings to increase clinical placement capacity (Buchanan, Jenkins, & Scott, 2014).

Health Care/Medical Social Work in Australia

Australia's health landscape is characterized by significant growth in the aging population, increased longevity rates, an explosion in chronic illness, and rapidly increasing costs of health care, which together contribute to current and future challenges for health social work. This section discusses the role of social work in critical hospital functions such as discharge planning, its role in the complex and chronic care delivery process, the challenge of changing medical priorities, mental health provision, bioethical issues, and primary care.

Hospitals play an important role in providing health services to Australians and have become increasingly busy and complex organizations throughout the decades. Social workers perform a range of activities in hospitals, such as psychosocial assessment, education, discharge planning, advocacy, counseling, case conferencing, crisis intervention, and community outreach. In addition, social workers use their expertise in enhancing the well-being of their patients through programs such as rehabilitation and subacute care, which includes palliative care support and group work for specific types of illnesses. In 2016, a special edition of the journal of the Australian Association of Social Workers (AASW) showcased a range of health social worker roles in a variety of settings. One article described how renal social workers support people with end-stage kidney disease—a life-threatening chronic disease—who are either on dialysis or awaiting a transplant. The role of the renal social workers was extensive, but their "top responses" were general psychosocial support, carer support, advocacy, general crisis and end-of-life counseling, as well as finding temporary and permanent accommodation (AASW, 2016).

Discharge Planning

Governments manage their health budgets on a "casemix" funding model whereby all costs associated with each inpatient "episode," or admission, are calculated (Cleak, 2002). This classification groups episodes with similar clinical conditions and similar use of hospital resources using information in the hospital records, such as diagnoses, procedures, and age of the patient. The average length of stay for different diagnostic groups is regarded as an indicator of the efficiency of hospitals and has become the focus of social work activity (AIHW, 2009).

Most studies throughout the world as well as in Australia report that discharge planning continues to be a key social work activity, which is based on a psychosocial assessment of the patient's situation and post-hospital support needs (Cleak & Turczynski, 2014; Judd & Sheffield, 2010; McAlynn & McLaughlin, 2008). The process of discharge planning includes early identification and assessment of patients likely to require services, coordinating the multidisciplinary health care team's discharge-related activities and resources necessary for post-hospital care, and providing information to patients and families to assist them in selecting and applying for services and follow-up of discharged patients (Soskolne et al., 2010). Social workers perceive that community issues such as insufficient resources in the patient's environment, lack of formal carers in the community, and length of time required to negotiate with appropriate services negatively impact on the discharge planning process. Effective discharge planning is akin to good case management in that it requires relationship-building skills as well as persistence and follow-through to achieve patient goals and enhance systems. Nonetheless, in the hospital context, in which bureaucratic systems and hierarchical relations mediate the exercise of professional autonomy, assertiveness and patient advocacy by social workers can be difficult (Giles, Gould, Hart, & Swancott, 2007).

Complexity and Chronicity

The elderly are overrepresented in the hospital system and are often considered "long stayers" due to the complexity and chronicity of their medical conditions and the inadequacy of the service system, in which their care needs exceed available resources. However, the relationship between aging and demand for health services is complex, and the extent to which the current growth in health expenditure can be attributed to population aging is the subject of much debate. However, increasing patient complexity, increasing numbers of patients with chronic health problems, and the emergence of risk assessment to minimize poor outcomes for the organization as well as the patient have led to social workers spending increasing amounts of time in negotiation and conflict resolution with patients, their families, and the health care system. The case complexity associated with serious medical conditions, along with an array of chronic social issues, can result in extended hospital stays, which can be further complicated by uncertainty regarding prognosis and the influence of existing or acquired disability on people's potential to resume their previous lifestyle (Redfern, Burton, Lonne, & Seiffert, 2016). In addition, the range of available community services does not always meet these complex needs; consequently, their discharge needs and level of post-hospital support is high, often necessitating long hospital stays. Others are discharged without the required level of support, placing them at risk of failed discharge and readmission (Cleak & Turczynski, 2014).

Dementia and cognitive decline are also strongly associated with nursing home discharges, and social workers report spending more time managing patients' complex legal and financial issues, including applications for administration and guardianship orders (Cleak & Turczynski, 2014). A study undertaken in one urban Australian hospital (Davis, Baldry, Milosevic, & Walsh, 2004) found that more patients received direct services of assessment, counseling, and liaison than discharge planning. A follow-up study by the same authors (Davis et al., 2004) showed that psychosocial assessment was the most common task performed. Another Australian study examining subacute services asked social workers to identify the cases that they considered to be complex (McAlinden, McDermott, & Morris, 2013). The results highlighted five key interrelated themes defining complexity: multiple competing demands, uncertainty, patient and family characteristics, pending breakdown, and systems challenges. It was found that these cases included difficult and challenging patient situations, in which decisions were unclear; complicated family and patient characteristics; and cases in which family and/or care system breakdown was imminent or had occurred (McAlinden et al., 2013).

The Role of Social Work Within Changing Medical Priorities

In addition to the major challenge presented by the complex needs of an aging population, evolving medical technologies and increased consumer expectations have necessitated health social workers to respond to a range of additional psychosocial needs that have been generated by these developments. This section discusses reproductive technology as an example, but the issues raised as well as the role of social work could easily be ascribed to other areas, such as organ transplantation, genetic testing, and some oncology diagnoses that stretch the boundaries of life and death and the legal definitions of father and mother.

The Issue

Infertility and its treatment are stressful and disruptive for women and their partners who are trying to have children. Assisted reproductive technology, although offering the hope of a successful pregnancy, can be emotionally as well as financially costly. The stigma of infertility, the demands of assisted reproductive technologies, the use of artificial insemination by donors, and the trauma of repetitive losses culminate to amplify the biopsychosocial issues for this group.

The Social Work Response

Infertility is one of the "newer" health diagnoses for approximately 9% of Australian women and has become an emerging setting for perinatal social workers. Social workers, with their holistic approach to health and understanding of the treatment process, work as members of a team to educate and help couples define their choices at each stage in the assessment and treatment, which can contribute to their sense of control and empowerment. Counseling and support are also offered to deal with the emotional distress that infertility provokes; the impact of infertility on the couples' relationship; as well as the sense of loss and mourning that they experience, particularly for those whose treatment does not result in a successful pregnancy (Greenfeld, 1997).

Mental Health and Health Care

In the past three decades, inpatient treatment for mental health and addictions has shifted from specialized facilities to community-based care. However, due to systemic underfunding of community mental health services and decreased psychiatric inpatient bed availability, emergency departments (EDs) are increasingly becoming points of entry for mental health patients. Visits to the ED for mental health reasons account for 10–15% of all visits, and the frequent use of ED services for mental health reasons has contributed to overcrowding and increasing wait times and demands on ED staff. These patients need intensive treatment planning and service mobilization.

People who frequently attend the ED usually have a range of other psychosocial factors, including homelessness, drug and alcohol abuse, lack of social supports, and being poor; despite these factors, they are often viewed by health professionals as uncooperative and demanding. Social workers assigned to the EE are likely to perform myriad tasks, many of which are not sufficiently recognized because of their nonmedical nature (Proctor, 2002). Interventions include assessing the social support needs of patients and families, counseling, and finding suitable referrals. Their role includes screening patients based on their psychosocial needs to help reduce hospital costs by reducing unnecessary admissions.

Bioethical Issues

The climate within health care has changed, and we have entered an era of patient rights, advanced directives, organ donation and surrogacy, and end-of-life decisions in which patients, families, and administrators question the values and assumptions underlying the decisions and practice of health care professionals. Medical advances and unprecedented access to health information have raised exceedingly complex questions that require ethical consideration that focuses on conflicts of interest between health care professionals, patients, and other large health care/welfare systems.

Social workers are trained to have a holistic view of patients so they are in a unique position to understand the dynamics involved in life-or-death decision-making and to expedite the deliberations that occur in an increasingly complex health care system. Social workers also have competence in information gathering and experience with and knowledge of family dynamics that can be used to identify resources and to represent the interests of those unable to participate in decision-making.

In a study undertaken in the United States by Foster, Sharp, Scesny, McLellan, and Cotman in 1993, hospital social workers were asked to respond to 21 practice situations in bioethics and to indicate the extent to which they encountered these ethical concerns, participated clinically, and felt prepared to handle the ethical concerns. The following items were the top seven situations that social workers encountered:

1. Discussing quality-of-life issues
2. Issues of privacy and confidentiality of patient information
3. Mediating interpersonal conflict between patient, family, and provider
4. Disclosure and truth telling such as in diagnosis and prognosis
5. Clarifying value conflicts between patient, family, and provider
6. Rationing health care resources
7. Discussing treatment options in terms of risk and benefit

Contrary to the authors' expectations, the social workers perceived themselves to be well prepared to respond to all these practice events, with the exception of rationing health care resources. Rationing is a complex situation, and it was suggested that it often involves medical decisions that raise issues of quality of life. This was viewed as a more biomedical than psychosocial issue and less open to social work's influence. This may involve discussing futile treatment of an irreversibly ill or considering options such as forgoing of artificial nutrition, hydration, dialysis, or discussing do not resuscitate orders.

Conflict of values can be a source of ethical stress that, unless mediated by the availability of supervision, consultation, and ethics education, can lead to social workers' dissatisfaction with their positions and careers. It has sometimes resulted in decisions by key professionals to leave the field.

Primary Health Care

Individual health can be understood as a general condition into which people are born and that develops over their life course, and these circumstances are in turn shaped by a wider set of social determinants and other influences, such as economics, social policies, and politics (AIHW, 2014). This holistic view of health incorporates physical, mental, and genetic dimensions, as well as cultural, socioeconomic, and environmental determinants. For example, Australians living in rural areas have less access to health services, travel greater distances to seek medical attention, and generally have higher rates of ill health and mortality compared with people living in larger cities (p. 24).

Primary health care refers to a broad range of health services most often delivered in community-based settings and thus has a direct connection to people's daily lives and management of their well-being (Australian Government Department of Health, 2013–14).

In Australia, the second largest component of health spending is for primary health care services ($50.6 billion, or 36.1% of total health expenditure). There is no coherent national approach to community health in Australia. Government-funded community health services in each state and territory provide a diverse range of services that are either provided directly by governments or funded by governments and managed by local health services or community organizations. Primary health care includes a range of frontline health services delivered in the community, such as services provided by doctors in general practice, dental services, and a range of other medical and allied health services. Allied health has become a well-developed concept in Australia and refers to clinical health care professionals who are distinct from medical and nursing staff. These professionals work in multidisciplinary teams and contribute their discipline knowledge to provide holistic and patient-centered health services. Team-based care is also considered a more effective way of meeting changing health care needs of a population that requires longer term management of chronic and complex illnesses.

Community work or community development is characterized by an organic "grassroots" engagement with communities, and the community discourse is consistent with the social work value base in emphasizing social justice, community empowerment, and the rights of marginalized groups. Primary care social workers use a biopsychosocial and ecological approach to frame and analyze issues that incorporates a social determinants model of health, grounded in a broader context of social and material inequalities. Community-based social workers undertake a myriad of tasks, including community outreach, community development, advocacy, and social policy.

In Australia, governments have invested heavily in expanding community-based health care options with a number of "substitution" programs that offer alternatives to using acute care beds as well as optimizing the functioning and independence of older people after a hospital stay. These programs include hospital in the home, community rehabilitation, home-based rehabilitation or therapy services, and transition care programs. They are usually goal-oriented, time-limited, and therapy-focused and are particularly focused on older people to enable them to return home after a hospital stay rather than enter residential care prematurely. The package of services includes low-intensity therapy such as physiotherapy and occupational therapy, as well as social work, nursing support, and personal care.

Looking Forward in Australia

Social workers in the health sector, particularly hospitals, face the many challenges of functioning secondarily to medical and nursing care. The multifaceted role of hospital social workers is not always readily evident to other professionals working in health care environments and for these reasons, health social workers may need to more vigorously articulate and promote their role in responding to the social dimension of health. Despite this, Australian health social workers' role in the discharge of patients within limited time frames now appears to be balanced with their additional role of negotiating and managing more complex medical conditions that have consequent psychosocial implications. Some of these challenges relate to shifts in the patterns of illness as new diseases have replaced infectious ones and lifestyle illnesses have resulted in a range of chronic illnesses that necessitate different approaches to their treatment and management. Social work can lay claim to a number of roles in responding to a wide range of these new and emerging social health problems. Post-traumatic stress disorder, disaster management, chronic fatigue syndrome, drug abuse, diabetes, and dementia are just some of the health issues that require a more holistic and client-centered response.

Social workers also face competition from other professionals, especially nurses, psychologists, and those in the allied health disciplines. As mentioned previously, social work is not usually the primary service, and social workers' expertise is not always evident, so social workers need to be more assertive in defining their role and to be more "insistent" about the contributions they can make. Patient-centered care models, with their presumed active engagement of the patient and family in decision-making, offer the potential for social workers to be key respondents to care needs, and the movement toward evidence-based practice and accountability has resulted in an encouraging increase in health social work research.

Health social workers have always located social and individual problems within a holistic framework, but they need to find opportunities to include the broader understandings of health inequalities within the core social work assessment and intervention processes. Research suggests that social workers generally have continued to overlook systems and structural pedagogy and have adopted the organizational focus on micro-based interventions directed at individual change (Parsell, Eggins, & Marston, 2017). As a value-based profession, social work explicitly advocates for marginalized and oppressive groups, and the health care setting offers a unique opportunity for social work to extend the health focus to include wider societal and global trends.

Heightened focus on nonmedical barriers to health care and the need to negotiate increasingly complex service delivery systems will, however, demand greater brokerage and collaboration skills.

Conclusion

Australian health social workers are in pretty good shape. They have been able to withstand periodic austerity policies that can marginalize their services and, indeed, social workers in public hospital settings are experiencing an upward trend in employment. They continue to play an important role in discharge planning and are pivotal team members in preadmission screening, short stay units, and medical/surgical wards, providing comprehensive assessments of patients' post-discharge needs. Likewise, a focus on reducing demand on inpatient services has increased the establishment of community-based, case management services involving social workers who work in multidisciplinary teams to optimize clients' health and well-being. However, increasing ethical and clinical complexity has led to social workers spending increasing amounts of time in negotiation and conflict resolution to assist patients and their significant others in negotiating the health care system and also in assisting them with difficult decision-making (Cleak & Turczynski, 2014).

In all these settings and roles, health social workers must remember their obligation to employ a client-centered and critical perspective that empowers patients to make decisions for themselves about treatment options. Health social workers must also continue to remind organizations that there are social determinants as well as individual determinants of health.

References

Australian Association of Social Workers. (2016, Autumn). Social work practice in the health sector. *Social Work Focus, 1*(1), 19–36.

Australian Government Department of Health, (2013–14). Annual Report. Retrieved from http://www.health.gov.au/internet/main/publishing.nsf/Content/annual-report2013-14

Australian Institute of Health and Welfare. (2009). *Australian hospital statistics 2007–08.* Health Services Series No. 33, Cat. No. HSE 71. Canberra, Australia: Author.

Australian Institute of Health and Welfare. (2014). *Australia's health 2014.* Health Services Series No. 14, Cat. No. AUS 178. Canberra, Australia: Author.

Browne, E. (2005). Social work in health care settings. In M. Alston & J. McKinnon (Eds.), *Social work: Fields of practice* (pp. 107–117). South Melbourne, Australia: Oxford University Press.

Buchanan, J., Jenkins, S., & Scott, L. (2014). *Student clinical education in Australia: A University of Sydney scoping study.* Sydney, Australia: University of Sydney.

Cleak, H. (2002). A model of social work classification in health care. *Australian Social Work, 55*(1), 38–49.

Cleak, H., & Turczynski, M. (2014). Hospital social work in Australia: Emerging trends or more of the same? *Social Work in Health Care, 53*(3), 199–213.

Daley, J. (2013, September). *Budget pressures and health spending.* RCH Grand Round, Grattan Institute, Royal Children's Hospital Melbourne, Melbourne, Australia.

Davis, C., Baldry, E., Milosevic, B., & Walsh, A. (2004). Defining the role of hospital social worker in Australia. *International Social Work, 47*(3), 346–358.

Department of the Prime Minister and Cabinet (Australia). (2016). *Closing the gap.* Prime Minister's report. Canberra, Australia: Author.

Foster, L., Sharp, J., Scesny, A., McLellan, L., & Cotman, K. (1993). Bioethics: Social work's response and training needs. *Social Work in Health Care, 19*(1), 15–38.

Giles, R. (2013). Contemporary issues in health social work. In M. Connolly & L. Harms (Eds.), *Social work: Contexts and practice* (3rd ed.). (pp. 243–261). South Melbourne, Australia: Oxford University Press.

Giles, R., Gould, S., Hart, C., & Swancott, J. (2007). Clinical priorities: Strengthening social work practice in health. *Australian Social Work, 60,* 147–165.

Greenfeld, D. (1997). Infertility and assisted reproductive technology. *Social Work in Health Care, 24*(3–4), 39–46.

Judd, R. G., & Sheffield, S. (2010). Hospital social work: Contemporary roles and professional activities. *Social Work in Health Care, 49*(9), 856–871.

McAlinden, F., McDermott, F., & Morris, J. (2013). Complex patients: Social workers' perceptions of complexity in health and rehabilitation services. *Social Work in Health Care, 52*(10), 899–912.

McAlynn, M., & McLaughlin, J. (2008). Key factors impeding discharge planning in hospital social work. *Social Work in Health Care, 46*(3), 1–27.

Mendes, P. (2005). The history of social work in Australia: A critical literature review. *Australian Social Work, 58*(2), 121–131.

Miller, C. J. (2015). *The predominance of American influences on the establishment of social work education at the University of Melbourne, 1920–1960.* PhD thesis, University of Melbourne, Melbourne, Australia.

Parsell, C., Eggins, E., & Marston, G. (2017). Human agency and social work research: A systematic search and synthesis of social work literature. *British Journal of Social Work, 47*(1), 238–255.

Proctor, E. K. (2002). Social work research: Informing the frontlines and taking the long view. *Social Work Research, 26*(3), 130–131.

Redfern, H., Burton, J., Lonne, B., & Seiffert, H. (2016). Social work and complex care systems: The case of people hospitalised with a disability. *Australian Social Work, 69*(1), 27–38. doi:10.1080/0312407X.2015.1035295

Soskolne, V., Kaplan, G., Ben-Shahar, I., Stanger, V., & Auslander, G. K. (2010). Social work discharge planning in acute care hospitals in Israel: Clients' evaluation of the discharge planning process and adequacy. *Research on Social Work Practice, 20*(4), 368–379.

Willis, E., Reynolds, L., & Keleher, H. (2012). *Understanding the Australian health care system,* New York, NY: Elsevier.

6

Health Care Social Work in China

Peter P. Szto

Introduction

China is a country of 1.34 billion people. A challenge for China is how to provide adequate health care to all its citizens. The challenge is difficult because China is the world's second largest economy yet still a developing nation—that is, it lags behind in terms of science, technology, and social development. With regard to health care, China is ranked 41st, with an average life expectancy of 76 years (World Health Organization, 2016), and according to the United Nations Human Development Index, China is ranked 90th on life expectancy, education, and income per capita. How China can improve its world ranking in health care is the focus of this chapter. Health care in China is important not only because of the sheer number of people involved but also because of the role that professional social work might play in advancing social development.

Social work is not indigenous to China. American missionaries imported it to demonstrate a Western model of charitable relief. Social work was first introduced in the 1920s at select Chinese university sociology departments. J. S. Burgess and D. W. Edward, members of the Princeton University Alumni Association in China, introduced social work in 1922 at Yenching University (today called Beijing University). Adding social work to the sociology curriculum was embraced at Yenching and other universities. At Soochow University, the president of the university praised the practical value of social work for China (as cited in Yamashita, Bosco, & Eades, 2004):

Our prime emphasis is not so much on social theories as on the training of social workers . . . our aim is not so much to train theorists who can write essays on social problems, but practical workers who can plan and direct programs of social service. (p. 164)

Burgess and Edward saw in social work a practical approach to solving social problems that worked in America, and so they believed it could also work in China. In addition to academic learning, they also believed that private philanthropy could help fund social service agencies. The link between academia and field education was important in applying social work knowledge to clients. According to Xia and Guo (2002), among the various agencies available in China in the 1920s, a health care field placement was possible at the Social Service Department of Xiehe Hospital. This placement is significant because it signals the availability of health care social work almost 100 years ago.

Prior to the introduction of social work, China had been practicing its own form of charitable relief. Over several millennia, clan associations and religious clerics had developed a sophisticated network of kinship-based care (Chan, 1993). Confucian social welfare philosophy informed this system of care and was resilient enough to survive thousands of years. When foreigners arrived—outside the university setting—social work did not widely impress the Chinese and was viewed as a Western novelty perhaps worthy of adapting. The novelty was short-lived because social work was formally banned from the university curriculum in 1952. Under the new communist regime, social work was deemed a remnant of Western bourgeois culture and a pseudo-science. In 1949, the new People's Republic of China adapted Marxism to eradicate social problems and to develop a socialist system of care. From a socialist perspective, professional social work practice was no longer necessary and was purged from the university curriculum. The Chinese communist leaders believed socialism, not social work, would provide social well-being for all of the country's citizens. After 1952, social workers in China found themselves out of favor and out of work so that their numbers gradually dwindled to zero (Xia & Guo, 2002).

China's new system of care was called the "Iron Rice Bowl" (鐵飯碗). The policy euphemism meant government paternalism vis-à-vis comprehensive cradle-to-grave provisions. The array of state-sponsored social welfare benefits was distributed through the danwei (單位), or place of employment. The distribution of benefits through the work unit ensured government control over employment. Administration of the danwei system also required a large cadre of "social workers" to distribute the government's largess—that is, income, housing, food, birth control, education, health care, and so on.

The Iron Rice Bowl policy proved far too difficult to realize and sustain than simply asserting slogans that the government would provide. After 1949, the Chinese had high hopes that Chairman Mao Tse-tung's ideals would usher in prosperity and an egalitarian society. Despite gallant efforts, Mao's promises never panned out. The state did try, however, by employing a large cadre of workers in a wide range of semi-government social welfare organizations, including the Women's Federation, the Communist Youth League, and neighborhood mutual aid services (Chan, 1993). By the 1980s, these organizations could no longer effectively respond to the new social problems that were emerging with the economic reforms. Still, in 1996, the Ministry of Civil Affairs reported that 186,666 local social organizations were registered with the central government. On the national level, there were 1,845 social organizations registered with the government (Saich, 1999). Unfortunately, the workforce providing services in these state-sponsored organizations was better versed in socialist ideals and Maoist aspirations than in professional social work knowledge and skills. After 30 years in pursuit of a socialist economy, Chinese leaders realized that they needed to change direction. However, despite the shortfall, China deserves credit for reducing poverty and addressing the basic health care needs of a billion people.

The death of Chairman Mao in 1976 gave China's leaders pause to consider alternative paths to modernize. They chose to reform the economy and to reopen China to foreign markets. The open-door policy of 1978 permitted the Chinese to engage foreign markets but only in designated space called special economic zones (SEZs). SEZs were highly successful in generating huge profits. Unfortunately, an unintentional consequence of the reforms was that they also generated extensive social problems—that is, crime, prostitution, overcrowding, urban congestion, corruption, and so on. Initially, the central government responded indifferently to the problems and preferred to focus on the economic gains. By 1984, the problems had become so severe that they could no longer be ignored. Government leaders were compelled to reevaluate the profession of social work and concluded that social work should be reestablished under the Ministry of Civil Affairs. In 1986, the Education Commission formally launched a social work program at Peking University to graduate a new cohort of professionals to confront the myriad of social problems. Finally, in 1988, the China Association of Social Workers was established as the new profession's own professional organization.

History of Social Work Health Care in China

A civilization that claims 5000–7000 years of continuous existence must know something about health care to have survived for so long. Since antiquity, the Chinese have maintained personal health and treated illnesses by relying on what is known as traditional Chinese medicine (TCM). Of course, in ancient times, the Chinese simply called it "medicine" and considered it normative. TCM is a holistic approach to health that involves multiple possible treatments—herbal remedies, acupuncture, dietary regimes, and massage. These various homeopathic cures seek to enhance a person's natural healing systems compared with more intrusive methods. It is important to note that in the West, TCM is labeled an "alternative medicine" and that the reference "alternative" is a Western bias. Chronologically, TCM actually precedes Western medicine, and so it actually is the true alternative to Western medicine. TCM. This distinction is critical because TCM has effectively sustained the health of billions of Chinese apart from Western medicine. What are its curative properties and how does TCM relate to social work?

TCM views the person as an integrated whole living in a dynamic relationship with the social environment. The aim of TCM is to maintain a harmonic balance between the person and the environment. Maintaining a proper balance is key to physical, mental, and spiritual health. Chinese physicians provide a variety of remedies to restore balance and fight diseases; these include herbs and different mind/body practices to enhance the person's immune system. The earliest medical text to outline TCM is the *Yellow Emperor's Inner Canon* (黃帝內經), published between 300 and 200 BC. The text is an imagined dialogue between the mythical Yellow Emperor and his court of physicians. The dialogue explains the core concepts of TCM, such as Qi (氣), which is the flow of energy, or life force, that animates humans. Qi flows in, around, and through the body. Qi is a sign of vitality, health, and measure of social relationships. The physician seeks to diagnose the quality of Qi to assess, harness, and heal the person.

It is argued here that the practitioner of TCM was a prototypical health care social worker. The reason is that health in China was understood in terms of an interaction between a person and the environment. This view is more than philosophical musing; it is a practical response and observation of everyday life. The ancients believed ill-health was symptomatic of disharmony, irregularity, and disruptions in the natural rhythms of life between a person and the social environment. Qi was the pathway along which discord, tension, or disease moved through the person. The goal of TCM was to restore the balance and maintain harmony through responsible living. For example, restraint in eating and exercise saved energy to augment balance. In addition, therapeutic restoration was an ethical necessity to maintain health. In TCM, the Chinese physician was less an authority figure and more an advisor. Similar to the Western notion of client self-determination, each individual was thus unique and deserving of respect. However, unlike Western medicine, TCM treats the whole person rather than reducing the person to a diagnosis or disease. TCM served China well because it sustained millions of Chinese for thousands of years.

TCM did not have any competition until Western merchants and missionaries arrived in the early 19th century. The medical missionaries believed Western medicine was not only scientific but also superior to TCM. In addition, they believed it could be a practical demonstration of divine love and compassion. The first Protestant missionary to China was Robert Morrison (1782–1834), who upon his arrival in Macao and Guangzhou struggled with how to effectively communicate the Christian gospel. Preaching and tract distribution showed little results in his early years. The idea of medical missions dawned on Morrison as being a more demonstrable expression of God's love to humanity. Medical missionary pioneers, Dr. Peter Parker (1804–1888), Dr. John G. Kerr (1824–1901), and hundreds more, in due time established Western-style hospitals and clinics throughout China (Szto, 2002). The missionaries set in motion a pattern of social technology transfer that competed with, and often replaced, traditional Chinese institutions.

Among the thousands of foreigners who came to China, one individual is noteworthy because of her contribution to health care social work. Ida Pruitt (1888–1985) was the first to practice health care social work in China. Born to Southern Baptist missionary parents in Shantung Province, Pruitt had studied social work at the Philadelphia Training School of Social Work, where she learned the value of community practice. She also trained at the renown Massachusetts General Hospital (MGH) in Boston before she returned to China in 1920. Her special interest in hospital social work caught the attention of the Rockefeller Foundation (a private philanthropic organization founded in 1913), which offered her the rare opportunity to help it establish a department of medical social work at the newly opened Peking Union Medical College Hospital. Pruitt was unduly qualified, having gained skills in medical social work at MGH under the tutelage of Ida Cannon (1877–1960). Cannon was widely recognized as the founder of medical social work practice. Pruitt's training at MGH equipped her with state-of-the-art know-how that she put to good use in China. Hospital-based social work in China owes its origins, and eventual expansion to Pruitt, who understood its practical value and positive impact on patient care.

Social Policies and Political Context of Health Care

Health care in China today is at a historic juncture. It lies somewhere between ancient practices and modern medical science. The health care delivery system is also in flux, lingering somewhere between the Iron Rice Bowl policies of the Mao years (1949–1977) and a transitional economy of the open-door years (1978 to the present). The system is moving away from statist-oriented health care practices toward a more market-oriented approach. The former embraces a total welfare state and the latter a welfare mix. In the midst of transitioning, the Chinese continue to value and practice kinship-based care, Taoist attitudes toward healing, and Confucian social mores, while admiring the health benefits of modern Western medical science.

China's demographics and political context play a significant role in shaping health care social policies. Providing affordable health insurance and health care to 1.34 billion Chinese is a daunting challenge for the Chinese leadership. One leading scholar on governing health care in China, Yanzhong Huang (2013), argues that health care should be given priority governance responsibility. He references Benjamin Disraeli's address to the British Parliament—"The public health is the foundation on which repose the happiness of the people and the power of a country" (cited on p. 1)—to make the case that China's post-reform political context is an opportunity for the government to take on a central role in health care. Whether the government's role is central or peripheral, this chapter argues that an analytical framework is necessary to explain the political context and particularly the strategic role that professional social work should play in health care delivery. Social welfare policy scholars Evers and Wintersberger (1990) suggest a "shifting welfare mix" to explain the structural relations between three distinct spheres or social structures: state, market, and households (the latter also known as third-sector or the voluntary private sphere). The welfare mix understands that the three spheres interact in an interdependent and reciprocal manner in the provision of welfare. This explanatory framework is important to analyze the shifting role between state and non-state resources as the sociopolitical context for health care social work to emerge.

China's health care practices changed significantly when the Iron Rice Bowl policy ended in 1978. The shift away from a total state welfare model created conditions conducive for an alternative health care scheme. Urbanization, industrialization, and fragmentation also helped destabilize the Iron Rice Bowl health care system. From 1949 until the 1980s, the danwei system guaranteed Chinese workers lifetime employment that included generous social welfare benefits, such as indefinite health insurance, housing, child care, schools, mail services, and free health care. By the late 1970s, the danwei system could no longer sustain total care (Bray, 2005). One option for the Chinese leadership was to liberalize the danwei by allowing nongovernment entities to provide the benefits instead. However, this posed the risk of the government losing its control and authority regarding social provisions. In Bray's words, the "decline of the danwei" (p. 158) meant the rise of individual identity and social organizations separate from state control. It also signified that the shift away from state-sponsored health care created the space for a "free-market" and private households to emerge in China. Saich (1999) observed that the political mood of the 1980s was ripe for the state to permit nongovernmental entities to fill the space previously occupied by the government. In other words, the times made professional social work an attractive alternative to solve China's social problems.

Despite the rise and fall of the Iron Rice Bowl policy, China's kinship–clan system never completely receded. One way to describe contemporary China is that it is a place where ancient health care practices such as TCM and modern Western scientific medicine coexist. Pregnancy offers a good illustration. When a family member becomes pregnant, the expectation is that the nearest of kin provide emotional, material, and moral support. This was done without asking or preconditions. Food was offered not only as material support but also as the source of health to replenish and nourish the body. According to Qi medical theory, the fetus drew blood and nutrition away from the mother and so food was critical to provide extra nourishment to the spleen and liver. It was vital to maintain an adequate flow of

Qi and to keep one's tendons strong to avoid leg cramps. Kin were expected to be especially mindful to the long-term consequences of pregnancy. Eating healthy food was therefore emphasized to yield lifelong benefits, from a healthy baby to, eventually, a productive member of society. This household approach to health care complimented TCM to provide a sustainable safety net.

Health Care Social Work in China

Health care social work in China today is an emerging area of practice. Multiple factors are shaping its emergence and are discussed here. The 1984 reestablishment of academic social work to the university curriculum was part political rhetoric and part policy change. The rhetoric involved slogans and lip service about social work. Policy change was incremental and lagged behind the rhetoric because few social work graduates could find employment due to the lack of a sufficient number of agencies to hire them. However, as the social problems increased, the rhetoric became sharper. For example, the sixth plenum of the 16th National Congress in October 2006 ("Communique of the Sixth Plenum," 2006) asserted,

> The plenum puts forward the main objectives and tasks for building a harmonious socialist society by 2020. . . . We must put more attention to developing social services and push forward economic and social development in a coordinated way . . . and train a large number of professionals who are good at dealing with social issues.

The Chinese Communist Party's embrace of professional social work practice was significant. Best estimates are that there were between 10,000 and 15,000 social workers in 2006. The estimate is inadequate to meet the needs of Chinese society, particularly with regard to health care. To address the workforce demands, the central government announced in 2013 the goal of training 3 million social workers by 2020. It has yet to be determined how many will specialize in health care delivery.

According to a January 4, 2015, *Wall Street Journal* article, 95% of China's 1.34 billion citizens have health insurance. This is good news, but only for those covered. The remaining 5%, or 6.7 million, are without coverage—this is a serious problem. Yip and Hsiao (2008) cite two basic reasons for the uninsured. The first is affordability due to "rapid health care cost inflation" (p. 1). When Premier Deng Xiaoping announced his economic reforms in 1978, he also announced that "To get rich is glorious." Deng's famous pronouncement motivated millions to seek a better life. An unintentional consequence of his endorsement to pursue wealth was the creation of conditions for illicit profit-seeking behavior (i.e., greed and corruption). The government's transition to a market economy also meant a significant loss in tax revenue and capacity to fund universal health care. In order to make health care affordable, the government imposed strict price controls at below market value. To make ends meet, hospitals and pharmaceutical manufacturers needed to operate at above costs in order for the government to make up for the loss in revenue. The new expectations thus created "perverse incentives" (p. 3) for health care providers to overprescribe and to favor patients who could pay. The second reason is that many of the uninsured lived in rural areas or became migrants without proper *hukou*—the household registration system used to assess Iron Rice Bowl benefits. The bias already against rural folk was exacerbated with the demise of the Iron Rice Bowl system. Furthermore, the collapse of the collectivist approach to health care left many uninsured and unprotected. Meanwhile, the government was slow to replace its health care resources for rural residents. To escape poverty, millions flooded into urban areas to fill factory jobs and for the promise of a better life. Rapid urbanization without proper hukou regrettably meant foregoing health insurance, housing, education, and other social welfare necessities. The peak of China's mass internal migration occurred from 2005 to 2008, with an estimated 250 million moving from country to city (China National Population and Family Planning Commission, 2015).

The previous scenario is a brief assessment of the health care system in China today. As an emerging profession and because of its holistic approach to health care, social work has much to offer the health care system. Social work's person-in-environment framework is advantageous in how it views the relationship between provider and patients. Health care social workers are in a strategic position to alleviate some of the pressures that hospitals experience—overcrowding, poor access to care, limited alternatives, and so on. China's health care system could benefit from the mediatorial function that is social work to bridge services between care provider and aftercare.

According to Wong (2016), the shift from welfare state to market reforms prompted hospitals to search for alternative funding. Hospital administrators could no longer rely on the government to finance their operations and had to look to the private sector. The scramble for market solutions meant that administrators were less inclined to view social services as a high priority. Social services were viewed more as a liability than an asset. Fortunately, there were exceptions; for example, the earliest hospital social work unit opened at the Beijing Bo Ai Hospital. Kind-hearted hospital administrators established the unit in the early 1990s, although it was not considered a professional unit until much later. In 2000, the Shanghai East Hospital also established a Social Service Department, followed in 2001 by the Shanghai Oriental Hospital and Shanghai Children Hospital. These hospitals came to be known as the "Shanghai Model" and were held up for other cities to emulate. In 2007, the Peking University Medical College established a Social Work Department, and in 2009 Beijing First People's Hospital added a professional social work unit. These examples underscore the preference given to urban areas and an institutional approach to health care. The advantage of an institutional approach is that hospitals offer multiple services in one location. The disadvantage is that people in rural areas or far from hospitals cannot easily access specialty care.

Another major factor shaping health care social work was the recent occurrence of major natural disasters in China. The disasters exposed the need for more hospitals, medical personnel, and social workers specially trained in disaster relief. In 2003, an outbreak of severe acute respiratory syndrome (SARS) in the Pearl River Delta region of south China made clear the connection between adequate medical resources and social services. During the crisis, social workers acted quickly and bravely to educate the public about appropriate hygiene and other precautionary measures to eradicate SARS. The massive 2008 earthquake in Sichuan Province was another dire emergency that demanded rapid mobilization of resources. Again, the social work response was quick, creating a positive image of social workers in health care.

Research on current health care in China reports major challenges for the government and for social work (Huang, 2013). A significant shortfall is the lack of formally trained social workers in health care. Responding to this shortfall, at a national meeting on health in Beijing on August 19 and 20, 2016, President Xi Jinping announced a call for full health protection. Xi reasoned that health maintenance is a precondition for economic and social development. Health should not be viewed in isolation subject to the negative effects of industrialization, rapid urbanization, and upward social mobility. The link between modernization and ill-health is not lost on Xi, who understands the importance of TCM as a preventative measure. He encouraged blending the two approaches as complimentary healing. Xi's understanding is significant given that the majority of doctors in China favor Western over Chinese medicine. Xi also underscored the role of capital markets to produce and disseminate medical innovations. His goal is to produce a health care system that minimizes the rural–urban divide and maximizes access to health care resources. The central government would therefore lend full support for local governments to develop basic medical services (i.e., clinics, hospitals, and rehabilitation). Although he did not explicitly promote health care social workers, the announcement is an opportunity for social work to increase its role in health care.

China today has approximately 25,000 hospitals. In 2003, there were approximately 18,000, but by 2013 the number had grown to the current 25,000. Total bed capacity is approximately 5 million, with approximately 10 million employed medical personnel (Statista, 2014). The hospitals vary in type, quality of service, and fit into two categories. The first category comprises community health centers, which offer preventative care and rehabilitation services in local neighborhoods. Physicians at these facilities typically have only 2 or 3 years of community college training. The second category comprises large-scale multistructure facilities that offer the full range of medical treatments. The Chinese prefer the second category, but unfortunately, preference for these facilities has resulted in extreme overcrowding, long wait times, and patient frustration. Making matters worse, the Chinese frown upon primary and preventative care and avoid the community health centers if possible. A solution to the overcrowding is for social workers to redirect patients through health education and prevention. Having simple medical procedures, such as vaccinations and well-baby checks, performed at community health centers alleviates overcrowding at hospitals. In addition, social workers can streamline services through case management and development of individualized aftercare plans. However, if the government only increases health care expenditures and builds more medical facilities—without increasing coordination of care—this will unfortunately not improve efficiency nor advance a harmonious society.

One telling anecdote experienced at the University of Nebraska at Omaha (UNO) illustrates the strategic role that social workers can play in improving health care delivery in China. For 3 weeks in the summer of 2016, 10 social workers from different provinces in China visited UNO for special training.

The goal of China's central government was to send select agency leaders to America with the aim of having them contextualize their experiences back in China. One training session involved participating in a UNO social work course on ethnic diversity. The UNO instructor divided the class into two groups: an American student group and a China social worker group. Both groups were instructed to create a skit that illustrated problems that social workers face involving access to health care in their respective countries. The Chinese skit dramatized striking health care inefficiencies, long delays, and the deep frustration that people experience just trying to see a doctor at a hospital. The groups role-played their skits with much energy, making the scenes appear as authentic and actual everyday experiences. Interestingly, the American skit portrayed almost the same difficulties as those shown in the Chinese skin. What was telling was not that both countries faced similar barriers but, rather, that the China group has the potential to effect real change upon its return to China.

Corroborating the previous classroom anecdote is a WeChat interview with a Chinese health care social worker in October 2016. The social worker works at a Beijing teaching hospital affiliated with Peking University. The hospital is an 1,800-bed facility with 40 clinical departments. The Department of Medical Social Work and Volunteer Service was established in 2009 and currently employs four full-time medical social workers. The two primary treatment modalities that the social workers use are individual and group work. Individual social services for patients and their families include emotional–social support, financial and social evaluation, and special support for low-income patients. Group work is primarily used with dialysis patients, children with leukemia, and women with breast cancer. Currently, child welfare cases involving abuse, neglect, grief, and loss are not major public health concerns, and thus no services are available. However, the social workers stated that they are starting to develop community service activities in an attempt to educate the public and promote outreach. They have already organized a variety of lectures as a continuing health education strategy targeting medical professionals. The idea is to hold at least 40 such activities on an annual basis.

Unfortunately, with only four full-time social workers to cover 1,800 beds, the social workers feel understaffed and overwhelmed. A typical day is therefore highly stressful and filled with different and unique challenges. The four social workers are resourceful, but it is nearly impossible to have an active presence in all clinical departments. To their credit, the social workers work well together as a team to prioritize and coordinate their daily responsibilities. Innovation and flexibility are skills they have culled to respond in an effective way to meet patient needs. One significant innovation has been recruiting and organizing volunteers to redistribute the workload. For example, volunteers have helped in the hospital's emergency room to support families and collect patient information. Because health care social work is still new in China, the social workers are continually seeking to design and develop new services to meet patient needs. Health care certainly presents an ongoing challenge for social workers in China. Perhaps the major challenge is to continually educate the hospital community as to the role and function of social work in health care.

Emerging Trends and Potential Future Issues

The trajectory of China's welfare mix will continue to shift toward nongovernment resources. Recent government policy pronouncements affirm that this trend will continue in the short term if not extend into the more distant future. The trend indeed affords the field of social work the opportunity to increase its role in health care. The government currently offers a three-pronged insurance scheme that impacts social work's role. First, in 2003, the government introduced a voluntary insurance scheme for rural areas called the New Cooperative Medical Scheme. The goal is to reduce catastrophic risk and to have 100% of rural residents insured by 2020. Second, for government and nongovernment organizations, Urban Employees' Basic Medical Insurance is available. This scheme will help social workers secure employment at urban hospitals. Third, nonsalaried individuals such as children and the elderly can attain insurance under the Urban Residents Basic Medical Insurance scheme. In all three insurance schemes, social workers can play a strategic role in educating the public about their availability and helping people enroll.

The future of health care social work is also tied to China's economic growth. Since 1978, China's gross domestic product (GDP) has risen to double-digit levels and lifted millions out of poverty into the middle class. In 1979, when Premier Deng Xiaoping initiated economic reforms, he unleashed a human potential movement that is near impossible to reverse. The Chinese have tasted prosperity and peace—and they like it. China's

GDP between 1960 and 1978 was 5.3%, whereas in 2010 it 10.4% ("China GDP," 2012). Clearly, the reforms ignited China's hard-driving private labor force into an almost unbridled capitalism. In 2009, China became the world's second largest economy after the United States. Economic growth, however, demands social innovation. Although government expenditures on health care are impressive, training a competent social work workforce demands investment and attention. The field of health care social work is in a unique position to advance social development in China. The waning of China's Iron Rice Bowl and shift away from statist social welfare provisions have not only occasioned the return of professional social work but also provided opportunity to reframe the role of social work in health care. President Xi has positioned health care as a centerpiece of government initiatives in its long march toward social development. Development of quality social work training must continue to meet the growing social needs of China's 1.3 billion people. Specific programs to train social workers to specialize in health care are small but critical to achieve President Xi's goal of full health protection.

Conclusion

Specialized training is highly recommended to develop health care social work in China. To attain a harmonious society, access to health care for 1.34 billion people is imperative. China has the workforce potential but needs to couple it with a relevant training model. The social welfare shift has created an opportunity to build upon traditional Chinese practices and incorporate "best practices" from overseas. It seems prudent to integrate the best of both worlds in the development of modern indigenous health care social workers.

References

Bray, D. (2005). *Social space and governance in urban China: The Danwei system from origins to urban reform*. Stanford, CA: Stanford University Press.

Chan, C. (1993). *The myth of neighbourhood mutual help: The contemporary Chinese community-based welfare system in Guangzhou*. Hong Kong: Hong Kong University Press.

China GDP: How it has changed since 1980. (2012). *The Guardian*. Retrieved from https://www.theguardian.com/news/datablog/2012/mar/23/china-gdp-since-1980

China National Population and Family Planning Commission. (2015). Retrieved from http://www.npc.gov.cn/englishnpc/NPCChina/2015-01/19/content_1894533.htm

Communique of the Sixth Plenum of the 16th CPC Central Committee. (2006). *China Daily*. Retrieved from http://www.chinadaily.com.cn/china/2006-10/11/content_706239.htm

Evers, A., & Wintersberger, H. (1990). *Shifts in the welfare mix: Their impact on work, social services and welfare policies*. New York, NY: Campus/Westview.

Huang, Y. (2013). *Governing health in contemporary China*. New York, NY: Routledge.

Saich, T. (1999). *Negotiating the state: The development of social organizations in China*. Unpublished manuscript.

Statista. (2014). *Number of hospitals in China from 2004 to 2014*. Retrieved from http://www.statista.com/statistics/279322/number-of-hospitals-in-china

Szto, P. P. (2002). *The accommodation of insanity in Canton, China: 1857–1935*. Guangzhou (China), UMI.

Wong, T. J. (2016). Corporate governance research on listed firms in China: Institutions, governance and accountability. *Foundations and Trends® in Accounting, 9*(4), 259–326.

World Health Organization, (2016). Retrieved from https://www.who.int/countries/chn/en/

Xia, X., & Guo, J. (2002). Historical developments and characteristics of social work in today's China. *International Journal of Social Welfare, 11*, 254–262.

Yamashita, S., Bosco, J., & Eades, J. S. (2004). *The making of anthropology in East and Southeast Asia*. New York, NY: Berghahn.

Yip, W., & Hsiao, W. C. (2008). The Chinese health system at a crossroads. *Health Affairs, 27*(2), 460–468.

7

The Role of the Social Worker
in Health Care in Cuba

Dolly R. Sacristan

Introduction

Cuba has been successful in developing a universal health care system that guarantees access to free health care for all citizens, despite an American economic blockade lasting five decades and the loss of financial support from the Soviet Bloc in 1991. Cuba's health care structure includes three levels of care: primary care clinics (consultorios), secondary care polyclinics (community health centers), and tertiary care hospitals and medical centers (Offredy, 2008). Services are delivered through the use of multidisciplinary teams and community-based models. Social work is a central component of this structure, and social workers hold multiple roles in the health care system of Cuba.

This chapter offers a review of the history of social work in Cuba, its role in the country's health care system, the sociopolitical context shaping social work practice, and possible future practice trends as the country transitions through new political, social, and economic changes.

The chapter integrates existing research and the author's exchanges with colleagues in Cuba and recent research during trips to Cuba in the past 3 years. The author's recent research in Cuba includes interviews with social workers employed by a polyclinic, or health center; a residential center for individuals with cognitive disabilities; the Center for Psychology and Sociology Research; a hospital for ear, nose, and throat disorders; the National Center for HIV/AIDS Prevention; and a senior citizen center.

The History of Social Work in Cuba

The genesis of social work in Cuba can be traced back to charity work activities done by the Catholic Church during the time of the

Spanish–American War in the late 1800s. In 1936, under Act No. 708, the government established the first National Corporation for Public Assistance (Corporacion Nacional de Asistencia Publica). The role of this entity was to oversee the charity activities carried out by existing private organizations, such as the Sociedad Liceum (1929), the Lawn Tennis Club (1913), and the Instituto Hispano-Cubano de Cultura (1926). In 1938, these organizations merged and became the Patronage of Social Services; it was this organization that introduced the idea of opening a school of social work. In 1943, the first school of social work, Ancillary School of Social Service, was developed. It offered a 2-year non-degree social work program at the University of Havana. In 1945, this program became the Institute of Social Services and was housed in the Social Sciences and Public Law Departments of the university. The curriculum included 30 courses, and the main admission requirement was to be a high school graduate (Mabel Molina, personal communication, June 2016). The graduates of this program belonged to the more affluent segment of society and played supportive roles with well-to-do individuals and families impacted by political turmoil during the Batista administration (Allen, Bailey, Dubus, & Wichinsky, 2015). Both the program and the university closed in 1956 during the political and social turmoil preceding the 1959 Cuban Revolution (Strug & Teague, 2004).

The triumph of the Cuban Revolution in 1959 marked a new period for the profession of social work. A new political system was instituted under socialist values of "cooperation, participation, community state intervention and international solidarity" (Lambie, 2011, p. 38). The new government emphasized ethical principles of equity and social justice for all Cuban citizens, and new welfare policies were created to increase access to services such as health care for all Cuban citizens (Mabel Molina, personal communication, June 2016). In 1959, the University of Havana reopened, but without the School of Social Work. Instead, the government established the Ministry of Social Welfare (Ministerio de bienestar Social) to carry out the new social policies intended to eliminate poverty and other social problems. In 1961, the Ministry of Social Welfare was dissolved after the government concluded that many of the initiatives for improving health care had been successful (Mabel Molina, personal communication, June 2016).

During the 1960s, the government created *las organisaciones de masas* (mass organizations) to mobilize people and encourage them to help; the leaders of these groups did not have any technical or professional training but played important social work roles in the community (Strug, 2006). Examples of these mass organizations are the Federation of Cuban Women and the Committees for the Defense of the Revolution, which are still in existence today and continue to represent essential components of the community-based social service system of the island. Based on the work of these mass organizations, the "communal ethos" was established (Strug, 2006), which would later become the landmark of social work practice in Cuba.

The professionalization of social work in Cuba and its role in health care began in the 1970s with the opening of technical training institutes for social workers. The Cuban Ministry of Public health (El Ministerio de Salud Publica), in response to many problems in health care due to a vast exodus of doctors from Cuba, decided to open these training institutes to train social workers in health care (Herman, Zlotnik, & Collins, 2014). Graduates went to work in hospitals, clinics, and public health settings assisting various health care professionals (Strug, 2006). In addition, during the 1980s, Cuba started the "family doctor and nurse system," in which doctors and nurses made home visits and were assigned to work in their own neighborhoods; social workers became part of this multidisciplinary approach and played important roles in health promotion initiatives and case management (Perez Montalvo, 2003).

In 1991, Cuba entered a phase of grave economic collapse following the loss of its protection by the Soviet Bloc and the intensified financial blockade by the United States; this period became known as the Special Period or *el periodo especial* (Uriarte, 2002). During this period, social problems increased significantly, and the government recognized the need to have a better trained social work workforce that could respond more effectively to the many problems that the country faced at that time. As a result, in 1998 the government developed policies to fund social work educational initiatives that resulted in the University of Havana starting a professional 6-year social work program intended to advance the training of the social workers who had graduated from the institutes and were working in health care. The graduates were conferred a degree in sociology with a specialization in social work (Strug, 2006). The curriculum during the first 2 years included general social science courses. In years 3–5, the students took social work courses on a community organization track; courses included practice with groups, communities, and organizations. Fieldwork requirements were fulfilled through their employment, taking breaks every

21 days to complete class requirements; completion of a thesis was required for graduation (Strug & Teague, 2004).

In addition to the professional social work program, in September 2000 a 1-year paraprofessional social work program was developed in Cojimar, a fishing town outside of Havana. This program was directed at youth aged 16–22 years who were unemployed or not in school. The program had an integrated curriculum, with courses in sociology, applied social work, communication, and psychology, among others, and a fieldwork component included canvassing activities in the community to identify the needs of youth. Students were trained to work with youth with behavioral problems within a family and a community context (Perez Montalvo, 2003). This program also prepared students to work with different entities in the community, such as family doctors and community leaders. Graduates from this program were called *emergentes* because their primary role was to do home visits to identify the emerging needs and problems of children, single mothers, and the elderly (Strug & Teague, 2004). They also worked very closely with other youth group organizations on health promotion programs and supporting civic and political activities (Perez Montalvo, 2003).

As Cuba continued to struggle with serious economic problems, the government developed new policies to fund professional studies in the hard sciences. These measures did not favor the profession, and in 2008 the University of Havana was forced to close its professional social work program. Today, the Ministry of Education offers a technical social work program and oversees training of new social workers (Strug, 2015b).

Social Work in Cuba Today and the Role of Social Workers in Health Care

Today, the social work workforce in Cuba is quite diverse. It is represented by social workers with different training levels; some hold a 6-year university professional degree or *licenciatura de Rehabilitacion Social y Ocupacional*, a great majority are middle technicians or *tecnico medio* and graduated from the technical training institutes where more than 2,000 social workers were trained, and the last group is the paraprofessional workers who came out of the *emergente* youth programs.

Social workers are employed in many settings, including polyclinics, hospitals, community-based organizations, schools, and governmental offices (Herman et al., 2014). A large number of social workers are employed in the health field and work as members of primary care health teams with a doctor and a nurse (*grupo basico medico*; Odalyz Gonzalez Juban, personal communication, June 2015). Primary health care teams are a part of the family medicine program established in 1984. A family physician and a nurse see approximately 150 families within an assigned geographic region in the community where they live. The family physician sees patients in the morning and does home visits in the afternoon. The primary care health team engages in health promotion initiatives and disease prevention; these are central components of clinical practice in Cuba (Dresang, Brebrick, Murray, Shallue, & Sullivan-Vedder, 2005).

To illustrate social work practice in Cuba today and its role in health care, the following discussion integrates some excerpts from the author's work in Cuba. The goal of the research was to learn about social work practice in Cuba. The study was qualitative and exploratory in nature, using semi-guided interviews. A nonprobability purposive sample was used with 24 volunteer participants. Participants were social workers (45% had technical degrees and 55% had professional degrees) with different levels of work experience. They were invited to participate in the study by two social work colleagues with whom the author had extended communication via email and phone after visiting Cuba for the first time in 2013. The interviews were conducted between July 2014 and May 2016. A case vignette of intimate partner violence that included demographic characteristics and living conditions that applied to many families in Cuba was used.

Some of the participants in the study worked with doctors and nurses in primary health care teams in their own communities. They reported that one of the main roles of a social worker is to complete an assessment that identifies the biopsychosocial needs of the individual and the family. A second role is to coordinate services for clients by making appropriate referrals and working with various community-based organizations to secure positive outcomes for the client system. These tasks are in line with case management activities done in the United States by social workers at the undergraduate and graduate levels.

One example of social work intervention on primary health care teams regards intimate partner violence. The referral for a home visit may come from the CDR, which may have received notification from a concerned neighbor or directly from the victim. The CDR is charged with functions in immunization projects, civil defense, and neighborhood safety (Perez

Hernandez, 2003). During the home visit, the social worker interviews the couple and other family members who may potentially be affected, such as children and the elderly. After the assessment of the case is completed, the social worker notifies the family doctor and nurse and a treatment plan is developed to address the social, psychological, and medical needs of the client system. In cases in which physical violence is present, the social worker notifies the CDR, which follows up with a report to the local authorities. The following is an excerpt of the course of action that one of the participants described with the case vignette; she is a social worker working with a primary care health team (translated from Spanish):

> The first thing I do is to carry out an in-depth interview with all family members involved to obtain all the related parts of the problem. This is important in order to come up with a social diagnosis. I respect the views of family members even if there is disagreement among them; this is central to developing a good relationship with the family. There are various alternatives; I refer the woman for assistance to one of the attention centers for women and families of the Federation of Cuban Women located in her neighborhood. A social worker there will provide psycho-education on the problem of violence and will persuade her to report the abuse to the police. In addition, upon completing my assessment our primary care health team may recommend that a child psychologist evaluate the children for any trauma issues that may be present as a result of domestic violence. The children should also be evaluated for any educational deficits that may be present due to family stress. With regards to the older adults living in the family, they too, should be assessed; I could link them with services at La Casa del Abuelo (senior day program). Not only the woman is at risk in a case of domestic violence but also the entire family is at risk. With regards to the housing problems and the electricity I will report the problems to the Popular Council of the neighborhood, they are in charge of providing assistance with these types of problems.

Polyclinics are a secondary level of care in which a significant number of social workers are employed. Polyclinics are specialized clinics staffed by multidisciplinary teams. Patients are referred to polyclinics when their medical and social needs are beyond the services that can be provided by the primary care health team in a local clinic or *consultorio* (Dresang et al.,

2005). In 2008, there were 470 polyclinics; specialty care in polyclinics often includes pediatrics, gerontology, internal medicine, social work, and physical therapy. Service provision is approached from a preventive and curative model that integrates the social needs of individuals and their families (Offredy, 2008).

One of the participants of the study related her experiences working at a polyclinic. The following excerpt illustrates the ethical challenges faced by many social workers as they struggle to provide the best care to patients with very limited resources. Most of the participants of the study shared similar experiences:

> As a social worker in a polyclinic I am faced every day with making decisions about the distribution of resources. One of the values of the social work profession is social justice. That means that I need to realize that I work with subjects not objects, clients are human beings and I need to show solidarity. Solidarity means I need to share what I have and understand what my patients feel. For example, yesterday an elderly woman came with her son to the polyclinic to pick up a wheelchair. She brought the authorization from her family doctor but I had to deny her request. I had giving the only wheelchair we had to a woman suffering from cancer that was very debilitated by the treatment and needed the wheelchair more than the elderly woman. The elderly woman understood and accepted the refusal, I told her she would be on the waiting list and she should call us in a few weeks. I'm face with decisions like this every day, we have very few resources and we need to prioritize. Scarce resources have to go to the people who need them the most, I cannot show favoritism and I need to be fair.

A smaller group of social workers at the technical and professional levels have advanced training in psychiatry, and they work in tertiary level of care settings such as hospitals. Although social work in Cuba does not prepare practitioners for advanced mental health practice like graduate programs do in the United States, social workers with some additional training in psychiatry are equipped to do crisis intervention, psychoeducation with couples and families, and support interventions such as talk therapy (Mabel Molina, personal communication, June 2016). The following is an excerpt from an interview with one of the participants working in a hospital:

With this case, I will complete a bio-psychosocial assessment (*historia social siquiatrica*). The woman in this case wants to stay with her abusive husband. Many women don't want to acknowledge a problem of domestic violence and look for reasons to justify their partner's violent behaviors. As I get to know more about the client's history I can help the woman understand her problem by using some therapeutic techniques such as motivational interviewing. In that case, where the woman has accepted that she is a victim of domestic violence and is willing to come forward as a victim, she usually goes to the police and reports it. If the woman accepts her problem I will be able to help her. I will also offer her couples counseling or family therapy, but it is her decision to accept the services.

The excerpts presented in this section highlight some of the functions that social workers perform in various roles and health care settings. A common theme is the emphasis placed on the family as the focus of the intervention rather than the individual and also the community-based programs as the main providers of services. This is true for social work and also for medicine. A concrete and interesting example of this is demonstrated by neighborhood clinics, in which only one medical record is kept for the entire family as supposed to an individual record per patient (Dresang et al., 2005). This community-oriented focus, in which different professionals and community members collaborate, is the foundation of health care delivery in Cuba, and it is in line with the tenets of socialist ideology.

Social Policies and the Current Political System

The life of a single human being is worth a million times more than all the property of the richest man on earth . . . far more important than good remuneration is the pride of serving one's neighbor. Much more definitive and much more lasting than all the gold that one can accumulate is the gratitude of a people. And each doctor, within the circle of his activities, can and must accumulate that valuable treasure, the gratitude of the people.

—Ernesto "Che" Guevara, "On Revolutionary Medicine" (1960; as cited in Andaya, 2009, p. 357)

This quote conveys an ideology of sacrifice and altruism. In Cuba, the sacrifice of the individual's material profits for the benefit of the whole and the "gratitude of people" is considered the essence of a true revolutionary. "The pride of serving one's neighbor" was evident in the enthusiasm and sense of duty to their work expressed by the participants of the study. It would be feasible to argue that the adherence to this socialist ideology has fostered and sustained resilience among social workers and other health care professionals who, despite the many challenges they encounter on a daily basis due to lack of resources, bureaucratic barriers, and systematic corruption, remain committed to their work. Study participants regularly cited values of social justice, solidarity, community, altruism, family, and love as their guiding principles for social work practice.

"Social Work Is a Labor of Love. Social Work Is a Calling, Not a Job"

As previously indicated, social work practice in Cuba is intrinsically tied to the health care system. As a result, economic, political, and ideological variables shaping Cuban public health policies have a direct effect on the livelihood of the social work profession and on its practice trends.

For more than 50 years under a socialist government, Cubans have received social protections that guaranteed universal and free health care, free education, a subsidized food program, guaranteed employment, and partially subsidized housing (Del Carmen Zabala Argüelles, 2010). This transformation post-revolution, some argue, was primarily the result of the significant financial support Cuba received from the former Soviet Union (Chaguaceda, 2013). With the loss of the support of the Soviet Union, Cuba's economy collapsed, the infrastructure of the health care system was barely operational, the supply of medicines diminished significantly, and many seriously ill patients were not able to receive treatment and were sent back to their homes (Goicoechea-Balbona & Conill-Mendoza, 2000). The government responded by developing health care policies that called for collaborative action to address the "collective needs." These policies led to the implementation of a community medicine model with the consolidation of mass organizations and the action and collaboration of professionals from different sectors (Backwith & Mantle, 2009).

This intersectoral approach to health care delivery has been identified as an important element responsible for Cuba's achievement of exceptional health outcomes (Spiegel et al., 2012). An example of this intersectoral work is the management of a case of intimate partner violence. As reflected in the excerpts presented previously, professionals from different sectors in the health field, such as family doctors, gerontologists, pediatricians, psychologists, and social workers, work together with representatives of mass organizations such as the Cuban Federation of Women, the Committee for the Defense of the Revolution, the Popular Council, and other community-based organizations, such as La Casa del Abuelo (a senior day program). Despite many economic and geopolitical challenges, this health care infrastructure has been shown to be effective and has allowed Cuba to continue to achieve health outcomes comparable to those of developed countries (Spiegel & Yassi, 2004).

Looking Forward

Despite the significant achievements in health care, today Cuba continues to suffer the economic sequel of the Special Period. Access to timely services and medical resources is poor, and full government subsidization of social services is at risk (Strug, 2015a). Although the infrastructure of health care and social services remains the same, the rise in social problems such as increased poverty, prostitution, drug use, and nutrition problems is significant and challenges the efficacy of the system. Lack of collaboration and miscommunication among sectors are becoming prevalent, leading to inconsistencies in program objectives and outcomes and thus causing overlap and competition for resources among service providers, affecting health care delivery at the community level (Uriarte, 2002).

An important change in the past 15 years that may have indirect negative consequences in the health outcomes of Cuban people is the widening of the income gap among Cubans. A new social class has slowly emerge as a result of economic reforms introduced in the 1990s that allowed individuals to operate in-home restaurants or *paladares* and rent rooms or apartments to tourists; other sources of income are family remittances from the United States and other countries, jobs in tourism that secure tips (Backwith & Mantle, 2009), and an underground economy of the sale of food imports in the Cuban convertible peso (CUC; dollar equivalent value) food market (Font, 2004).

Although new economic policies in Cuba are improving the financial status and living standards of some citizens and also improving the overall economy of the country, these changes may create conflict and tension among citizens because not everyone is benefiting from these policies in the same manner. The rise of social classes as a result of new economic policies contradicts the principles of equity and social justice that have been the foundation of the socioeconomic and political structure of socialist Cuba. These new socioeconomic trends could potentially lead to a health gap among Cubans as well as changes in the entire health care and social service infrastructure of the country. For instance, studies have identified income inequality as a social determinant of negative health outcomes. This has been demonstrated by mortality rates in children and a higher incidence of cirrhosis (Lynch et al., 2001), life expectancy differences between White and African American men in the United States (Marmot, 2001), and an association between income inequality and poor or fair self-reported health (Sturm,& Gresenz, 2002).

As Cuba continues to grapple with economic challenges, social stratification by income, and an increase in social problems, social service structure and practice delivery may require changes in order to continue to secure positive health outcomes for the Cuban people. Social justice from a social work practice standpoint may need to be redefined to include the many intersections of clients' socioeconomic status, ethnicity, gender, religion, sexual orientation, and ability and how these contribute to the overall health and social conditions of the individual (Suárez, Newman, & Reed, 2008). Cuba may have to adopt a social work practice approach similar to that used in the United States, in which a major focus is placed on the diversity of individual clients within the context of the working relationship with the social worker rather than focusing on the overall needs of the collective (Rothman, 2008).

Conclusion

Cuba has generated significant interest among researchers in medicine, and there seems to be a growing body of literature focused on Cuba's success in sustaining a functional health care system under very precarious economic conditions. Spiegel and Yassi (2004) argue that Cuba's success with regard to health outcomes has challenged the assumption that "generating wealth is the fundamental precondition for improving health" (p. 85). On the other hand, there is little literature available on social work practice in Cuba, and the literature on the role that social workers play in the health care system is almost nonexistent. This provides an opportunity for meaningful research on these topics.

This chapter offered a brief examination of social work practice in Cuba. Social work is a fundamental element of the community-based infrastructure of the health care system of the country, and social workers are key contributors to the overall success of disease prevention efforts, health promotion initiatives, and direct social work services. The profession as an entity has become resilient, just like the Cuban people, and despite many socioeconomic and political challenges, the social work profession in Cuba remains a model of grassroots labor for the social work world.

As Cuba's economic and social infrastructure frames continue to be transformed by internal policies and external factors such as globalization, new approaches to health care delivery and social work practice may be implemented. Further research to better understand Cuba's evolution and the role of the social work profession in contributing to a social justice-informed approach to health care delivery is needed.

In closing, Cuba and the United States can learn from each other's successes and failures in the delivery of health care. Social workers in the United States could benefit from considering more social work models that emphasize family and community involvement. Similarly, Cuban social workers could gain from giving more consideration in their practice models to the diversity of the individual.

References

Allen, J. A., Bailey, D., Dubus, N., & Wichinsky, L. (2015). The interrelationship of the origins and present state of social work in the United States and Cuba: The power of a profession to bridge cultures. *Journal of Human Behavior in the Social Environment, 25*(1), 18–25.

Andaya, E. (2009). The gift of health. *Medical Anthropology Quarterly, 23*(4), 357–374.

Backwith, D., & Mantle, G. (2009). Inequalities in health and community-oriented social work: Lessons from Cuba? *International Social Work, 52*(4), 499–511.

Chaguaceda, A (2013). Cuba: What social justice are we speaking of? *Havana Times*. Retrieved February 20, 2017, from http://www.havanatimes.org/?p=99380

Del Carmen Zabala Argüelles, M. (2010). Poverty and vulnerability in Cuba today. *Socialism and Democracy, 24*(1), 109–126.

Dresang, L. T., Brebrick, L., Murray, D., Shallue, A., & Sullivan-Vedder, L. (2005). Family medicine in Cuba: Community-oriented primary care and complementary and alternative medicine. *Journal of the American Board of Family Practice, 18*(4), 297–303.

Font, A. M. (2004). *Cuba today: Continuity and change since the "período especial."* New York, NY: City University of New York.

Goicoechea-Balbona, A., & Conill-Mendoza, E. (2000). International inclusiveness: Publicizing Cuba's development of the "good life." *International Social Work, 43*(4), 435–451.

Herman, C., Zlotnik, J. L., & Collins, S. (2014). *Social services in Cuba.* Washington, DC: NASW Press.

Lambie, G. (2011). Healthcare in Cuba: A model for sustainability? *Journal of Holistic Healthcare, 8*(2), 38.

Lynch, J., Smith, G. D., Hillemeier, M., Shaw, M., Raghunathan, T., & Kaplan, G. (2001). Income inequality, the psychosocial environment, and health: Comparisons of wealthy nations. *Lancet, 358*(9277), 194–200.

Marmot, M. (2001). Inequalities in health. *New England Journal of Medicine, 345*(2), 134–136.

Offredy, M. (2008). The health of a nation: Perspectives from Cuba's national health system. *Quality in Primary Care, 16*(4), 269–277.

Perez Hernandez, L. (2003). Education as protagonist of social policies. *Journal of the Cuban American Alliance, 2*(2), 10–14.

Perez Montalvo, L (2003). Social work experience in Cuba. *Journal of the Cuban American Alliance, 2*(2), 15–18.

Rothman, J. C. (2008). *Cultural competence in process and practice.* Boston, MA: Pearson.

Spiegel, J., Alegret, M., Clair, V., Pagliccia, N., Martinez, B., Bonet, M., & Yassi, A. (2012). Intersectoral action for health at a municipal level in Cuba. *International Journal of Public Health, 57*(1), 15–23.

Spiegel, J. M., & Yassi, A. (2004). Lessons from the margins of globalization: Appreciating the Cuban health paradox. *Journal of Public Health Policy, 25*, 85–110.

Strug, D. (2006). Community-oriented social work in Cuba: Government response to emerging social problems. *Social Work Education, 25*(7), 749–762.

Strug, D. (2015a). A faculty development program in Cuba for American social work academics. *Journal of Human Behavior in the Social Environment, 25*(1), 3–13.

Strug, D. (2015b). *Cuba and Cuban social work at a time of change*. Alexandria, VA: Council of Social Work Education.

Strug, D., & Teague, W. (2004). Cuba's social work education initiative. In M. A. Font, S. Larson, & D. Xuereb (Eds.), *Cuba Today* (pp. 271–275). New York, NY. Bildner Center for Western Hemisphere Studies.

Sturm, R., & Gresenz, C. R. (2002). Relations of income inequality and family income to chronic medical conditions and mental health disorders: National survey. *BMJ, 324*(7328), 20.

Suárez, Z., Newman, P., & Reed, B. G. (2008). Critical consciousness and cross-cultural/intersectional social work practice: A case analysis. *Families in Society, 89*(3), 407–417.

Uriarte, M. (2002). *Cuba, social policy at a crossroads: Maintaining priorities, transforming practice*. Boston, MA: Oxfam.

8

Health Care Social Work in England

Malcolm Payne

Introduction: Structure and Legal Basis of English Social Work

England is the largest of four nations in the United Kingdom of Great Britain and Northern Ireland. Northern Ireland, Scotland, and Wales have national parliaments. The UK Parliament at Westminster in London is responsible for shared matters as well as policy and law covering England. The United Kingdom and Ireland are the two nations that make up the British Isles, an archipelago situated off the northwest coast of Europe. Both countries are members of the European Union, a regional economic bloc, although in a referendum in 2016, the UK electorate voted to leave the Union.

Under European and UK law, social work is a regulated profession with protected title, meaning that nobody can describe themselves as a social worker in a professional context unless they have been registered as such by the national regulatory authority (Hussein, 2011). In England, that regulatory agency is the Health and Care Professions Council (HCPC), which registers a number of therapeutic professions (although not clinical psychology and counseling) and approves social work education programs as suitable qualifications. Social work is the largest profession regulated by the HCPC. In 2016, 93,444 social workers were registered (Health and Care Professions Council, 2016). Proposals for changing the English registration arrangements are currently before Parliament.

Many social workers, both in the UK and in England, are employed in local government "social care" agencies. Social workers concerned with children and families usually work in departments providing education and children's services. As of September 2014, 26,810 were employed by English local authorities, with a vacancy rate of 15% (Department for Education, 2015, p. 1). Social workers concerned with adults usually work in adult social care departments. As of September 2015, 14,700 social workers were employed by these departments, with a vacancy rate of 13% (Health and

Social Care Information Centre, 2016, Table 4.5). Occasionally, these departments are joined with each other or with other local government departments such as housing.

Private companies provide social services mainly by contract to local government social care agencies. Charitable voluntary or not-for-profit agencies also do this but provide alternative types of service in some areas. Social work in England is essentially a local government profession. The few social workers in private practice are usually dual qualified in a psychotherapeutic and counseling profession and would not describe themselves as social workers. There have been successful experiments in contracting local government social care services to small professional companies formed by social workers (Le Grand, 2012). Currently, there is debate about whether this would be a good model for future development, fostering professional independence from local government structures while continuing local government accountability for important public services.

Registered social workers are a small proportion of employees in the adult social care sector, which covers the main areas of health care social provision and provides approximately 1.3 million jobs. More than two-thirds of employees are in the private sector, approximately one-fifth in the voluntary sector, and 10% in local government. Approximately 38% are employed in residential care (Skills for Care, 2015).

There are three main legal bases of social work responsibilities in local government. The Children Act 1989 is concerned with the care and safeguarding of children, including adoption and foster care. Social workers are responsible for investigating concerns about abuse and neglect of children and for managing any care and supervision considered necessary. The Care Act 2014 is concerned with social care services to adults. Provisions include care homes, day care, home care, assistive technology and equipment, and support and social work for people with intellectual and physical disabilities, mental disorders, and those in later life. The Mental Health Act 1983, which was significantly amended by the Mental Health Act 2007, is concerned with legal protection of and providing services to mentally ill people. All of this legislation accords local authority social workers legal powers to intervene in people's lives—for example, taking children into care and ensuring compulsory care for people with mental disorders. Various other pieces of legislation are relevant to the structure of services and service provisions for particular groups of people.

The crucial legal and administrative distinction between health care and social care is responsibility for paying the cost. Health care is a free national service, paid for from general taxation, and social care is a local government service, for which service users pay charges toward the cost. The policy principle behind this distinction is that whereas health care needs are considered exceptional in people's lives, social care services substitute for the normal activities of daily living, for which people remain responsible even if they are unable to carry them out. For example, where parents are found to have neglected or abused their children, they remain responsible for contributing toward the cost of local authority care. Adults who require social care services are similarly assessed for ability to pay, up to a significant proportion of their wealth, including the value of their house if they own one. These distinctions have been inhibitors of integration between health and social care services.

Policy for children's social care is formulated through the Westminster government's Department for Education, and that for adult social care is formulated through the Department of Health. Both issue guidance and manage the implementation of policy in their respective fields. Because most private and voluntary sector social care depends on local government contracts, government policy sets the main parameters of social work practice. Services are financed by local taxes, charges, and a grant provided through the Department for Communities and Local Government. Legislation, policy development, administration, and finance of both children's and adults' social care are therefore organized through separate lines of accountability from health care, which is financed through the Department of Health.

The main professional association, the British Association of Social Workers (BASW), has special interest groups that organize conferences and policy work; currently, there are groups for renal disease and for alcohol and other drugs (BASW, 2016). In the past, there have been groups for social workers interested in other medical specialties and in aging (Payne, 2002). BASW's structure includes a "reference group" on social work with adults, which covers many health care interests. BASW is linked with a small trade union for social workers, but many local government and health care social workers are members of the local government employees' union, Unison.

Up-to-date information about UK social work can be obtained from the websites of the organizations cited in this section.

The Social and Political Context of English Health Care Social Work: The National Health Service

Health care in the United Kingdom is provided by a range of locally managed services responsible to national parliaments but branded across the United Kingdom as the National Health Service (NHS). Free health care provision through the NHS is a politically sacrosanct social policy.

Residents of the United Kingdom are registered with a local group of primary care doctors, called general practitioners (GPs), of their choice. GPs employ administrative support and professionals on a primary health care team (PHCT), which may include social workers and counselors. PHCTs are financed by annual payments to the GP for each registered patient, funded from taxation. People seeking health care approach their GP for consultation and treatment. When diagnostic or treatment requires resources beyond GPs' capacities, GPs refer patients to a hospital or other health care facilities. Commissioning groups of PHCTs have contracts with local health care facilities for most common provision, but they can pay for services anywhere, even abroad. All treatment and care is funded, through the commissioning groups, by taxation. Prescriptions for medication and equipment are free in hospitals and for children, older people, and people with disabilities; there is a standard charge for others. In emergencies, anyone in the United Kingdom may go to the urgent care/accident and emergency center of any local hospital for treatment, free of charge. Accidents and medical emergencies are attended by the local NHS ambulance service, with paramedics who provide immediate assessment and treatment.

Social Work in Health Care Services

Each area has a variable pattern of connections between local authority social care and health commissioners. The Health and Social Care Act 2012 requires local authorities to establish a Health and Wellbeing Board responsible for local coordination, future planning, and preventive health care. This still-developing innovation may become a future basis for integrated planning for health and social care provision.

Hospitals are organized in departments by medical specialty. Many specialist teams have one or more social workers attached. These social workers usually work together as part of a social work department. Since the 1970s, most hospital social workers have been employed by the adult social care department and outposted to local hospitals. In recent years, however, pressure on local government finances has sometimes led to hospital teams' responsibilities being limited to managing child protection referrals and assessment for adult social care packages, mainly for older people on discharge from the hospital. Some specialist medical teams have therefore obtained funding to employ social workers from health care budgets, and the pattern of social work provision has become more varied.

Home health care is coordinated by GPs and the PHCT, but commissioning groups employ teams of health care staff for specialist work—for example, in geriatrics or for long-term conditions. End-of-life care is provided by a network of charitable hospices, most with inpatient facilities and community palliative care services and which coordinate their work with patients' GPs. By tradition, they employ social workers to provide psychosocial care and family and bereavement support. In the absence of a local hospice, end-of-life care provided by local health care services often continues this tradition. The Association of Palliative Care Social Workers (2016) is a specialized professional group within social work that is not connected to BASW.

Where social care services are required, PHCTs refer patients to local authority services, and they refer hospitals to their own social workers or directly to the local authority. Local agreements coordinate these arrangements and integrate social care with health care provision. The pinch point is discharge from hospitals. Patients no longer requiring hospital medical treatment have to wait sometimes for days or weeks while community care is put in place by PHCTs and adult social care departments.

History of Health Care Social Work

Hospital-based social work in England dates from the appointment in 1895 of Mary Stewart, a worker with the London Charity Organization Society (COS), to reduce abuse of charitable funding for treatment and overcrowding in the outpatients' department (Willmott, 1996). Many charitable hospitals developed this role, particularly helping with the practical and relationship consequences of extreme poverty among working people.

Guilds of help in many northern industrial towns formed a different tradition, focusing on the public health objectives of reducing infant mortality and tuberculosis. More collectivist than the COS, they often worked along-side local authority public health professionals. An aftercare service established in 1909 at St. Thomas's Hospital London for tuberculosis patients was so successful that it became a national statutory service in 1919. This raised the profile and built acceptance of the profession. As the local authorities took over Poor Law hospitals in the 1930s, with their large populations of poor elderly and disabled people, they extended the use of medical social work into these institutions. With the creation of the NHS in 1948, the charitable and Poor Law hospitals were merged into a single system, and medical social work became increasingly widespread (Payne, 2005, p. 39). As the NHS developed, attempts were made to include social work in PHCTs, either by attachment of social workers to GPs or by liaison systems between local authorities and GP practices (Collins, 1965; Gilchrist et al., 2009; Goldberg & Neill, 1972). It was found that the most effective strategy was to employ well-planned services working directly with patients (Corney, 1980).

Following the reorganization of local authorities and the NHS in 1974, all responsibility for social work was transferred from the NHS to local authorities. Community care emerged as the central policy for all adult care. During the 1980s, deinstitutionalization policies aimed to close large geographically isolated hospitals for geriatric patients and mentally ill and intellectually disabled children and adults, transferring funding from hospital to community health and social care services. In an influential experiment, Davies and Challis (1986) employed American case management processes to develop "care management" in which social workers created tailored packages of care involving public, private, and voluntary sector care organizations and informal caregiving from a variety of sources. The innovation sought to make more flexible and economical provision for all adult groups, particularly older people. This was adopted nationwide as assessment and care planning for community care became the main function of local authority adult social care (Lewis & Glennerster, 1996; Payne, 1995).

The first specialized professional organization in British social work, the Hospital Almoners' Committee, was created by health-related social workers in 1903. It eventually transmuted in the early 1920s into the Institute of Almoners and later the Institute of Medical Social Workers. The institute developed a well-regarded 1-year training course in the 1920s and maintained control of the curriculum of medical social work education until 1970, when it merged with other organizations into the BASW.

Social Work Practice in Health Care

Social workers in health care services provided by the NHS and in palliative care are an important focus of health care social work. Their main responsibilities are helping people manage the financial, practical, and relationship consequences of treatment in hospital for serious or long-term conditions. This includes advocacy for social security benefits for disabled people and informal caregivers and for discretionary financial benefits. Other issues are emotional responses to physical illness and disability, such as anxiety about survival being dependent on machinery, or relationship concerns, such as adjustment to changes in sexual relationships at the onset of disability. Increasing numbers of older people in the population have stimulated interest in gerontological social work because "the particular skill and knowledge set of social workers uniquely equips them to manage the intersection of issues that currently challenge health and welfare services: complex needs, risk, transitions, end of life, carer stress and frailty" (Ray et al., 2015, p. 1296).

An important focus of this work is the concept of loss, including grief and bereavement as a result of the death of a loved one, and the impact of the loss of a limb or sensory capacity, well-being, leisure-life, personal development, and work opportunities that results from illness and disability (Currer, 2007). An example is working with the relatives of an older person whose personality and identity have been severely altered by dementia. Another important theoretical concept is attachment, considered important across the life course in understanding children's behavioral difficulties, marital and relationship difficulties in adulthood, and bereavement (Howe, 2011).

Outside clinical settings, the main focus of the social work role continues to be assessment for packages of community care services. A "single assessment process" was introduced for older people in 2002 (Department of Health, 2002). Local services agreed to share tools and formats for assessment so that information could be exchanged more easily. Another important aspect of the assessment role is intervention to safeguard vulnerable adults from abuse and mistreatment. Local authority social workers play a central coordinating and interventive role.

Since the 1990s, following campaigns by informal caregivers' groups (the British terminology is "carer"), the value of informal care of disabled and older people by friends, relatives, and local networks has been increasingly recognized. Legislation has been developed, and further strengthened by the Care Act 2014, to require assessment of informal caregivers' needs when adults receive a community care assessment, but this is weakened by poor resources to provide services and inconsistency in planning (Mitchell & Glendinning, 2017). Nevertheless, a network of carers' organizations makes group work and mutual support available in many areas, including for adult and child bereavement. Recently, this network has also begun to work with schools and community organizations to raise understanding of death and dying (Paul, 2016; Sallnow & Paul, 2015).

Practice developments in care management led to concepts of "person-centered care" or personalization, implemented first in local government social care and then extended to NHS home health care provision (Burton, Toscano, & Zonouzi, 2012; Coalition for Collaborative Care, 2016; Gardner, 2014). The "independent living" movement, mainly of disabled people, was an important source, seeking greater independence from "care" by others. It emphasized "self-directed care," with practitioners acting as brokers between "service users" and services. Personal assistants would be directly employed and managed by the disabled person or a relative or by mutual aid organizations of disabled people. The second source was the related concept of "direct payments" or "independent budgeting." Rather than organize community care packages of services, social workers took part in a process of "co-production" of services. Consideration of options to meet users needs led to the development of a budgetary estimate, negotiated by social workers, informal caregivers, and service users. Cash payments based on the budget allow users and caregivers to manage their own services. These developments are part of an international trend toward "cash for care" schemes (Arksey & Kemp, 2008; Timonen, Convery, & Cahill, 2006). An important philosophical element is an emphasis on dignity as a principle in providing care for people who might otherwise be provided with services in a mechanistic way (Skills for Care, 2013).

Critique of this innovation suggests that it promotes withdrawal from public responsibility for care of others. Also, governmentality, ensuring that arrangements are efficient and well managed, is displaced from public organizations to members of the public (Scourfield, 2007). Older people and those without relatives to help are less willing to participate in co-production (Ellis, 2007). Moreover, social workers still exercise control over arrangements, and flexibility depends on the resourcing and policy of the agency, as well as the practitioner's advocacy and brokerage skills (Gilchrist et al., 2009).

An important aspect of end-of-life care that has influenced social work more widely is advance care planning, a process of discussing plans for care when illness or increasing disability reduces a clients' capacity for independent decision-making. Official guidance on practice under the Care Act 2012 proposes that all adults receiving health and social care should be involved by social workers not merely in assessment but also in a process of "person-centered care and support planning" (Department of Health, 2016, Chapters 10–13), which extends discussion of future care options across the care career from the first contact with social care services (Payne, 2013). The source of this process is discussion of end-of-life care plans in palliative care, leading to the possibility of making advance decisions ("advance directives" in American terminology) to refuse treatment at the end of life (Henry & Seymour, 2011). Projects such as "preferred priorities of care" sought to help patients express their preferences in wider aspects of care, and projects aimed at "anticipatory care planning" in Scotland demonstrated that helping people think through and keep a record of their hoped-for "personal outcomes" made it more likely that their preferences could later be honored (Cook & Miller, 2012).

Government policy continues to experiment with coordinating integrated services to provide for patients with complex health care needs and those with long-term conditions (Goodwin, Sonola, Thiel, & Kodner, 2013). McGregor, Mercer, and Harris's (2018) systematic review of empirical research on the role of primary care social work found that patients with complex health and social needs derived measurable health benefits from social work intervention in primary care, with improved subjective health functioning and self-management, reduced psychosocial morbidity, and reduced barriers to treatment and health maintenance. Interventions with a dual focus on individual and social factors measurably improved psychosocial well-being and enabled patients to make better health decisions. The advantages of the interventions were that patients believed that their concerns were heard and accepted and that their health and illness were understood in the context of their lives. There were also gains in practical assistance, education, and empowerment. Beneficial impacts on clinical care and continuity of care were found, reducing the need for clinicians to concentrate on psychosocial issues and contributing to identifying at-risk groups in populations for which GPs were responsible. In this way, developing social work in primary care is thought likely to contribute to intervention to combat health inequalities. A focus on health inequalities is an increasingly important feature of health care social work, stimulated by the Marmot Review (2010), which drew attention to the social determinants of health care inequalities. A research seminar series, a network of practitioners and academics, and publications have followed (Bywaters, McLeod, & Napier, 2009).

The history of administrative, financial, legislative, and, consequently, professional division between health and social care has stimulated policy and practice initiatives to promote joint and integrated collaboration between the professions and services involved. Past initiatives involved joint service planning processes, teamwork development, and financial transfers from the well-funded health care services to patchily funded social care provision. Recently, there has been a greater emphasis on identifying and measuring jointly agreed outcomes. Evidence suggests that collaboration can result in improved subjective health and well-being of patients and reduce inappropriate admissions to acute and residential care; in addition, joint intermediate care designed to rehabilitate people from acute to home care can reduce costs. Nevertheless, both professional and public understanding of the aims of integrated care are lacking, and studies have not assessed how integrated care is different from "usual care" systems, so it is difficult to form firm conclusions about the effectiveness of attempts to integrate services (Cameron, Lart, Bostock, & Coomber, 2014).

Conclusion: The Future of Health Care Social Work in England

This chapter has set out the dual aspects of health care social work in England: the traditional role of medical social work in health care institutions, mainly hospitals but also PHCTs, and the assessment and care management role in local government social work. Social care, and social work within it, is a well-established feature of British social provision, but its health care role remains marginal. This is because the administrative, financial, legal, and professional divisions between health and social care place social work on the boundary between poorly integrated service systems. Although the role of psychosocial help is recognized, it does not have a clear place in health care, with social work to represent it, and the social work profession has not established a clear identity and role for social work in broader community health and care services. Partly, this is because local government social care services, always underfunded in comparison with acute health care, have been under political and financial pressure for much of the past decade since the global financial crisis in 2008 placed public finances at risk. The new Health and Wellbeing Boards may provide a useful forum for stronger preventive practice and better integration in the future.

The work of hospital and hospice social workers in specialized medical fields continues to provide a strong basis for interpersonal and group work practice in social work. Much innovation in social care services in the 21st century has focused on the care management role, person-centered care planning, and service users' participation in co-production of services. Innovations in engagement with and support for informal caregivers are allied to this. There is criticism of mechanistic public service functioning and restrictive financial and policy demands. However, the opportunity is available to promote flexible, respectful practice within the limitations of a public service framework.

Notwithstanding uncertainty about the role of social work, imaginative innovations and developments in practice are taking place in health care social work. Advance care planning across the care career, community and group work with informal caregivers, collaboration with schools and community groups with regard to providing bereavement support, the development of advocacy and brokerage roles, the emphasis on dignity in care, and a strong focus on the need for social justice in responding to health inequalities all lay foundations for future opportunities to advance a social work contribution to health care provision. That these possibilities are present in a divided health and social care system that is under constant financial pressure speaks much for the imagination and commitment of practitioners to find new ways of responding to health and social need.

Division between health and social care services in England remains a central factor in the critique of poor coordination and lack of integration between various aspect of provision. Although this continues to be a focus of government concern and intervention, it is inherent in the legal and administrative divisions between free health care and fee-based social care. The identity and strength of social work can only be enhanced if practitioners continue to demonstrate good work at the intersection of health and social care, listening carefully and responding to the needs and wishes of patients, informal caregivers, and communities.

References

Arksey, H., & Kemp, P. A. (2008). *Dimensions of choice: A narrative review of cash-for-care schemes.* York, UK: Social Policy Research Unit.

Association of Palliative Care Social Workers. (2016). *The role of social workers in palliative, end of life and bereavement care.* London, UK: Author.

British Association of Social Workers. (2016). *Special interest groups.* Retrieved from https://www.basw.co.uk/what-we-do/groups-and-networks/special-interest-groups

Burton, J., Toscano, T., & Zonouzi, M. (2012). *Personalisation for social workers: Opportunities and challenges for frontline practice.* Maidenhead, UK: Open University Press.

Bywaters, P., McLeod, E., & Napier, L. (Eds.). (2009). *Social work and global health inequalities: Practice and policy developments.* Bristol, UK: Policy Press.

Cameron, A., Lart, R., Bostock, L., & Coomber, C. (2014). Factors that promote and hinder joint and integrated working between health and social care services: A review of research literature. *Health and Social Care in the Community, 22*(3), 225–233.

Coalition for Collaborative Care. (2016). *Personalised care and support planning handbook: The journey to person-centred care—Core information.* London, UK: NHS England. Retrieved from https://www.england.nhs.uk/wp-content/uploads/2016/04/core-info-care-support-planning-1.pdf

Collins, J. (1965). *Social casework in a general medical practice.* London, UK: Pitman.

Cook, A., & Miller, E. (2012). *Talking points: Personal outcomes approach: Practical guide.* Edinburgh, UK: Joint Improvement Team. Retrieved from http://www.jitscotland.org.uk/resource/talking-points-personal-outcomes-approach-practical-guide

Corney, R. H. (1980). Factors affecting the operation and success of social work attachment schemes to general practice. *Journal of the Royal College of General Practitioners, 30*(212), 149–157.

Currer, C. (2007). *Loss and social work.* Exeter, UK: Learning Matters.

Davies, B., & Challis, D. (1986). *Matching resources to needs in community care: An evaluated demonstration of a long-term care model.* Aldershot, UK: Gower.

Department for Education. (2015). *Children's social work workforce during year ending 30 September 2014.* Retrieved from https://www.gov.uk/government/uploads/system/uploads/attachment_data/file/406660/Children_s_Social_Work_Workforce_2013-14_SFR.pdf

Department of Health. (2002, November 19). *Tackling health inequalities—2002 cross-cutting review.* Retrieved from https://webarchive.nationalarchives.gov.uk/20110321235115/http://www.dh.gov.uk/en/Publicationsandstatistics/Publications/PublicationsPolicyAndGuidance/DH_4098280

Department of Health. (2016). *Care and support statutory guidance.* Retrieved from https://www.gov.uk/guidance/care-and-support-statutory-guidance

Ellis, K. (2007). Direct payments and social work practice: The significance of "street-level bureaucracy" in determining eligibility. *British Journal of Social Work, 37*(3), 405–422.

Gardner, A. (2014). *Personalisation in social work* (2nd ed.). London, UK: Sage.

Gilchrist, I. C., Gough, J. B., Horsfall-Turner, Y. R., Ineson, E. M., Keele, G., Marks, B., . . . Littlechild, R. (2009). *Direct payments and personal budgets: Putting personalisation into practice.* Bristol, UK: Policy Press.

Goldberg, E. M., & Neill, J. E. (1972). *Social work in general practice.* London, UK: Allen & Unwin.

Goodwin, N., Sonola, L., Thiel, V., & Kodner, D. L. (2013). *Co-ordinated care for people with complex chronic conditions: Key lessons and markers for success.* London, UK: King's Fund.

Health and Care Professions Council. (2016). *Statistics—Current.* Retrieved from http://www.hcpc-uk.org/aboutregistration/theregister/stats

Health and Social Care Information Centre. (2016). *Personal social services: Staff of social services departments, England as at September 2015.* Retrieved from https://digital.nhs.uk/data-and-information/publications/statistical/personal-social-services-staff-of-social-services-departments/personal-social-services-staff-of-social-services-departments-at-30-september-england-2015

Henry, C., & Seymour, J. (2011). *Advance care planning: A guide for health and social care staff.* London, UK: Department of Health.

Howe, D. (2011). *Attachment across the life course.* Basingstoke, UK: Palgrave Macmillan.

Hussein, S. (2011). *Social work qualifications and regulation in European Economic Area (EEA).* London, UK: General Social Care Council.

Le Grand, J. (2012). *Public service mutuals: The next steps.* London, UK: Cabinet Office.

Lewis, J., & Glennerster, H. (1996). *Implementing the new community care.* Buckingham, UK: Open University Press.

Marmot Review. (2010). *Fair society, healthy lives.* London, UK: Author.

McGregor, J., Mercer, S. W., & Harris, F. M. (2018). Health benefits of primary care social work for adults with complex health and social needs: A systematic review. *Health and Social Care in the Community, 26*(1), 1–13. doi:10.1111/hsc.12337

Mitchell, W., & Glendinning, C. (2017). Allocating personal budgets/grants to carers. *Journal of Social Work, 17*(6), 695–714. doi:10.1177/1468017316651994

Paul, S. (2016). Working with communities to develop resilience in end of life and bereavement care: Hospices, schools and health promoting palliative care. *Journal of Social Work, 30*(2), 187–201. doi:10.1080/02650533.2016.1168383

Payne, M. (1995). *Social work and community care.* Basingstoke, UK: Macmillan.

Payne, M. (2002). The role and achievements of a professional association in the late twentieth century: The British Association of Social Workers 1970–2000. *British Journal of Social Work, 32*(8), 969–995.

Payne, M. (2013). Extending advance care planning over the care career. *European Journal of Palliative Care, 20*(1), 34–37.

Payne, R. K. (2005). *A framework for understanding poverty.* Highlands, TX: Aha! Process, Inc.

Ray, M., Milne, A., Beech, C., Phillips, J. E., Richards, S., Sullivan, M. P., Tanner, D., & Lloyd, L. (2015). Gerontological social work: Reflections on its role, purpose and value. *British Journal of Social Work, 45*(4), 1296–1312.

Sallnow, L., & Paul, S. (2015). Understanding community engagement in end of life care: Developing conceptual clarity. *Critical Public Health, 25*(2), 231–238.

Scourfield, P. (2007). Social care and the modern citizen: Client, consumer, service user, manager and entrepreneur. *British Journal of Social Work, 37*(1), 107–122.

Skills for Care. (2013). *Delivering dignity in care services—The common core principles toolkit.* Retrieved from http://www.skillsforcare.org.uk/Topics/Dignity/Dignity.aspx

Skills for Care. (2015). *The state of the adult social care sector and workforce in England.* Retrieved from http://www.skillsforcare.org.uk/NMDS-SC-intelligence/Workforce-intelligence/publications/The-state-of-the-adult-social-care-sector-and-workforce-in-England.aspx

Timonen, V., Convery, J., & Cahill, S. (2006). Care revolutions in the making? A comparison of cash-for-care programmes in four European countries. *Ageing and Society, 26*, 455–474.

Willmott, P. (1996). 1895–1945: The first fifty years. In J. Baraclough, G. Dedman, H. Osborn, & P. Willmott (Eds.), *100 years of health related social work 1895–1995: Then–now–onwards* (pp. 1–20). Birmingham, UK: BAQSW Trading.

9

Health Care Social Work in India

Nemthianngai Guite

Introduction

Social work's response to a rapidly changing health care system requires an empirical approach to practice because dramatic changes in health care delivery have been stimulated by advances in technology and new approaches to the financing of health care. Currently, India has one of the highest disease burdens in the world. Many die of preventable diseases, and India's health crisis is driven by the unavailability of doctors and nurses, the high proportion of out-of-pocket expenditures on health care because of low insurance coverage, and weak public health systems. High health care costs often lead people to delay treatment, thus aggravating health problems. Emphasis on public health in India has increased in the past decade, but public health standards still remain among the lowest in the world. The poorest income classes benefit less from the public health system than do better-off sections of society. Therefore, structural changes that have led to the health care crisis have major implications for health care social work practice and education.

In India, social work emerged as a profession early in the 20th century and is now charged with supporting the country's social welfare mandate to promote well-being and quality of life. Thus, social work encompasses activities directed at improving human social conditions and alleviating human distress and social problems. There are many fields of social work practice; however, professional social work practice began in the health care field. In the health care field, practitioners work in medical settings such as hospitals, nursing homes and public health agencies, mental health institutions, and the community to raise awareness and promote health care.

Health care social work is the application and adoption of the method and philosophy of social work in the field of health and medical care. It is the branch of social work that deals with the social, physical, and psychological aspects of the patient. Social work in a medical setting uses relevant social skills and knowledge to help patients. However, in India, less importance has been given to this essential branch of health promotion. Although the Tata Institute of Social Sciences continues to pioneer the practice of social work in health care, the benefits of the profession's involvement in health care delivery have often not been widely appreciated. Most of the national health programs are operating at a snail's pace due to non-use of this field of medicine. Medical social work is a very powerful and essential branch of social medicine that studies the relationship between society, disease, and medicine in order to help provide comprehensive health care. As long as it is considered an offshoot of social work, it will draw little attention by medical personnel and health planners. This is the problem in India. The time has come to consider it as part and parcel of medical and health care.

History of Health Care Social Work in India

The nature of contemporary health care social work practice in the Indian health care system was not only driven by practical considerations but also heavily influenced by those with power (i.e., Western values and practice) within this health system and broader society. The most prevalent and visible practice was care provided in hospitals by medical and associated staff. The original development of Hospitals was through charitable care (often linked to religious organizations or, more recently, philanthropy); the responsibility of the state for such care is a more recent development, and care is often provided through local authorities. In India, social workers were recommended to be an integral part of the multidisciplinary health team by the Bhore Committee as early as 1946, and its history can be traced back to England and the United States. In addition to hospital care, a variety of professional (and nonprofessional) workers provided care in what became (more or less) a primary care system. Such primary care operated in parallel to hospital care, and the link between these two approaches in the form of formalized patient referral and coordinated approaches is relatively recent. The third arm is public health, with an initial focus on sanitation, water, and the control of infection. Public health was viewed as requiring state responsibility, in part because of the difficulty of encouraging or enforcing interventions that might be seen to favor wider society compared to individuals and in part because of the "public good" of such interventions.

Before the arrival of the British in India, the traditional systems of medicine were prevalent. Medical services largely remained primitive and unorganized. The advanced medical knowledge of the Vedic period (between 1500 and 500 BC) was gradually lost during subsequent centuries. Monasteries served the poor and the sick, but gradually they too plunged into anarchy. During the medieval period (i.e., the 8th to the 18th century), the medical services in India continued to deteriorate. They failed to keep pace with advances made in other areas of the world. They also failed to meet the needs of vast sections of the population. With the arrival of the British, new advances in medicines were gradually introduced in India through doctors who studied either in Britain or in newly established medical colleges in India (Varma, 2015). There is less documented evidence of voluntary organizations working in health care in India. Individuals carried out much of the charitable and philanthropic activities in the field of health. On a small scale, organized activities were confined to Christian missionaries who came to India. Perhaps the first voluntary health agency in India was the Indian Red Cross established in 1920. Today, it has a network of more than 400 branches. Following the end of British colonialism (Britain ruled India from 1858 to 1947), every health planning committee since the Bhore Committee has emphasized a primary health care approach and comprehensive health care for India's vast population.

As mentioned previously, the history of health care social work in India can be traced back to the first British hospital almoner and American medical social worker (1895 and 1905, respectively). During those times, when mental patients were discharged, acquaintances and nurses were asked to counsel them. In 1905, Boston physician Richard Cabot opined that medical science should also include the study of emotional and social problems. He suggested that medical students should work as volunteers for charities and agencies. The same year, a Boston medical institution appointed a social worker for the first time.

It is from Britain and the United States that reference was taken for the establishment of medical social workers in India. In India, the Tata Institute of Social Sciences took the lead in offering a course in medical social work in 1946. It remained one of the most sought-after specializations among students despite several limitations in practice settings. Social workers experienced only limited success in asserting their professional autonomy and assimilating into the medical professional world. Unfortunately, with the current turmoil of change in the health care system in India, social work appears to be losing ground in the hospital sector.

Until 1975, students who graduated from social work educational institutions with specialization in medical and psychiatric social work were employed predominantly in medical settings such as state governments, and most Indian states accepted their qualifications for work in physical health settings. Since then, health care settings throughout the country have followed a multidisciplinary approach, and the need for social workers to aid patients with psychosocial problems has been acknowledged. In meeting the health needs of India's more than 1.3 billion people—more than one-sixth of the world's population—the role of social workers is critical, especially with regard to grassroots-level workers. In urban areas today, medical social workers are an integral part of health care delivery. The number of voluntary agencies working in the field of health has increased significantly. Huge international funds are flowing into voluntary agencies working in areas related to AIDS, reproductive health, and so on. In India, where resources are limited, meeting the health needs of the vast population is not possible without the assistance of private and nongovernmental organizations.

The Social Policies and Political Context of Health Care Social Work

Beginning in the 1940s, the health care system, which had previously focused exclusively on the treatment of individual patients, began to consider a broader spectrum of influences on disease. Health care was not only about individuals but also includes its surroundings, environment, and society. When Anderson, Smith, and Sidel (2005) used the expression "socially minded physicians," it clearly indicated the political orientation of physicians who moved beyond clinical practice and tried to approach ill-health through social medicine, in which community was made the functioning unit of health care. Change in health care focus from individual to social care led to the development of the community medicine movement. Sidney and Emily Kark set up such a model in South Africa in 1940. Based on the principles of social medicine, the model worked with social intervention: "non-traditional health interventions, such as a milk distribution program for children and the planting of a community garden" (Anderson et al., 2005, p. 28).

Unlike the revolutionary movement in Latin America, Europe, and England toward strengthening the basic structure of society and linking health with the larger development issues in the 19th century, there was no strong political will to change the social structure and economic inequalities in India. The caste system in India is a social evil that was not abolished in the true sense but instead perpetrated by politicians for vote bank politics. The social medicine perspective adopted in Latin America by Virchow and Che Guevara, in which politics was mixed with the field of medicine on a large scale, was never adopted by Indian social and political thinkers and revolutionaries to fight for equality at the grassroots level. The relationship between socioeconomic conditions and health was never addressed to solve the health crisis. Most of the health policies and programs aimed to suit the political agenda and interests of the ruling political party.

The social and political context in which health care social work exists and is practiced in India today reflects that the profession is not able to address the health crisis. As discussed previously, historically, health care social work in India began with an individual- and institution-centric approach adopted from the West. An indigenous method of practice based on societal health needs and problems was not given the required attention by professionals and academicians. A systematic study of the relationship between society, disease, and medicine is required in order to develop a better and relevant intervention. Given the health crisis in India, health care social work is not able to address the issues at the grassroots level. In the past, health care social work had to go beyond the limitations of the paradigm of "scientific medicine" and expand to a more inclusive and holistic understanding of health by improving health literacy at a societal level. It will need to do so again.

In India, there are well-formulated guidelines in terms of national policies for health, nutrition, education, children, and so on. These policies provide an overall framework for health and development, and they reflect political commitment. The constitution of India and its directive principles, in addition to national policies, provide the broad guidelines for mobilization and distribution of resources in such a way as to meet the health needs of the masses. However, because health care is under state control, implementation of health care policies is the responsibility of the government, and implementation at the ground level has frequently failed, with taxpayers' money reaching only a few corrupt officials. Occasional constitutional amendments and their ratification by state assemblies have also provided guidelines for planners and administrators to direct resources to priority areas. Inadequate resource availability in the states may have affected policy implementation. Decentralization in health and development planning was envisaged under the 73rd Constitutional Amendment Act, better known as the Panchayati Raj Act (1993), and it provides an opportunity for community participation in developmental programs in rural areas. Recognition of social workers as important agents of change at the policy level is required for effective evaluation and monitoring of various development programs.

The resources allocated to the health sector form an important determinant of health services in the country. The outlay in health and health-related sectors has increased during the Five Year Plans. However, because the percentage of total outlay for the health sector has remained constant during the successive Five Year Plans at approximately 2% or 3% of gross domestic product compared to 10% in developed countries, the major financial expenditure (approximately 60%) is toward the payment of salaries of health personnel (Kapilashrami, 2000).

With the backdrop of the social policies and political context in which health care social work exists, the following section highlights the broad areas of health care social work practice in present-day India.

Health Care/Medical Social Work in India

Virtually every specialty area in the health system—including emergency room services, oncology, pediatrics, general medicine and surgery, intensive care, rehabilitation, substance abuse programs, public health, community health, and mental health—employs social workers. With the increased emphasis on cost containment, health system planners are placing more emphasis on primary community-based and home health care (Keigher, 2000).

The health care system is a complex, comprehensive, interdisciplinary network of services comprising diagnosis, treatment, rehabilitation, health maintenance, and prevention activities for people of all ages and circumstances. Of specific interest to social work are those people who require additional social supports when confronting issues of health, illness, and disability—the frail elderly; pregnant women; people with physical and mental disabilities or addictions; and people who are chronically ill, poor, homeless, or medically uninsured. Social work students in Indian universities are placed in a variety of health systems, including public health, community health, hospitals, counseling clinics, health organizations, mental health institutions, and rehabilitation services. Therefore, existing and emerging roles of professional social workers within broad health domains such as social work in public health, social work in community health, social work in hospital-based services are examined in the following sections.

Social Work in Public Health

Social work's association with public health dates to the early 20th century when social workers were involved in communicable diseases control, settlement houses, and maternal and child health. Social work and public health share a social justice mission to improve, defend, and enhance well-being as they both work together to ameliorate social health problems. Both fields borrow from one another. For example, social work researchers use epidemiology to frame interventions in areas such as HIV/AIDS, substance abuse, violence, and maternal and child health.

In addition to community-oriented services, social work has an important role to play in public health. In general, public health is "primarily concerned with the promotion of health and prevention of illness and other disabling conditions" (Moroney, 1995, p. 1967). As members of interdisciplinary teams, which include doctors, nurses, engineers, educators, business administrators, and lawyers, social workers focus on the social aspects of health and address social conditions in health and wellness. In India, public health settings include health-planning agencies, the National Institutes of Health, the Ministry of Health and Family Planning, and, at the international level, the World Health Organization and corporate establishments such as Public Health Foundation of India.

An increasing number of private institutions and universities have introduced a Master of Public Health and Social Work (MPHSW) program. PHSW is defined as social work practice that uses an epidemiologic approach to preventing, addressing, and solving social health problems. By emphasizing prevention through health promotion, PHSW is multimethod and transdisciplinary, making it especially relevant to contemporary practice. Social workers with a degree in public health or with a Masters of

Philosophy degree in social medicine and community health work in the field of illness prevention and health promotion. They work with interdisciplinary colleagues to identify and modify social, psychological, and environmental factors that contribute to health problems or that influence the use of health services. The emphasis of social work in public health depends on the particular nature of the agency's mission and the pressing health needs of the community.

In general, public health social work is on the cutting edge of prevention and promotion of health. Public health social work can focus on numerous functions of public health, resulting in a unique blending of roles: researcher, policy analyst, program planner, provider of direct services, evaluator, and administrator. Public health's focus on multiple determinants of health and disparities enables social workers to apply time-tested social work methods, including group work, community organization, social action, and administration and research adopting ecological approaches (Van Pelt, 2009). In a society of rapid change and pressing new complexities with a double burden of disease (the rising incidence of both communicable and noncommunicable diseases), public health social work can be one of public health's best transdisciplinary responses to improving the health and well-being of the whole society.

However, the current public health scenario in India is similar to that of 19th-century England, where there were major inequalities in terms of accessing health services and providing basic infrastructure for the labor class. When the needs of the people are not taken into account, development with equal distribution cannot be achieved due to faulty planning and policy of the government. Therefore, public health social workers can bridge the gap from the individual to the community to policy by helping develop policies and legislation that more effectively provide services for individuals and the community. For example, a public health social worker should have the skills to apply the science of diabetes prevention not only in educating individuals about diabetes but also in setting up community programs to reach urban Indian populations with a high prevalence of diabetes.

Professional public health social workers in India work in the field as program coordinators, policy analysts, and researchers at the macro level. They are also involved in the implementation of health programs in partnership with community-based organizations. Health activism is one area in which health care social workers are involved. For instance, with regard to advocacy and raising awareness among the masses, social workers are involved in public health issues such as drug policy and pricing of life-saving drugs, the rights of surrogate mothers, fighting against corrupt practices concerning health services and schemes for child nutrition such as Integrated Child Development Services (ICDS) schemes, and striving to provide decent workplace and living conditions for the migrant labor population working in unorganized sectors.

Social Work in Community Health

Whereas the term "community" can be broadly defined, community health tends to focus on geographical areas rather than people with shared characteristics. It is a discipline that is concerned with the study and improvement of the health of biological communities.

Community health may be studied within three broad categories, and social worker interventions can be implemented for each of these. First, primary health care refers to interventions that focus on the individual or family, such as hand-washing, immunization, circumcision, personal dietary choices, and lifestyle improvement. Social workers mainly work in the area of illness prevention and health promotion activities at this micro level, using various techniques of communication and methods of social work practice. Secondary health care refers to activities that focus on the environment, such as sanitation drives, clearing of waste and drainage, and spraying insecticides to control vector-borne diseases such as malaria. Tertiary health care refers to those interventions that focus more on the curative aspects in hospital settings. Private hospitals operated by charitable institutions provide both primary care and curative care at the community level. For example, at St. Stephen Hospital in Tiz Hazari, Delhi, social workers are employed and trained to provide services, which are both preventive and promotive in nature, in the Community Health Centre in "Sunder Nagri," an urban slum of Delhi. Throughout the country, many community-based organizations operated by religious/nonreligious charitable institutions are supported and funded by state governments to implement various national health programs at the community level.

With respect to community-oriented services in India, emerging roles for social workers are as follows:

- Getting involved in programs for raising awareness of health issues and healthy practices in communities
- Assessing people's knowledge, attitudes, and practices pertaining to health
- Designing programs concerning sociocultural determinants of health care utilization patterns
- Enhancing health care utilization patterns
- Learning techniques of behavior change communication
- Forming community-based organizations to deal with health issues or equipping such organizations to take up health issues
- Networking with organizations and promoting intersectoral collaborations with government-run programs and schemes, such as ICDS schemes, the National Rural/Urban Health Mission, and schools
- Getting involved in training of grassroots-level health workers
- Initiating independent innovative health programs
- Participating in forming institutional, community, state, and federal health policies
- Planning and administering health care services
- Conducting research to further document and develop empirical evidence on health scenarios

Social Work in Hospital-Based Services

Based on the work of almoners in 19th-century London hospitals, American hospital-based social work originated in the early 20th century at Massachusetts General Hospital when physician Richard Cabot hired Ida Canon with the idea that a social worker could assist in conveying essential information about patients' living environments and circumstances to hospital staff—and in doing so support the patients' treatment. In India, social workers were recommended to be an integral part of the multidisciplinary health team by the Bhore Committee as early as 1946, which categorically mentioned the term "social worker" and social workers' specific role in strengthening the services in hospitals. Medical social work began in the hospital with holistic care of the patient in conjunction with a medical team. However, throughout the years, their role has expanded to other settings, such as rehabilitation centers, public welfare agencies, and community health programs. For example, the role of social worker in one of

India's most reputed tertiary care hospitals, the All India Institute of Medical Sciences (AIIMS) in New Delhi, is worth mentioning here. The medical social worker at AIIMS works under the designation of a medical social service officer (MSSO). Currently, AIIMS employs 51 MSSOs working in various departments of the hospital. The first medical social worker in the hospital was appointed in 1960. Throughout the years, their role and responsibilities have evolved. According to Shekhar (2015), the Chief MSSO in AIIMS, the major tasks performed by MSSOs can be summarized as follows:

1. Multidisciplinary teamwork: A therapeutic network among the patient, doctor, family, and community is created for the management of the psychosocial and economic aspects of the illness. The network is also involved in discharge planning and creating protocols.

2. Management of patient welfare services: These services include dispensation of free medicines and surgical items to poor patients, exempt hospital levy charges of BPL (below poverty line) and indigent patients, providing railway concession facilities for outstation patients as per government rules to ensure regular follow-ups with patients, and providing accommodation facilities to outstation patients.

3. Facilitation of services available for EWS (economically weaker section) patients: Awareness is created about the Delhi High Court Order for free treatment of EWS patients in more than 46 notified private hospitals. Advocating and coordinating the referral of EWS patients should also be done.

4. Management of financial assistance: MSSOs help arrange financial support for carrying out patient treatment where needed from governmental schemes. They also tap financial resources through nongovernmental organizations, corporate social responsibility units, and voluntary donors for patients who are not eligible under the government scheme.

5. Casework and counseling: Psychosocial support is provided to persons with mental illnesses or drug addictions by way of counseling, therapy, psychological tests, and so on. Casework is also conducted to empower and enable patients to cope with illness/disability.

6. Group work and community organization: MSSOs disseminate health education and health awareness through information, education, and communication materials; organize health camps such as blood

donation camps and AIDS awareness camps; create awareness among the public to stimulate people's participation in health care programs; and conduct group activities for specific groups of patients and their attendants.

7. Transplant coordination and authorization: MSSOs motivate and coordinate organ donations and transplantations through the Organ Retrieval Banking Organization (ORBO), and they coordinate Renal Authorization Committee meetings and assessment of unrelated kidney donors as per the Transplant of Human Organ Act of 1994.

8. Emergency medical social services: MSSOs provide medical social services 24 hours a day, 7 days a week in trauma centers and ORBOs; coordinate referrals of patients to other hospitals due to non-availability of beds; and provide specialized services during epidemics, disasters, and natural calamities.

9. Rehabilitation: MSSOs provide patients assistance in the rehabilitation process.

Small hospitals often employ a single social worker who is responsible for all aspects of social services. Large hospitals, such as AIIMS and Safdarjung Hospital, usually employ several social workers who specialize in fields such as pediatrics, trauma centers, orthopedic rehabilitation, nephrology, neonatal intensive care, oncology, women's health, and emergency room services.

Looking Forward

The social, political, and cultural context in India largely influences the current status of health care social work professionals in the country. Traditionally, the Indian health care system was based on a welfare state concept and model in which out-of-pocket expenditures were not encouraged. However, due to structural changes resulting from economic policies implemented in the early 1990s, this model is inappropriate. Currently, India has one of the highest disease burdens in the world. Therefore, contemporary social work practice in Indian health crisis situations/health settings must evaluate and take into account the effectiveness of social work interventions. It must be questioned whether the current practice of social workers meets the demands of the changing health care system. The existing and emerging domains of social work practice in health care that can address the health crisis must be identified.

The methods of social work can be explored and applied at different levels, with different target populations and health issues. The implications of the rapidly changing health care system on social workers' activities need to be examined. The future of a healthy India lies in mainstreaming the public health agenda in the framework of sustainable development. In many ways, some of the profession's most important work in the years to come may involve supporting this agenda by working to address the social determinants of health. For example, the rural–urban divide needs to be reduced so that all people have adequate access to clean energy and safe water; the best health care is available to all; governance is responsive, transparent, and corruption free; poverty and illiteracy are eradicated; and crimes against women and children are eliminated.

Public health social work may be the future of social work in India. Political changes, such as the increased influence of the political right, are expected to affect the future delivery of health care in India, possibly leading to more emphasis on preventive health care and integrated health care and wellness services. The ability of public health social workers to bridge prevention and intervention, individual and community, and practice and policy will be increasingly valued by India's changing society.

References

Anderson, M. R., Smith, L., & Sidel, V. W. (2005). What is social medicine. *Monthly Review, 56*(8), 27–34.

Kapilashrami, M. C. (2000). Review of the present health status of India, emerging health problems and their solutions. *Health and Population Perspectives and Issues, 23*(1), 1–10.

Keigher, S. M. (2000). The challenge of caring in a capitalist world. *Health and Social Work, 25*(2), 83–86.

Moroney, R. M. (1995). Public health services. In R. L. Edwards (Ed.), *Encyclopedia of social work* (19th ed., pp. 1967–1973). Washington, DC: NASW Press.

Shekhar, B. (2015, February). *Medical social work practices: Some perspectives.* Paper presented at the Field Work Supervisor Meeting held in the Department of Social Work, University of Delhi, Delhi, India.

Van Pelt, J. (2009). Social work and public health—Perfect partners. *Social Work Today, 9*(1), 28.

Varma, D. R. (2015). *Medicines, healthcare and the Raj: The unacknowledged legacy.* Gurgaon, India: Three Essays Collective.

10

Health Care Social Work in Nigeria

Uzoma Odera Okoye

Introduction

The importance of health to all humans transcends concerns of just individuals and their families. Currently, health care is inclusive of governmental structures and significant bodies. The growing concern for the health care of citizens has compelled health-related professionals and others to consider ways in which health care can be effectively provided to everyone. Given the fact that many factors influence the health status of people, health care has become multidisciplinary (Bichi, 2015). One of the disciplines that plays a prominent role in the health sector is the social work profession. Social work professionals offer psychosocial care as a compliment to chemotherapeutic services provided by medical practitioners. This multidisciplinary approach to health care has permeated the health sectors of nations throughout the world, including Nigeria (Bywaters, Mcleod, & Napier, 2009).

However, nations throughout the world have implemented the multidisciplinary framework of health care to different degrees, so professionals must remain focused on their specific areas of patient health care . Social work is a relatively new profession in Nigeria; as such, its professional mandate has been contentious (Ogundipe & Edewor, 2012). It is in this context that it is important to explore health care social work, the focus of this chapter. Relevant to this discourse is the policy context within which health care social work is performed in Nigeria and the challenges that arise in the course of practicing health care social work in the country.

History of Social Work in Nigeria

In Nigeria, there are both formal and informal forms of social work. The formal structure and practice of social work are traced to the colonial era, whereas the informal practice dates back to the pre-colonial era as inherent in African cultures. The philosophy of filial and collective responsibilities has guided the interactions of community members in Africa. Before the colonial era, Africans took upon themselves the responsibilities of social orderliness, self-help, problem-solving, and enhancement of social functioning of community members. This is captured by Okafor (2004), who opined that Africans had a comprehensive welfare system that aided various members of their societies. They communally provided for their aged, barren, orphans, widows, pregnant mothers, children, physically challenged, and other vulnerable, poor, or oppressed groups (Idyorough, 2008).

The evolution of traditional Nigerian society toward urbanization and capitalism brought with it urban crime and an increasing divide among people for access to resources and opportunities, leading to a plethora of social problems. Ekpe and Mamah (1997) note that it was during this period that the Guardianship of Infants Acts of 1886 was introduced. Social change disrupted traditional welfare approaches and created the need for formal social work in Nigeria (Kazeem, 2011). Voluntary organizations and clubs such as the YMCA (Young Men's Christian Association) played important roles in advancing social development and cohesion in Nigeria (Ajayi, 1965). The Salvation Army Church and Green Triangle Group in the Lagos colony were also vital to the introduction of formal social work services. Their initial focus was rehabilitating juvenile delinquents and young offenders who were negatively affected as a result of seeking to emulate the lifestyles of men returning from World War II as well as by the effects of capitalism (Iwarimie-Jaja, 2002).

To give more impetus to the services of the missionaries, recommendations by Dr. Donald Faulkner in the 1940s resulted in child welfare legislation and the establishment of remand homes and approved schools at strategic locations in Nigeria. This was followed by other acts and ordinances that sought to improve the welfare of the people. These acts by the colonial government focused on labor and child welfare, providing free services for the disabled, and the establishment of boys' clubs to prevent delinquency among both rural and urban migrants (Eze, Ezea, & Aniche, 2000). The broad causative factors of juvenile delinquency led to the establishment of a variety of social work services. Thus, social welfare agencies began to provide services for marriage guidance, family planning, unemployment, indigence, community development, and adoption and foster care (Anucha, 2008). However, these services were patterned after those in

Britain without accounting for cultural differences. Also, the services were available only in urban areas (Anucha, 2008).

At the dawn of independence, the Nigerian government continued to provide the same social services as those provided during the colonial era. However, the Social Development Directorate Decree 12 of 1974 was a major milestone. This led to the establishment of the Ministry of Social Welfare, which subsequently at several times has been subsumed under the Ministries of Labor, Youth and Sports, Culture, and Women Affairs. Following reports and recommendations by Dr. A. H. Shawky, institutions charged with the responsibility of training social workers were created in 1976. The Social Development Policy was formulated in 1989 and revised in 2004, providing more impetus to health care social work in Nigeria (Federal Republic of Nigeria, 2004).

History of Social Work in Health Care in Nigeria

The history of social work in health care in Nigeria has not received much attention and thus is not well documented. Social work in health care in Nigeria owes its origin to the missionaries who took over health care delivery from the colonial government in northern Nigeria. As a result of the outbreak of communicable disease epidemics and illnesses such as hypertension and ulcers in northern Nigeria in the early 20th century, it became obvious to the colonial administration that medical investigations alone could not provide complete remedies for such illnesses (Idyorough, 2008). This led to the concession of the health care delivery system to missionaries, who had the wherewithal to offer social services and care to patients as a complement to the medical care they also provided these patients. However, provision for health care social workers was not made until the 1950s, when the almoners began to provide care.

Following an increase in indigent patients who could not pay their medical bills, in 1950 the Director of Medical Services wrote to the government of the Lagos colony, demanding the employment of ex-nurses as almoners to help with the provision of social welfare services for patients. In response to the letter, Mallam Abba Namtari was appointed as the first almoner for the Government Hospital in Yola in 1952. Other hospitals made their own appointments from first-class clerks as directed by the government. Further recruitment of almoners in western Nigeria was performed by

Mrs. Omitowoju beginning in 1957 (Idyorough, 2008; Ityavyar, 1985; Schram, 1971). The introduction of almoners into the health care delivery system in Nigeria was the precedent on which health care social work in Nigeria was introduced. Today, federal government-owned medical facilities usually make provision for health care social work services through the departments of social work, social welfare, or public health social work. Many state-owned medical facilities do not employ social workers.

Health Care Social Work in Nigeria: A Policy and Political Perspective

The practice of social work in Nigeria's health care system is anchored by various policy goals. A principal policy orientation that led to the establishment of social work can be found in the policy sanction that first led to the recognition of the social work profession. This is stated in the 1974 Social Development Directorate Decree and the 1989 Social Development Policy. The Federal Ministry of Women Affairs and Social Development captured it in two of its obligations (Federal Republic of Nigeria, 2004):

- Training of professional social workers and the organization and co-ordination of training facilities for government and nongovernmental social welfare agencies
- Care and support of all vulnerable groups (destitute, the indigent, the sick and their families)

The previously mentioned policy documents obligations that are regarded as justifications for the practice of social work in Nigerian health care settings, which has institutional backing from the Ministry of Women Affairs and Social Development. Specifically, two policies that have bolstered the sanction of social work services within health care facilities in Nigeria are the National Strategic Health Development Plan (2010–2015) and the Task-Shifting and Task-Sharing Policy for Essential Health Care Services in Nigeria (Federal Ministry of Health, 2014). These policies are directives that social workers must work in collaboration with medical personnel to effectively provide family planning, premarital counseling, HIV/AIDS counseling and care, community extension services, psychotherapeutic services, and other services (Federal Ministry of Health, 2014).

In furtherance, the Association of Social Workers of Nigeria (AMSWON) was formed as an arm of its parent body, the Nigeria Association of Social Workers (NASoW), which was established in 1975 (NASoW, 2016). The health care social workers wing, formed more than three decades ago, serves as a supervisory group for social workers in the country. Generally, social workers in health care receive recognition in medical facilities in Nigeria, particularly those owned by the federal government. However, this recognition tends not to be sufficient because the law backing the general practice of social work is not an act of parliament but merely a policy (Idyorough, 2013). This has led to a consistent push to professionalize social work in Nigeria, which will serve to consolidate services provided by social workers, including those in the health care setting.

Theoretical Orientation Backing Health Care Social Work in Nigeria

Currently, social work in health care in Nigeria is guided by experience. As such, Kolb's theory of experiential adult learning provides a useful framework for understanding social work in the health care setting. Kolb, Boyatzis, and Mainemelis (2000) argue that learning is a continuous process grounded in experience. According to them, adults learn through concrete experiences, reflective observation, abstract conceptualization, and active experimentation. This is the case with social workers in health care settings in Nigeria. On entry into the health care setting, the majority of social workers possess only undergraduate-level generalist social work knowledge; consequently, they learn on the job, developing basic skills that enable them to provide support for their clients. There is currently no specialized training in health care social work in Nigeria, but there is an urgent need for their services. Patients in Nigeria commonly face psychosocial and economic issues. It is the responsibility of the health care social worker to help patients deal with and recover from these types of problems. This is done through motivational and psychotherapeutic counseling, linkage to resource systems, enhancing cohesion among immediate support systems, advocating the rights of patients, mediating patients' needs and the responsibilities of medical practitioners, and so on. Social workers perform all these actions based on the experience they have acquired during the course of their practice.

Focusing on Social Work Health Care in Nigeria

Social work in Nigeria has been an integral part of medical care since the colonial era. It has gone through a series of developmental stages with regard to its practice, policy descriptions and motivations, personnel constituents, and community sanctions. These factors have had a major influence on current social work in Nigeria. They are also yardsticks by which social work practice in Nigeria can be appraised as effective or not.

The roles of the social worker in health care in Nigeria are similar to those of social workers throughout the world. Social workers focus primarily on the psychosocial well-being of patients, with little oversight of other areas that may affect patients' psychosocial functioning. This is corroborated by Oyeniyi (2010), who states that social work in health care is an arm of social work, practiced within the health care delivery setting to help remedy the numerous social and psychological problems of patients in order to alleviate their distress while receiving treatment. The health care social worker in Nigeria works in a multidisciplinary team comprising other professionals, as is done in other areas of the world. Such professionals include medical doctors, nurses, psychologists, dieticians, midwives, and others. The health care social worker in Nigeria is domiciled within a unit in the health facility's department that is variously called social welfare, social work, public health social work, volunteer service, and so on. Due to the unpopularity of social work in this area of the world, most medical facilities choose to go by the name social welfare unit because most persons are more conversant with this term (Ezeh & Mbah, 2004). The roles of the social worker in health care have been substantively delineated by the Task-Shifting and Task-Sharing Policy for Essential Health Care Services in Nigeria (Federal Ministry of Health, 2014).

These roles and services are adopted from the curriculum and texts that are used to train social workers at various institutions of social work studies and also from experiences they have gathered during the course of their practice. These are similar to policy directives and role recommendations of the country's health care providers (Bichi, 2015; Idyorough, 2008; Oyeniyi, 2010). The roles that underscore the practice of social work in health care in Nigeria are evident in the mission statement of the Nigeria Ministry of Women Affairs and Social Development (2016), which states that "the Mission is to ensure the provision of integrated and quality Social Services such as relief of distress—material and financial support for the poor, vulnerable, needy and provision of enabling environment for social progress" (p. 1). Thus, social workers in health care are sanctioned to help patients improve their psychosocial well-being while they deal with their medical conditions.

In Nigeria, social workers are readily employed by health facilities owned by the federal government and some tertiary health facilities owned by state governments, such as those of Lagos, Ekiti, and Kaduna states. It is very rare for social workers to be employed by privately owned facilities (Bichi, 2015). Due to the absence of quality social welfare institutions and health insurance in Nigeria, citizens are exposed to a wide range of social anomalies and dysfunction. Some citizens admitted to medical facilities may be coming into contact with social workers for the first time. Patients with severe psychosocial problems tend to overwhelm social workers with their many problems, believing that social workers are experts in their field when in fact many have only elementary training. Many patients are reluctant to talk for fear that they will be accused of sharing their family secrets with an "outsider." Nevertheless, social workers in health care settings must take on the roles of brokering, mediating, advocacy, and enabling to help link patients to services that will be of use to them. These are explored next.

Counseling Services for Psychologically Depressed Patients

It is generally normative for patients to experience bouts of psychological depression. The effects of psychological disturbances on health conditions are well explained as the consequences of psychosomatic disorders (Barber, Brown, & Martin, 2016). In Nigeria, financial difficulty is the prominent issue that leads patients into such a depressed state. This is due to the absence of quality social security measures to help citizens meet the financial demands of their treatments and even those of their dependents. Other common issues include academic challenges, relationship challenges, religious conflicts, internal displacements, loss of property as a result of accidents or natural disasters, unfavorable diagnoses, and a diagnosis of HIV/AIDS. Health care social workers in Nigeria have been sanctioned to counsel patients who are depressed and help them return to normal functioning.

At some point, counseling is performed in conjunction with other services, such as referral to resources such as religious ministers. In addition, Nigerians are very culturally and religiously minded people. Patients often respond positively to counseling by social workers when their cultures and religions are accorded some level of respect. For instance, many patients respond better if the social worker prays before starting a counseling session. Also, when counseling female Muslim patients, male social workers are expected to give some them significant space because it is against their culture to have close contact with males who are not their husbands or brothers. Counseling in the Nigerian medical setting tends to be demanding and requires social workers to be extremely competent and knowledgeable of the values and principles of the profession.

Palliative Care

Terminally ill patients in Nigerian hospitals are offered palliative care by social workers. The social worker attempts to help the patient accept death and the dying process as normal. In Nigeria, death is not discussed because it is believed that doing so will make it happen. Therefore, social workers often collaborate with religious ministers in this regard. The religious approach of many Nigerians usually pits faith against fate. For example, the average Nigerian believes that a patient on renal dialysis can be cured by a miracle from some undefined supernatural means. Social workers who try to offer palliative care might be presumed as potential killers of their kin. Thus, social practitioners try to offer palliative care based on the ready acceptance of the dying condition by patients and their family members or other close associates. Often, palliative care in Nigeria is done in conjunction with religious clerics and legal professionals in cases in which there are legal implications of the death, such as when the property of the dying patient is to be divided among the family.

Soliciting Financial Assistance
for Indigent Patients

Although Nigeria is an oil-rich nation, it is ranked as a poor country by the World Bank (2016). There is no comprehensive health insurance program for all. Therefore, medical care is expensive, and many Nigerian citizens face challenges paying medical bills. As such, social workers in Nigeria tend to grapple with the challenge of assisting clients to find ways to pay their medical bills. The websites of four hospital social work units indicate that soliciting financial assistance for indigent and abandoned patients is one of the major services they render. The health care social worker works with the client to identify resource systems and also determine the amount the client can contribution to pay medical bills. Resource systems include relatives, high-profile persons in the society, philanthropists, faith-based organizations, nongovernmental organizations, and other incorporated trustees. With the help of the social worker, the client will determine whether to pay on his or her own enlist debtors, sell valuable property, take out loans or micro-credits, or utilize another option to help pay medical bills. As a last resort, social workers may help clients apply for a bill waiver, which may be granted.

Repatriating Abandoned Patients

This is a common issue faced by social workers in health care settings in Nigeria. Patients are brought to medical facilities and abandoned by those who brought them. Reasons for abandoning patients include poverty, cultural inclinations (banishment, the patient is an outcast, or the belief that the patient's medical condition represents a bad omen), spiritual issues (e.g., a belief that a spiritual instruction has been given to the household of the patient's to abandon him or her), terminal illness, and old age (the person is unproductive and difficult to care for). Social workers are expected to carry out investigations to ascertain the reasons that led to the abandonment of patients. It is often difficult for practitioners to trace the family of such persons because Nigeria does not have a comprehensive citizen identification system. Social workers in Nigeria must also deal with issues of spirituality because spiritual forces are accorded respect in Nigerian culture. Hence, in extreme cases, security agencies are employed to force supposed caregivers to pick up their abandoned family member from the medical facility. In some cases, the abandoned are returned to their homes and communities after investigations identify their addresses. In other cases, the abandoned are taken to institutional care settings such as orphanage homes, homes for the elderly, and rehabilitation centers. The social worker is responsible for completing the submission process to these facilities.

Home Visits and Follow-Up in Special Cases

Undergraduate social work education in Nigeria includes training in community care and follow-up services. This training is important for social workers in health care settings. Some patient cases may require community reconciliation and reintegration. In these cases, social workers must visit the homes and communities of the patients to broker and facilitate their reconciliation and reintegration. Examples include patients treated for vesicovaginal fistula or patients who have issues regarding rules guiding marital sanctity. The social worker works collaboratively with the patient to gradually eliminate the stigma. In addition, when a patient is diagnosed with an illness that may lead to the patient becoming physically challenged, the social worker follows up with the patient until the family accepts the reality of the diagnosis.

Creating Contributory Fund Projects and Encouraging Blood Donors

Health care social workers in Nigeria help raise funds in anticipation of indigent patients. They do so by encouraging high-profile people in the state to donate funds, influencing multinationals to contribute funds as their corporate social responsibility, and partnering with nongovernmental organizations. These funds are used to assist indigent patients. In addition, social workers in Nigeria sometimes take on a public relations role. They encourage the public to participate in blood donation and offer moral support.

Other responsibilities of health care social workers in Nigeria include the following:

- Public sensitization toward public health
- HIV/AIDS and other related disease campaigns
- Supervision of student generalist practitioners/social workers with regard to fieldwork practice and internships

- Communication of policies and practices of the medical facility to patients and their support networks
- Recommendation of policies and practices to the facility's management that will enhance the well-being of patients
- Participation in ward rounds to ascertain the psychosocial conditions of patients and exchange ideas with other professionals
- Provide friendship to patients and their support networks

Conclusion

Social work practice in the health care setting in Nigeria faces many challenges. The major challenge is the fact that social work in Nigeria has not been professionalized by any act of parliament, and so there is no obligation to employ social workers in every health facility in the country. Also, few institutions offer undergraduate social work training, and in those that do offer it, enrollment in social work programs is relatively low because people do not regard it as a profession but, rather, as charity work (Okoye, 2008). As a result, there are very few astute social workers to fill key positions in health care settings; hence, professionals from related fields often must fill these position.

In addition, it is important for social work associations in Nigeria to hold more professional conferences and provide continuing professional development focused on improving social work services in health care settings in Nigeria. This will be more effective if social work associations collaborate with relevant international representatives. AMSWON must be more proactive in getting the government at the federal, state, and local levels to involve more social workers in the management of tertiary, secondary, and primary health centers throughout the country. This will go a long way toward providing the needed support for patients dealing with psychosocial problems.

In summary, there is a need to expand the postgraduate program of social work in tertiary institutions in Nigeria to offer programs in medical social work. This will provide practicing social workers in the health care setting an opportunity to acquire core medical social work knowledge. The passage of the social work bill into law by the Nigeria House of Representatives on June 7, 2016, provides hope that the social work profession in Nigeria will gain its long-awaited professionalization (Adebayo,

2017). With an increasingly larger well-trained workforce and the professionalization of social work by an act of parliament, the quality of social work practice in Nigeria will likely match that of social work practice in countries throughout the world.

References

Ajayi, J. F. (1965). *Christian mission in Nigeria*. London, UK: Longman.

Adebayo M. (February 9, 2017). Social Workers lament delay in passage of Council of Social Work Bill by Senate. Retrieved at http://dailypost.ng/2017/02/09/social-workers-lament-delay-passage-council-social-work-bill-senate/

Anucha, U. (2008). Exploring a new direction for social work education and training in Nigeria. *Social Work Education, 27*(3), 229–242.

Barber, P., Brown, R., & Martin, D. (2016). *Mental health law in England and Wales: A guide for mental health professionals*. Exeter, UK: Learning Matters.

Bichi, A. A. (2015, November 4). AMSWON makes case for increased social workers in hospitals. *Vanguard*. Retrieved from http://www.vanguardngr.com/2015/11/amswon-makes-case-for-increased-medical-social-workers-in-hospitals

Bywaters, P., Mcleod, E., & Napier, L. (2009). *Social work and global health inequalities: Practice and policy developments*. Bristol, UK: Policy Press.

Ekpe, C. P., & Mamah, S. C. (1997). *Social work in Nigeria: A colonial heritage*. Enugu, Nigeria: Unit Oriental Press.

Eze, C. A., Ezea, P. C., & Aniche, A. (2000). *Fundamentals of social work*. Nsukka, Nigeria: Liberty Printing Press.

Ezeh, P. J., & Mbah, F. U. (2004). *Social work and social worth*. Enugu, Nigeria: Lifegate.

Federal Ministry of Health. (2014). *Task-shifting and task-sharing policy for essential health care services in Nigeria*. Abuja, Nigeria: Author. Retrieved from http://www.health.gov.ng/doc/TSTS.pdf

Federal Ministry of Women Affairs and Social Development. (2016). *Social welfare department*. Retrieved from http://www.womenaffairs.gov.ng/index.php/department/social-welfare

Federal Republic of Nigeria. (2004). *Social development policy for Nigeria*. Abuja, Nigeria: Author.

Idyorough, A. E. (2008). *History and philosophy of social welfare services in Nigeria 1900–1960*. Makurdi, Nigeria: Aboki.

Idyorough, A. E. (2013, March). *Social work administration in Nigeria: Challenges and prospects*. Keynote address presented at a 2-day stakeholders' meeting on professionalization of social work in Nigeria.

Ityavyar, D. A. (1985). *The development of health services in Nigeria, 1960–1985*. Unpublished doctoral thesis, Faculty of Graduate Studies, University of Toronto, Toronto, Ontario, Canada.

Iwarimie-Jaja, D. (2002). *Understanding social work*. Owerri, Nigeria: Springfield.

Kazeem, K. (2011). An integrated approach to social work practice in Nigeria. *College Student Journal, 45*(1).

Kolb, D. A., Boyatzis, R. E., & Mainemelis, C. (2000). Experiential learning theory: Previous research and new directions. In R. J. Sternberg & L. F. Zhang (Eds.), *Perspectives on cognitive, learning, and thinking styles* (pp. 227–248). Mahwah, NJ: Erlbaum.

Nigeria Association of Social Workers. (2016). *Welcome to NASoW*. Retrieved from https://nasowlagos.org.ng/

Ogundipe, A., & Edewor, P. A. (2012). Sociology and social work in Nigeria: Characteristics, collaborations and differences. *African Sociological Review, 16*(2), 40–55.

Okafor, D. I. (2004). *Social work in Nigeria: A historical perspective*. Onitsha, Nigeria: Mid-Field.

Okoye, U. O. (2008) *Awareness of social work profession in Nigeria: A challenge to social workers*. Paper presented at the Second International Social Work Day Celebration on the theme Social Work: Making a World of Difference, Abuja, Nigeria.

Oyeniyi, O. J. (2010). *About the social work department*. Dala-Kano, Nigeria: National Orthopedic Hospital.

Schram, R. A. (1971). *History of the Nigerian health services*. Ibadan, Nigeria: Ibadan University Press.

World Bank. (2016). *World development indicators 2016*. Retrieved from https://openknowledge.worldbank.org/bitstream/handle/10986/23969/9781464806834.pdf?sequence=2&isAllowed=y

11

Health Care Social Work in Saudi Arabia

Abdulaziz Albrithen

Introduction

Social work was introduced in Saudi Arabia with assistance from social work experts from other Arab countries. The Ministry of Education was established in 1953; a year later, the organization created the Department of Education and Social Activity. The functions of this department were to undertake supervision of the various aspects of school activities throughout the kingdom of Saudi Arabia and to develop plans and programs that would help improve social activity (Al-Saud, 1996; Tash, 2001).

In 1965, the Ministry of Education employed 44 social experts from Egypt, 19 of whom were employed as counselors at the Ministry and in various provinces, and 25 were employed at different schools. The Ministry continued to hire social experts to work in schools until, in 1981, there were 668 of them; this included 29 counselors in the provinces and 5 at the Ministry (Al Saif, 1991; Al-Saud, 1996; Tash, 2001).

In addition to the Ministry of Education, social workers also worked at the Ministry of Social Affairs. Moreover, through the General Department of Social Welfare, which is responsible for planning and implementing social welfare programs, a group of social experts were employed to work with the blind; prisoners and their families; and juveniles, orphans, and the disabled. They were also engaged in activities at the Department of Social Security (Alsadhan, 2004; Alselmy, 2007).

As a profession, social work within the Kingdom of Saudi Arabia is in its infancy compared to that in most Western countries. The majority of social services are still deeply rooted in traditional social care institutions, specifically those that cater to the needs of children, adolescents, orphans, and other vulnerable members of society. The number of social security-related assistance programs within Saudi Arabia continues to grow.

History of Health Care Social Work in Saudi Arabia

There is a very strong need for social workers in Saudi Arabian medical institutions, in both private and public sectors (Ragab, 1995; Saleh, 2002). The Saudi Arabian Ministry of Health is the second largest employer of social work professionals in the country, facilitating their availability in state hospitals throughout the country. These hospitals range from general practice facilities to those focused on specialized fields such as psychiatry. In addition to the Ministry of Health, numerous other agencies, including the Ministry of Defense and Aviation, the National Guard, and the Ministry of Education, operate medical facilities in which the services of social workers are also needed.

Because social work in health care is considered an important service in hospitals in Saudi Arabia, certified human resources experts ensure that there are sufficient numbers of qualified and well-trained practitioners. The promise of a good salary has also helped ensure there are enough practitioners to provide special services to patients and their families. In addition, these practitioners have organized specialized seminars, thus advancing the field (Albrithen, 2013).

In 1973, the Ministry of Health employed 35 social experts from Egypt to work in the medical field. Because the tasks and duties of these social experts were not defined and there was no oversight in placing them in different facilities, they were all employed at the psychiatric hospital and a hospital that specialized in chest diseases in the city of Taif. It was thought that social work in the medical field should be confined to these two health areas (Albaz, 2010; Yalli, 2008). In 1974, realizing that social experts were concentrated within these fields, comprehensive regulations were developed to govern the tasks of these experts. Offices of social work in the medical field were established at the Ministry of Health, which separated social workers from those practicing in specialized fields, such as the psychiatrists engaged in medical social work (Tash, 2001).

During the following decade, social experts were distributed to general hospitals, maternity and childcare centers, and health clinics, in addition to hospitals that specialized in psychiatric and respiratory diseases. By 1982, there were 150 social workers in the medical field (Tash, 2001).

Currently, the Saudi Ministry of Health (SMoH) employs approximately 80% of all social workers in Saudi Arabia. Of the remaining social workers, 11% are employed by quasi-governmental health facilities, 7% are employed by Saudi governmental agencies, and 2% are employed by for-profit private institutions (Yalli, 2008).

Social Policies and Political Context

The centralized political system in the Kingdom of Saudi Arabia is an absolute monarchy, headed by a king from the royal Al-Saud family. In the founding of the Kingdom in 1936, the government took it upon itself to bring about fundamental changes in various sectors of the society throughout the country. Income generated from the country's oil production was viewed as one of the major factors that made this possible (Abu-Alia, 1986). The huge revenues derived from the sale of oil from deposits discovered in 1938 were the major catalyst that transformed the Kingdom. Payments received from foreign companies involved in developing concessions in the country likewise enabled the government to launch a great number of large-scale development programs by the 1960s. Such programs were focused on the creation of infrastructure in transportation, telecommunications, electric power, and water industries. Programs also addressed the modernization and expansion of the armed forces in terms of new equipment and training and the creation of petroleum-based industries (Abu-Alia, 1986; Metz, 1992).

These initiatives by the government thrust the national economy in a different direction and also impacted individual lifestyles in various ways. Modern infrastructure created a shift from traditional to modern agriculture. Small-scale trading gave way to industry-based employment, especially in oil and related service industries. Education flourished, as evidenced by the number of universities and vocational institutions that were created and that have become increasingly valued and viewed as important for providing better opportunities in peoples' lives. In the field of medicine, Saudis have shifted to modern medicine for common ailments, although some use it in conjunction with traditional herbal remedies, which together contribute to make life better and have resulted in a reduced mortality rate (Abu-Alia, 1986). Most citizens attend school in order to gain employment in the government, which provides better salaries, job security, and working conditions in general compared to companies in the private sector.

Despite the previously mentioned improvements in people's lives due to the introduction of modern medicines, the national rates of various health problems such as infant mortality and diseases such as malaria, yellow fever, cholera, plague, and bilharzia, as well as acute illnesses such as diabetes, kidney and heart diseases, mental disorders, and terminal diseases such as cancer remain on the rise and demand more medical/social services (SMoH, 2004). Other health-related socioeconomic and behavioral problems have also been on the rise, such as those associated with traffic accidents leading to disability and death and those related to drug smuggling and illegal drugs use (Al-Nahedh, 1999; Metz, 1992).

To address the problems brought about by rapid social and industrial changes, in the early 1960s, the Ministry of Labor and Social Affairs established information programs designed to improve living standards and quality of life in general and also to stimulate citizen participation in community development (Saudi Ministry of Culture & Information, 2005).

In 2004, the Ministry of Labor was separated from the Ministry of Social Affairs (MoSA), which currently has more than 60 centers and institutions under its supervision. These centers provide a complete range of services and are located throughout the country to support individuals and families with social, economic, physical, and mental health problems (Yalli, 2008).

In addition, MoSA also administers more than 20 projects aimed at social development of neighborhoods and communities in the Kingdom. Of these, approximately 16 Social Development Centers provide social services in rural areas, and 7 Social Services Centers operate in urban areas. MoSA is aided in the administration of all these centers by the Ministry of Education, the Ministry of Health, and the Ministry of Agriculture, Water, Principality and Village Affairs (Yalli, 2008). MoSA also supports the 162 multipurpose cooperative societies working in the fields of agriculture, consumption, and public services.

The Social Insurance Program represents one of the aspects of care that the government focuses on. The Ministry Secretariat for Social Insurance Affairs, through its 76 offices, conducts field research (case assessments) and funds all those deserving of social insurance in the form of pensions given periodically or as temporary relief assistance. Eligible groups include unemployed persons, widows and widowers, females who have no living family members to support them, orphans, people with disabilities, female dependents of those serving custodial sentences, and victims of natural disasters (Saudi Ministry of Culture & Information, 2005).

The Ministry of Health supervises the establishment and operation of general and specialized hospitals, infirmaries, and health institutes throughout the country. It also supervises the supply and distribution of medicines and the approval of sales, including control of the prices of medicine and fees in the private health care sector (Yamani, 2000). In recent years, an improved health care system has been a major development in Saudi Arabia; the Kingdom has expended a lot of effort to improve its citizens' lives. The provision of health care services is also shared by the private sector under the supervision of the Ministry of Health (Yalli, 2008).

Organized in 1950, Saudi Arabia's health care system has slowly evolved to the present system, similar to those in other countries, in which services are delivered by government or public health institutions as well as the private sector. In the public sector, the state assumes the responsibility of providing complete health care to all Saudi citizens free of charge (Yamani, 2000).

According to the Saudi Ministry of Health, there are more than 365 hospitals with a total capacity of 51,130 beds and 2,891 health care centers in Saudi Arabia and an estimated 1,848 primary health care centers throughout the Kingdom. These centers provide free primary health services as well as auxiliary services such as child and mother care, dental health, and medical checkups. Free medicines are also dispensed to citizens through these centers. In addition, there are 39 hospitals run by the National Guard, various universities, Aramco, armed forces, public security, the Ministry of Interior, the Ministry of Defence and Aviation, and many others (SMoH, 2006). Most hospitals in the Kingdom are located in urban areas, whereas health care centers meet the health care needs of people in rural areas (SMoH, 2002). The majority of medical facilities, including hospitals with large bed capacities, are located in the cities of Riyadh, Jeddah, Makkah, and Medinah, where the Holy Islamic centers are located, and in Dammam, Al-Khubar, and Dhahran—cities with a major oil industry presence (SMoH, 2002).

In Saudi Arabia, the minimum entry requirement for employment as a hospital social worker is the possession of a bachelor's degree in social work or in any related field obtained either in the United States (Gibelman, 2004) or elsewhere within the international community (Ragab, 1995). Students in this field obtain their degrees in social work either from universities in the home country or abroad through various sponsorship programs. Thus, educational requirements for health care social work practitioners in Saudi Arabia generally align with or are comparable to those of their Western counterparts with regard to employment requirements, contracts, and practices in full-time employment.

Health Care/Medical Social Work

Saudi Arabia has the largest and fastest growing population of all the Gulf Cooperation Council countries. The Central Department of Statistics and Information estimated that the total population was 31.6 million in 2016, of which 22.8 million were Saudi nationals as Colliers estimated that for 2016, 22 of 30 million residents were Saudi (Colliers International, 2016). The fast-growing population and rising average incomes will increase the demand for services and infrastructure in energy, water, telecommunications, housing, education, and health care and social services, among others.

According to data from the International Monetary Fund (IMF) released in July 2013, 1.5 million of the 2 million new jobs created during the previous 4 years went to non-Saudis. The IMF also found that the unemployment rate among Saudi nationals was 12%. Youth (30%) and females (35%) were particularly affected by the country's unemployment problem.

Companies have traditionally been reluctant to employ Saudis, who are paid more than foreigners and enjoy better job protection. In addition, many Saudis prefer to work in the public sector because private employers offer comparatively lower salaries, unattractive benefits packages, and demand longer work hours. According to data from the Saudi Arabian Monetary Agency, in 2011 only a small percentage of Saudis—10.9% of the native population—were employed in the private sector (Saudi Arabian Monetary Agency, 2011).

The Saudi government has always given high priority to the development of health care services for all its workers, which poses challenges for the health care system because as the labor force has increased, there has been a shortage of Saudi health professionals. Problems have also arisen from other sources, such as the Ministry of Health's multiple roles with perceived limited financial resources, changing patterns of diseases, and a high demand for free services. Usually, government employees are provided health care and needed social services from government hospitals, whereas those in the private sector receive services from private firms.

In the health care context, family loyalty, for example, is linked to a person's health because the family is an important sociocultural institution that plays a significant role in its members' practices. An individual family member cannot make decisions related to his or her medical care, such as seeking, accepting, or rejecting any medical intervention, on his or her own. Such decisions are made by the head of the family after consultation with the rest of the family members. This form of decision-making is highly influenced by the idea of a tribal configuration, with the tribal leader guiding and looking after the welfare of his group (Abu-Alia, 1986; Al-Saif, 2004; Metz, 1992). An individual derives support and financial security from his or her family and is expected to return the same with his or her services and loyalty.

Gender separation is also a very important part of Saudi culture, which reflects traditional values related to chastity and sexual modesty. These values are not only tied to family honor but also held to be a religious obligation. Specific traditions supported by Islamic guidelines encourage modesty for both women and men; however, women are generally viewed as being responsible for avoiding sexual temptation (*fitna*). In Saudi Arabia, gender segregation is considered as a mechanism to ensure sexual modesty and to avoid temptation. These values and practices remain strong in Saudi culture and can also be found to some degree throughout Arab and Islamic countries as modesty has taken on religious significance in Islam through interpretations of Muslim theologians (Metz, 1992).

Gender equality is maintained to the highest possible degree through ensuring equal access to quality buildings and facilities and a legal framework for equal access to services and employment opportunities (Abu-Alia, 1986; Al-Saif, 2004). In the health care context, for example, each gender is offered separate and suitably designed facilities where they can be employed and/or cared for by personnel of the same sex.

The previously discussed cultural characteristics of Saudi society were presented in this chapter to illustrate the need for cultural sensitivity in the practice of social work health care. The examples show that despite the rapid growth in population with expatriates comprising 45% of the workforce, a growing number of locally and internationally educated youth, and the need for reforms brought about by these social concerns, innovations in areas such as social health care practice must take into serious consideration traditional cultural values that are held in high regard in Saudi society.

Looking Forward

Although social work is a relatively young profession in Saudi Arabia, it has made remarkable progress. The field of social work is separated into two distinct categories: those who deliver professional services in the field and those in academia who teach social work to produce more professionals. Even with the recognition this sector has gained, it is undeniable that there is still room for improvement as well as a need for recommendations to help those who practice in the field and those who are in the area of education.

Above all, the recent developments in the field of health care and social work in Saudi Arabia make a strong case for the creation of a professional organization among health care social work practitioners that represents practitioners and at the same time serves as a regulating body to screen credentials of potential members and update knowledge and experience through local and international conferences and seminars. This new association could issue professional licenses to prospective practitioners and renew these licenses on a regular basis based on established official requirements created by the association, including the updating of skills by requiring attendance of professional seminars. This association, with its rules and regulations in the issuing of licenses to social work practitioners, distinct from other associations for professionals such as sociologists and psychologists, might present unwanted competition among practitioners in Saudi Arabia. The association and its licensing function might also regulate the practice within the profession and minimize ethical violations that exist within the field. The major aim of such an association would be to improve the delivery of services and professionalize the field of social work as a whole in Saudi Arabia.

Regarding the educational aspect of social work in Saudi Arabia, the creation of an education council or the establishment of a Saudi Council on Social Work Education might deliver the needed corresponding improvements. The council should focus on social work education and its policies and unify social work education in the country. This agency would be tasked with updating recent knowledge, developing curriculum, publishing research results, monitoring degrees and their requirements, and providing academic accreditation for all social work departments and colleges within the country.

The two entities of social work could influence each other, improving both through their respective organizations. Surely this would improve social work as a whole within Saudi society. When the "association" and the "council" fulfill their roles and functions properly, social work will have capable professionals (i.e., social workers, educators, and researchers).

Health care social work is one of the earliest recognized professions in Saudi Arabia and is currently considered one of the most popular among practitioners. There are more than 1,000 social workers in primary health care centers, government hospitals (both general and specialist hospitals), as well as private hospitals. Nonetheless, its full potential has not been completely developed, and it is still far from the envisioned concept of clinical practice of social work, which is why the creation of the previously discussed associations is strongly encouraged.

By 2030, when Saudi Arabian society as a whole is envisioned to have advanced and to be further recognized internationally as envisioned in Saudi Arabia Vision 2030 endorsed by the Council of Ministers, chaired by the Custodian of the Two Holy Mosques, King Salman, the field of health care social practice in the country is likewise envisioned to have progressed in parallel with its partners in progressed. The education system based on the Saudi Council of Social Work Education will be capable, with its unified programs, of preparing qualified field practitioners, and the professional organization will bring together all qualified practitioners and better train its members in adjusting to the improved governmental health care programs, with the invigorated public sector participating in the delivery of these services in cities and rural areas throughout the country.

In summary, there is an urgent need for a concerted effort among practitioners and academia to address the current and ever-growing demand for services and to become an active partner of the government in order to achieve the goals of Saudi Arabia Vision 2030.

References

Abu-Alia, A. (1986). *Al islah el egtemai fi ahdi el malik Abdul-Aziz* [*The social revolution in the era of King Abdul-Aziz*]. Riyadh, Saudi Arabia: Al-Marikh Press.

Albaz, R. S. (2010). *Social work in the medical field*. Riyadh, Saudi Arabia: Imam Muhammad Ibn Saud Islamic University.

Albrithen, A. (2013). Social work history and features of the social security system: Saudi Arabia. In H. Soliman (ed.), *Social work in the Middle East* (pp. 95–109). New York, NY: Routledge.

Al-Nahedh, N. (1999). Relapse among substance-abuse patients in Riyadh, Saudi Arabia. *Eastern Mediterranean Health Journal, 5*(2), 241–246.

Alsadhan, A. (2004). *Social welfare in Saudi Arabia: The origin and reality*. Riyadh, Saudi Arabia: King Abdulaziz Foundation for Research and Archives.

Al-Saud, A. (1996). *Social work in Saudi Arabia society: Educational reality and requirements for authentication*. Riyadh, Saudi Arabia: Obekan.

Al Saif, A. (1991). *Social work in Saudi Arabia: The development of a profession*. Doctoral dissertation, Florida State University, Tallahassee, FL.

Al-Saif, A. (2004). *Al-medikhal le dera'sat el mojtam'ah el Saudi* [*An introduction to studying the Saudi society*]. Riyadh, Saudi Arabia: Al-Khereeje Press.

Alselmy, A. (2007). *Professional roles of social workers in shelter care agencies: Between the expected and reality*. Riyadh, Saudi Arabia: Ministry of Social Affairs.

Colliers International. (2016). Kingdom of Saudia Arabia Healthcare Overview. Retrieved from https://www.colliers.com/en-gb/saudiarabia/insights/market-news/2016

Gibelman, M. (2004). *What social workers do* (2nd ed.). Washington, DC: NASW Press.

Metz, H. (1992). *Saudi Arabia: A country study*. Washington, DC: Federal Research Division, Library of Congress.

Ragab, I. (1995). Middle East and Egypt. In T. D. Watts, D. Elliott, & N. Mayadas (Eds.), *International handbook on social work education* (pp. 281–304). Westport, CT: Greenwood Press.

Saleh, A. (2002). *Social work and fields of practice*. Westport, Egypt: Darul-Ma'arefah Al Jamaih.

Saudi Ministry of Culture & Information. (2005). *The Saudi Arabian information resource*. Retrieved July 23, 2005, from http://saudinf.com/main/c6.htm

Saudi Ministry of Health. (2002). *Health statistical year book*. Riyadh, Saudi Arabia: Department of Statistics.

Saudi Ministry of Health. (2006). *Statistics book*. Retrieved October 5, 2006, from https://www.moh.gov.sa/en/Ministry/Statistics/Book/Pages/default.aspx

Saudi Arabian Monetary Agency. (2011).Retrieve from http://www.sama.gov.sa/en-US/EconomicReports/AnnualReport/6500_R_Annual_En_47_2011_10_27.pdf

Tash, A. (2001). *Social work*. Cairo, Egypt: Egyptian Cultural Assembly for Publishing and Distributing.

Yalli, N. (2008). *Hospital social work in Saudi Arabia: An investigation of practitioners' perceptions of the common workplace issues that influence their position and role in health care.* Doctoral dissertation, University of East Anglia, Norwich, UK.

Yamani, M. (2000). *Aspects of drug misuse in the Kingdom of Saudi Arabia.* Unpublished PhD thesis, Cardiff University, Cardiff, UK.

12

Social Work in Health Care in South Africa

Charlene Laurence Carbonatto

Introduction

Social work in South Africa has been shaped by the country's colonial past, an era of Apartheid, and efforts to become a democratic society since 1994. The challenges facing social work in health care are formidable in South Africa, a country that is both first and third world; that has health trends ranging from diseases of civilization to diseases of life; in which Western and indigenous health systems function side by side; and that has diverse cultures, religions, beliefs, and practices. These factors, together with high rates of HIV and AIDS, the dual disease of HIV and tuberculosis (TB), poverty, and unemployment and a high incidence of violence against women and children in this predominantly patriarchal society, make South Africa a unique country in which to practice social work. Social workers in health care have to be trained to deal with these unique and demanding circumstances. This, against the backdrop of an unpredictable future with the current political climate, influences the status of the country and the health care system.

Social Work in South Africa

South Africa was first under Dutch rule from 1652 until 1795 and then under British rule until 1910, becoming a union with four separate colonies. It became a self-governing nation state within the British Empire in 1934. In 1961, it became a sovereign state, named the Republic of South Africa (RSA; South African History Online, 2011).

Colonialism, Patel (2015) states, shaped the evolution of the nature, form, and content of social welfare policy in South Africa:

> Colonial administrations adapted the socio-economic organization of the colonies to their own interests, with the primary aim of establishing and sustaining the conditions necessary for economic activity. Indigenous inhabitants in the colonies had to adapt their technology, methods of production, forms of social organization, culture, political, legal and welfare systems to meet the demands and world views of the colonial powers. They further aimed to "civilize" the indigenous people and acted as trustees of what they perceived to be civilization. (pp. 44-45)

Social welfare was at a critical stage in the early 20th century, launching a commission of enquiry on the challenges and problems among Whites, namely the "poor White problem." Two major recommendations from the Carnegie report and a conference led to the establishment of a state Department of Social Welfare in 1937, followed by various welfare organizations. Social work training commenced thereafter at seven South African universities (McKendrick, 1987, p. 12). There was an almost total adherence to models of training developed in Europe and the United States (Potgieter, 1998, p. 21), which, Midgley (as cited in Patel, 2015, p. 48) mentions, led to the adoption of approaches inappropriate to the conditions in poor countries.

The Apartheid system came into effect in 1948, soon after the National Party came into power. This White-only government introduced the Apartheid policy, aimed at racial discrimination, its argument being that integration of various races would impose a threat to peace and freedom and that development could only be attained through separateness or "apart-ness." Social welfare during this period was characterized by inequality and unfairness. The Population Registration Act of 1950 classified the population into four groups—namely White, Black, colored (people of mixed race), and Indian. The act stipulated different access to and benefits from social welfare resources based on race, with the White community enjoying better access to social welfare compared to other races. Separate welfare departments were also established with the aim of addressing the social welfare issues of each racial group separately (Mbedzi, 2015, pp. 51–52; Patel, 2015, p. 49; Potgieter, 1998, pp. 21–22).

Racial differentiation was an explicit principle of the South African welfare system and was tied to the political and economic objectives of the ruling elite (Patel, 2015, pp. 49–50). Patel summarizes it as follows:

The history of resistance in South Africa is characterized by the opposition of the indigenous people to colonialism and apartheid. Over many different generations, opposition grassroots organizations and social and political movements advocated the political, economic, and human rights of all South Africans in a common society and drew attention to the effects of this deprivation on their well-being. Alternative social development initiatives emerged throughout the 20th century in response to the neglect of basic services by the state for the black population and as part of the general political activities of opposition movements to apartheid. (p. 58)

The first legislation granting social workers full professional status was the Social and Associated Workers Act (Act 110 of 1978), later amended to the Social Services Profession Act (Act 110 of 1978), which enabled the creation of a council to regulate the training, registration, and conduct of social workers, namely the South African Council for Social Service Professions (SACSSP; Lombard, 2015:

The SACSSP serves as an umbrella body for the various categories of personnel in the welfare field and makes provision for the Professional Body for Social Work (PBSW). The requirement for a social worker to register with the SACSSP is a four-year Bachelor of Social Work (BSW) qualification. Social work students have to register from their second-year level at the SACSSP as student social workers in order to engage in social work practice training. (p. 2)

In 1994, after the election of Nelson Mandela in a democratic government, the process of developing a white paper for social welfare, through a democratic consultative process, was initiated. Leila Patel, a social worker and social policy specialist, was appointed to manage and lead the process of drafting the *White Paper for Social Welfare* (RSA, Ministry of Welfare and Population Development, 1997). This white paper is aligned with the declaration of the United Nations World Summit for Social Development adopted in Copenhagen in 1995 (Patel, 2015, p. 77).

Lombard (2008) states that this legislation marked a turning point in the history of social welfare service provision and paved the way to bring social work into alignment with national and international goals and thus positioning social work to play a relevant role in democratic society in South Africa.

In 2013, there were 16,164 registered social workers with the SACSSP (Waters, 2013) and 18 universities with undergraduate generalist social work and postgraduate training. There is a 77% shortage of social workers, with the Minister of Social Development, Ms. Dlamini, emphasizing the need for 66,329 social workers just to implement the Children's Act, Older Person's Act, and the Prevention of and Treatment for Substance Abuse Act (Waters, 2013).

Social workers are employed in various state or public departments— namely the Department of Social Development, Department of Health, and Department of Correctional Services—and also in nongovernmental organizations (NGOs) and church-based organizations.

History of Social Work in Health Care in South Africa

The Dutch settlers were the first White Europeans to settle in the Cape in 1652 when the Cape of Good Hope became a mid-voyage refreshment station for the long voyage between the Netherlands and the Far East (McKendrick, 1987, p. 6). Employees of the Dutch East India Company (DEIC) settled here to operate the refreshment station, bringing with them their European beliefs, practices, and way of life.

They erected the first hospital in a tent-like structure for the sick sailors from their ships, who suffered mainly from dysentery, malaria, respiratory infections, smallpox, TB, tetanus, cholera, scurvy, and typhus. In 1656, a permanent structure was erected outside the fort to serve as a hospital, and it was often overcrowded (Van Rensburg, 2012, p. 63). It was initially staffed by a master surgeon, assistant and apprentice surgeon, and a sick comforter. Nursing activities existed in the form of folk nursing, practiced by relatives, neighbors, and well-known elderly women. Institutional nursing was practiced by slaves, who were nursing assistants and bedside attendants. Later, freed Black slaves also held these positions (Van Rensburg, 2012, p. 70). By 1670, more Dutch and French Huguenot immigrants had arrived, and a Dutch Colony was formed. The DEIC provided the first relief to poor White "Boers" and the indigent, leading to the establishment of the first welfare organization—the Dutch Reformed Church in 1665. *Boer* is a Dutch and

Afrikaans word for "farmer," used to refer to the descendants of the Dutch-speaking settlers in South Africa during the 18th century.

Within the first 10 years of the Dutch settling in Africa, three changes came about that are still evident today: racial conflict, racial intermingling, and poverty (McKendrick, 1987, p. 6). The racial intermingling or relationships across racial lines led to the formation of a mixed race, referred to as "coloreds."

The settling of the Dutch led to the displacement of the first inhabitants of the southwestern African region, namely two groups of indigenous peoples: the San people, known as Bushmen, who were hunter–gatherers; and the Khoi, Khoikhoi, or Nama people, also known as the Hottentot people, who practiced nomadic pastoral agriculture. Collectively, these two groups of indigenous people are referred to as the Khoisan people. During this period, the practice of Western medicine by Europeans in the Cape coexisted with the practice of indigenous medicine among the Khoisan and African people.

In 1699, Simon Van der Stel's Cape Hospital opened, which could accommodate between 500 and 750 patients. With the arrival of French Huguenots in 1688, doctors began practicing in rural areas. In 1765, a hospital in Simon's Bay was erected. Smallpox epidemics from 1713 to 1767, followed by leprosy, killed thousands of settlers and slaves. In 1795, the Dutch rule ended with the first British occupation (Van Rensburg, 2012, p. 65).

Indigenous medicine later formed the basis of the practice of folk medicine among the Boer people due to a lack of medical care in rural areas (Van Rensburg, 2012, p. 64).

Away from the Cape, the rest of South Africa had no exposure to Europeans and their philosophies. Beginning in 1795, the British attempted to bring orderliness to "White" land by imposing British rule of law and subjugating slaves, Khoisan, and Africans to it. This caused a deep resentment for the British by the Boers, who moved north and east to get away from British law, only to find the land occupied by African tribespeople. The Boers and the Africans, both farmers and herders, soon were competing for land, grass, and water, causing conflict because the only way to obtain land was by force, treaty, or cession. For both these groups, the family remained the pivotal organization in meeting their needs (McKendrick, 1987, p. 8).

With the discovery of diamonds in Kimberly in 1870 and gold in Witwatersrand in 1885, many immigrants arrived. Laywomen and diggers' daughters were employed to nurse the sick, with 'colored' bedside attendants. In 1840, Robben Island became an institution for the mentally ill, and in 1845 it also became an institution for lepers. It remained the only institution for the mentally ill until 1875 (Van Rensburg, 2012, pp. 70–72).

In 1930 in Somerset Hospital in Cape Town, the first almoner, a person who helps people in hospitals with financial and social problems, was introduced to help the sick poor. In 1938, a request from the SA Association for Trained Nurses was made to the Department of Welfare to establish a Department of Social Work in hospitals due to lack of finances. However, no action was taken. On May 1, 1940, a member of the Research Unit of the Department of Welfare was tasked with performing research to determine the need for social workers in hospitals. The research report made the following recommendations:

- Social work can make a very important contribution to support the patient in crisis.
- Social workers must have a basic degree in social work.
- Social workers in the hospital must have more specific knowledge.

In July 1941, the first social worker was appointed at Pretoria General Hospital, followed by the first social worker appointed at Groote Schuur Hospital, Cape Town, shortly thereafter. From then onward, medical social workers were slowly appointed in public teaching hospitals, linked to universities, as well as smaller regional and district hospitals. Private hospitals began developing and utilizing social workers primarily for in-patient referrals to private medical practitioners.

The University of Stellenbosch initiated specialized training for medical social workers in 1969, with a postgraduate diploma in Medical Social Work and practical training at the Karl Bremer Hospital. This diploma course changed to a Bachelor of Social Work Honors degree in Medical Social Work in 1973 and to a master's degree in Medical Social Work in 1987; unfortunately, this program ended in the late 1990s. Other universities followed, with the University of Cape Town offering a Bachelor of Social Work (Honors) degree in Medical Social Work beginning in 1977 and later changing it to a psychiatric social work degree and a master's degree in Clinical Social Work, which it still offers. The University of Pretoria was the first institution to offer a master's degree in Medical Social Work in 1982, and today the program, MSW (Health Care), is still the only specialized degree in social work in health care in South Africa.

Social Policies and Political Context Within Which Health Care Social Work Exists

Beginning in 1948, racial inequality in access to health care services was enforced by the apartheid government. The health departments were divided, rendering separate health services to Whites, coloreds, Indians, and Blacks and thus leading to inequalities in access to health services (Hassim, Heywood, & Berger, 2007, p. 12). Roestenburg, Carbonatto, and Bila (2016) note that

> in 1994 after the African National Congress (ANC) came into power, the process of restructuring the health services in South Africa received urgent attention. This involved the amalgamation of the 14 different fragmented departments of health into a single National Department of Health. The aim was to create a new integrated National Health System organized at national, provincial and district level. This involved the dismantling of the apartheid structures and the creation of new ones, which could deliver services to all South Africans, regardless of race or ethnic group. The White Paper for the Transformation of the Health System (1997), based on the ANC National Health Plan (1994) and the Reconstruction and Development Plan (1994), set out how this new national Department of Health would function on national, provincial, district and community levels. (p. 179)

Hassim et al. (2007, p. 97) emphasize the importance of the *White Paper for the Transformation of the Health System* (RSA, Ministry of Health, 1997) in guiding health sector transformation to where it is today. The Patients' Rights Charter (RSA, 1999) encouraged health workers to understand and respect the rights of patients and for patients to take responsibility for their health and respect the rights of health care workers (Hassim et al., 2007, pp. 98–99).

Unfortunately, colonialism stigmatized and marginalized African health systems and, together with the subsequent apartheid government, prevented indigenous health systems from developing. Some cultures, most notably African and Khoisan, still give preference to indigenous health systems.

There were 43,277 medical practitioners registered at the Health Professions Council of South Africa in May 2016 compared with approximately 300,000 indigenous traditional health service providers registered with organizations for traditional medicine. These healers are in the communities, assessable to the people, trusted by the people, and, if recognized by the health sector, could be incorporated as health service providers into the health system to provide a support system for health professionals who are overworked and understaffed. With some training, they could play a role in assisting with certain health services, such as monitoring of adherence with directly observed treatment, short course, treatment for TB, diabetes, and HIV patients. Hassim et al. (2007, pp. 204–205) cite the World Health Organization as reporting that 80% of Africans still make use of traditional African medicine and that there is a gap between healers and practitioners of biomedicine.

The following are important legislation and policies in health care in South Africa:

- The Traditional Health Practitioners Act 35 of 2004 ("No. 35 of 2004: Traditional Health Practitioners Act," 2005) aims to regulate traditional medicine and traditional healing, with four categories of traditional health practitioners identified: traditional surgeons (*iingcibi*); traditional birth attendants (*ababelekisi*); herbalists (*iinyanga* or *izinyanga*), and diviners (*sangomas* or *izangoma*). Provisions have been made for a new statutory body for the regulation of traditional healers, namely the Interim Traditional Health Practitioners Council of South Africa.
- The Constitution of the Republic of South Africa 1996 and the Bill of Rights focus on fairness, respect, equality, dignity, and accountability, like the values and principles of social work, and emphasize
  - the right to human dignity; and
  - the right of access to health care, food, water, and social security.
- The National Health Act (Act 61 of 2003) (RSA, 2003) provides a framework for a structured uniform health system by uniting various elements of the national health system, taking into account the obligations imposed by the constitution and other laws, on the national, provincial, and district levels.

- The National Health Amendment Bill (2011) (RSA, 2011a) introduces the Office of Health Standards Compliance and the implementation of the National Core Standards at public health facilities to enhance quality services, accountability, and improved monitoring and evaluation.
- The Patients' Rights Charter (RSA, 1999) serves to ensure realization of the right to access of patients to health services as guaranteed in the constitution and specifies the obligations of both patients and health workers.
- The National Developmental Plan 2030 (RSA, The Presidency, 2011) focuses on improved health care for all in Chapter 10.
- The *National Health Insurance in South Africa Policy Paper (2011)* (RSA, 2011b) is in line with prevailing international thinking and trends, particularly the goal of achieving universal health coverage.
- Choice on termination of Pregnancy Act 92 of 1996 (RSA, 1996) makes provision for termination of pregnancy for women aged 14 years or older without consent of their parents. Circumstances under which pregnancy may be terminated are stipulated in the first, second, and third trimester until week 20.
- Criminal Law (Sexual Offences and Related Matters) Amendment (Act 6 of 2012) (RSA, 2012) comprehensively reviews and amends all aspects of laws and legal aspects of sexual offenses.

Knowledge of the previous legislation and policies is essential for social workers in health care, enabling them to advocate for quality health services for their clients.

With regard to the political context, a lack of basic service delivery in mainly impoverished communities remains one of the major primary health care problems. Unfortunately, the political climate remains volatile, with protests nationwide due to lack of housing, electricity, water, sanitation, and refuse removal as a result of corruption and blatant misuse of state funds and resources for personal gain among local government officials. Constant empty promises by the president and the ruling political party have led to community protests, often resulting in damage to state property including schools and clinics being set ablaze, in a desperate effort to end ongoing corruption and make government officials listen and deliver on their promises. The shortage of social workers makes advocating for these communities difficult. The most recent plans for equal land distribution without compensation, in addition to constant cabinet reshuffling in parliament (e.g., the Minister of Finance was replaced three times in 4 months), have resulted in South Africa being downgraded to "junk status" on a global financial level. Thus, challenging times lie ahead.

Focus of Social Work in Health Care in South Africa

The focus of social work in health care is first on primary health care, awareness, and prevention of illnesses with the highest incidences, namely HIV, TB, and malaria. Next, it focuses on interventions with vulnerable populations: Women, children, the elderly, people with disabilities, and those with chronic, life-threatening, and acute diseases and mental illness are prioritized, with emphasis on maternal and child health because women and children are most at risk for HIV, sexual abuse, and intimate partner violence. Last, environmental and community sustainability is of utmost importance, in line with the Global Agenda for Social Work and the 17 Sustainable Developmental Goals (SDGs; United Nations Development Programme and United Nations Research Institute for Social Development, 2017), to ensure healthy lives and promote well-being for all at all ages (SDG 3).

The priority focus areas for social workers as stipulated in various policies include children, youth, women, people with disabilities, people with chronic diseases, people with HIV/AIDS, mental health, and substance abuse (RSA, Ministry of Welfare and Population Development, 1997, pp. 58–91); HIV/AIDS, sexually transmitted diseases, maternal health, child health, women's health, nutrition, communicable diseases, chronic diseases, disability and gerontology, mental health, and substance abuse (RSA, Ministry of Health, 1997, p. 23); and maternal and child health, nutrition, communicable diseases, violence, women's health, occupational health, rural health, mental health, chronic diseases, rehabilitation, disability, and gerontology (ANC Health Plan, 1994, pp. 84–87).

Furthermore, a broad-based knowledge of and respect for diversity and also Western and indigenous health care systems functioning side by side are important for holistic practice. The latest trend is to decolonize social work education to be more relevant.

In 2016, the population of South Africa was 55,653,654, with 50.5% of the population female and 49.5% male (Countrymeters, n.d.). The African/Black population of 44,891,603 (80.48%) was largest, followed by people of mixed race/colored (4,869,526; 8.79%), White (4,516,691; 8.25%), and Indian/Asian (1,375,834; 2.48%). Those younger than age 15 years comprised 28.5%, whereas 65.8% were aged 16–64 years and 5.7% were aged 65 years or older. The median age was 25 years (Countrymeters, n.d.). Total dependency ratio was 51.9%, with large numbers of children and elderly dependent on the workforce, whereas the child dependency ratio was 43.3%. Life expectancy at birth was 49.3 years, with 676,245 deaths and 1,139,909 births in 2015. The adult literacy rate was 94.3% (RSA, 2016; Statistics South Africa, 2016). It is evident that due to the large number of African citizens, the indigenous health care system is widely practiced; the emphasis is on the health of women, children, and the elderly; and there is a low life expectancy due to HIV and AIDS.

Social workers in health care practice in public and private hospitals and in private practice, with referrals from medical practitioners. In public teaching hospitals, social workers are assigned to a department or area as part of the interdisciplinary team—for example, gynecology; obstetrics; the neonatal intensive care unit; pediatrics; infertility; urology; surgery; ophthalmology;   hematology–oncology–chemotherapy–radiotherapy; internal medicine; cardiology; pulmonology; immunology–HIV; geriatrics; ear, nose, and throat; gastroenterology; psychiatry; orthopedics; neurology; neurosurgery; and the rehabilitation unit. In-depth knowledge and understanding of medical conditions and treatments in their assigned areas are necessary because social workers attend ward rounds, conduct psychosocial assessments of patients' circumstances, determine their understanding and experience of their illness, and assist in preparation for and adherence to treatment. Feedback is provided during ward rounds, advocating for the patient and family. Psychoeducation with the patient and family and special intervention strategies with regard to the psychosocial impact, coping and support, discharge planning, and adaptation or rehabilitation are implemented. Interdisciplinary team members usually include the medical specialist, a registrar, a medical practitioner, medical student interns, registered nurses, a physiotherapist, an occupational therapist, a health social worker, and a dietician, all of whom supervise student interns. At smaller regional provincial hospitals with less specialized services, there are fewer social workers, whereas at district or community hospitals, one social worker may serve the entire hospital and community.

The SACSSP is in the process of registering a specialization in social work in health care. The draft regulation for a specialty in social work in health care defines social work in health care as follows (SACSSP, 2017):

Social work in health care focuses on health promotion, prevention, intervention and research regarding the psychosocial assessment of the implications of illness, disability, chemical dependence, medical treatment, care and support, hospitalization, rehabilitation and reintegration of patients with significant others and the community from a holistic perspective.

The Department of Social Work and Criminology, University of Pretoria, is currently the only university with specialized postgraduate training in social work in health care in South Africa. It has remained dedicated to this specialized program in social work in health care since 1982. This is a 2-year master's coursework program, with theory and practice modules in the first year, followed by research and mini-dissertation in the second year. Staff capacity allows for selection of 10 students per year, who are mainly qualified part-time students, mostly from South Africa and Southern African Development Communities (i.e., Angola, Botswana, Democratic Republic of Congo, Lesotho, Madagascar, Malawi, Mauritius, Mozambique, Namibia, Seychelles, South Africa, Swaziland, United Republic of Tanzania, Zambia, and Zimbabwe) and Kenya. Graduates work in public sector hospitals, of which there are approximately 400, including 10 teaching hospitals, and in smaller regional, district, and community hospitals and psychiatric hospitals. The 4,100 public sector primary health care clinics in the community, including antiretroviral clinics, are other employment sites of the Department of Health. Other graduates are employed by the Department of Social Development, in the directorates disability and substance abuse, and some work in geriatric frail care centers, substance abuse rehabilitation centers, and NGOs.

Looking Forward: Emerging Trends and Potential Future Issues

In the wake of the specialization of social work in health care in South Africa, soon to be approved by the SACSSP, it is envisaged that more universities will initiate postgraduate programs in health care, increasing recognition of social workers in the health care industry.

The decolonializing of social work and social work education, with the focus on transformation, Africanization, and indigenization of social work, will incorporate locally relevant content into the social work curriculum, bringing exciting challenges.

With its envisaged National Health Insurance (NIH), the health system might provide more positions for social workers in hospitals, especially private hospitals. With regard to the Office of Health Standards Compliance and the National Core Standards (NCS) for health institutions, the challenge for social workers is in advocating for patients and their right to receive quality health care.

Other challenges for social work in health care involve collaboration with alternative, complementary, and indigenous health service providers in the interest of holistic patient care.

Conclusion

South Africa is a country with a unique background that influences its people, its health system, socioeconomic development, relationships, politics, social welfare, and health services and policies. Social work and social work education have historically been influenced by South Africa's colonial history and apartheid policies. In the past, social work education was based on European models. Currently, the decolonization of social work and transformation at universities create challenges, but there is optimism that a locally relevant social work curriculum will eventually be developed.

The indigenous beliefs and practices ignored and set aside in the past must now be acknowledged and incorporated into the health system. Legislation and a changing health system have placed the emphasis on reengineering primary health care, focusing on principles such as equity. South Africa is entering a new era of health care, with NHI and NCS aiming to improve all health facilities with the goal of better health for all, as envisaged in the National Development Plan 2030.

Lack of basic service delivery in mainly impoverished communities remains one of the major primary health care challenges; corruption and the current political climate negatively affect efforts to improve health care services. Health care continues to evolve, as demonstrated by the increasing recognition of indigenous medicine, which is used to treat the largest portion of the population, and healing that is culturally appropriate. At the same time, efforts to decolonize both the profession of social work and social work education have commenced, creating new challenges.

References

ANC Health Plan. (1994). pp. 84–87. Retrieved from https://www.sahistory.org.za/sites/default/files/a_national_health_plan_for_south_africa.pdf

"Constitution of the Republic of South Africa." (1996, December 18). *Government Gazette, 378*(No. 17678).

Countrymeters. (n.d.). "South African population." Retrieved November 27, 2016, from http://countrymeters.info/en/South_Africa

Hassim, A., Heywood, M., & Berger, J. (Eds.). (2007). *Health and democracy: A guide to human rights, health law and policy in post-apartheid South Africa.* Cape Town, South Africa: SiberInk.

Health Professions Council of South Africa. (2016). *Statistics: Summary of registered persons on 3 May 2016.* Retrieved April 30, 2017, from http://www.hpcsa.co.za/Publications/Statistics.

Lombard, A. (2008). The implementation of the white paper for social welfare: A ten-year review. *The Social Work Practitioner–Researcher, 20*(2), 154–173.

Lombard, A. (2015). Internationalizing social work education: The South African experience. *Indian Journal of Social Work, 76*(1), 41–56.

Mbedzi, P. (2015). The history of social welfare and social work. In C. J. Schenck, R. P. Mbedzi, L. Qalinge, P. Schultz, J. Sekudu, & M. Sesoko (Eds.), *Introduction to social work in the South African context* (pp. 59–71). Cape Town, South Africa: Oxford University Press.

McKendrick, B. W. (Ed.). (1987). *Introduction to social work in South Africa.* Pinetown, South Africa: Owen Burgess.

"No. 35 of 2004: Traditional Health Practitioners Act." (2005, February 11). *Government Gazette, 476*(27275).

Patel, L. (2015). *Social welfare and social development* (2nd ed.). Cape Town, South Africa: Oxford University Press.

Potgieter, M. C. (1998). *The social work process: Development to empower people.* Cape Town, South Africa: Prentice Hall South Africa.

Republic of South Africa, Department of Social Development. (2016). *Population trends and social development*. Retrieved from http://www.population.gov.za/index.php/documents/send/76-population-trends-and-social-development-gender-and-the-empowerment-of-women/174-south-africa-population-trends

Republic of South Africa, Ministry of Health. (1994). *Towards the national health system* (Vol. 1, No. 2, pp. 1–4). Cape Town, South Africa: Government Printer.

Republic of South Africa, Ministry of Health. (1996). Choice on termination of Pregnancy Act No. 92 of 1996. *Government Gazette, 377*(1762).

Republic of South Africa, Ministry of Health. (1997). White paper for the transformation of the health system in South Africa. *Government Gazette, 382*(17910).

Republic of South Africa, Ministry of Health. (1999). *Patients' rights charter*. Cape Town, South Africa: Government Printer.

Republic of South Africa, Ministry of Health. (2003). The National Health Act (Act 61 of 2003). *Government Gazette, 469*(26595).

Republic of South Africa, Ministry of Health. (2011a). The National Health Amendment Bill (2011). *Government Gazette, 547*(33962).

Republic of South Africa, Ministry of Health. (2011b). *National health insurance in South Africa policy paper (2011)*. Cape Town, South Africa: Government Printer.

Republic of South Africa, Ministry of Health. (2012). Criminal Law (Sexual Offences and Related Matters) Amendment (Act 6 of 2012). *Government Gazette, 564*(35473).

Republic of South Africa, Ministry of Welfare and Population Development. (1997). White paper for social welfare. *Government Gazette, 386*(18166).

Republic of South Africa, The Presidency. (2011). *National developmental plan 2030*. Pretoria, South Africa: Government Printer.

Roestenburg, W., Carbonatto, C. L., & Bila, N. J. (2016). Mental health services in South Africa. In M. A. Sossou & T. Modie-Moroka (Eds.), *Mental health conditions and services in selected African countries: Implications for social work and human services professions* (pp. 167–198). New York, NY: Nova Science.

South African Council for Social Service Professions. (2017). *Draft regulation for a specialty in social work in health care*. Pretoria, South Africa: Author.

South African History Online. (2011). *The Dutch settlement*. Accessed December 12, 2016, from http://www.sahistory.org.za/article/dutch-settlement

Statistics South Africa. (2016). *Community survey 2016: Statistical release P0301.* Retrieved from http://cs2016.statssa.gov.za/wp-content/uploads/2016/07/NT-30-06-2016-RELEASE-for-CS-2016-_Statistical-releas_1-July-2016.pdf

United Nations Development Programme and United Nations Research Institute for Social Development. (2017). *Global trends UNDP: Challenges and opportunities in the implementation of the Sustainable Development Goals.* New York, NY: United Nations Development Programme.

Van Rensburg, H. C. J. (Ed.). (2012). *Health and health care in South Africa* (2nd ed.). Pretoria, South Africa: Van Schaik.

Waters, M. (2013). SA has a 77% shortage of social workers. Retrieved April 29, 2017, from https://www.politicsweb.co.za/party/sa-has-a-77-social-worker-shortage--mike-waters

13

Health Care Social Work in Sweden

Manuela Sjöström

Introduction

The institutionalization of social work as an independent academic discipline in 1977 can be perceived as a milestone in Swedish social work's professionalization. Today, it is taught at a dozen universities, at undergraduate, graduate, and postgraduate levels (Brante, 2003). Although undergraduate education is supposed to focus on general social work, Dellgran and Höjer (2003) show that research in the area has rapidly differentiated into many subfields.

Graduated social workers work in different areas of the welfare system: Approximately 95% work in public organizations, such as social administration and social care organizations, health care services, schools, and the penal system; a minority of social workers work in nonprofit and for-profit private organizations as voluntary organizations and the church; and a small number are employed in companies' human relations departments or at revision bureaus. According to information from the labor union, approximately 40,000 graduated social workers are employed throughout the country (SSR, 2016). They work with different sorts of social problems and conditions that have caused or could cause social or health problems: poverty, poor housing, child abuse, all forms of addiction, migration, aging, psychiatric and physical illness, social deviation, criminality, disability, and so on. Depending on the size of municipalities and health care organizations, social workers often specialize in a subfield, with health care being one of them. Social work's formal jurisdiction is not clearly defined in legislation. Social workers are not licensed, which means that they cannot claim autonomy over a legally protected work field, and there are no work tasks that only they can perform (Sjöström, 2013).

Health care social workers in the Swedish context are employed in private or county-driven health care services: They often specialize in specific medical subfields, in- or outpatient care at medical and psychiatric care units; and pediatric or geriatric care. They also have an unquestioned place in municipality-driven youth health clinics and in schools.

This chapter focuses on social work in health care and describes its scope of practice or, more precisely, its publicly claimed but informal jurisdiction in Sweden (Sjöström, 2013). A short introduction on Swedish health care social work history is given, and some elaboration is made on the political context and social policies currently affecting Swedish health care social work practice. Contemporary health care social work is then examined, and conclusions drawn regarding the profession's future jurisdiction and challenges.

History and Professionalization of Health Care Social Work in Sweden

According to Olsson (1999), the first pioneer of health care social work in Sweden, Gertrud Rohde, a dedicated teacher, started to organize social services for psychiatric patients in the capital of Stockholm in 1914. Jane Norén expanded this work to other health care fields in the 1920s. The two largest cities in the country, Gothenburg and Malmö, subsequently followed Stockholm's example. Later, social services were also implemented for patients in specialized wardens for cancer, tuberculosis, and functional disabilities. In the 1940s, social services also spread to hospitals in minor cities, other medical specialties, and health care teams in schools (Isaksson, 2016; Olsson,1999). Often, health care social workers possessed a background in nursing. During this period, debate about the most appropriate form of professional training for these duties—social work or nursing—occurred.

In contrast to other Western countries, health care social workers in Sweden were assigned to a specific hospital or warden but had their offices in their homes. Some patients they met at their offices, and they met with others at hospitals or in their homes. Health care social workers also had varying employers: Some were hired by hospitals, whereas others were sponsored by municipalities, philanthropic organizations, or private donations (Olsson, 1999).

In the early days of health care social work, social workers were tasked with supporting health care by helping patients with their social problems, advocating for patients' rights, and increasing health care's efficiency and effectiveness by cooperating with other support systems—public and private. Work tasks included helping patients apply for funds or insurance benefits; engagement as guardians for specific patients; storage of patients' private belongings during hospital visits; investigation of patients' homes and social situations; and counseling or supporting patients and their relatives in relation to employers, landlords, banks, and so on. Social workers were also involved in discharge management: planning further rehabilitation and care, organizing for education and work, as well as patient follow-up after discharge. They actively engaged in social policymaking in order to impact on the future development of the social welfare system. During the 1930s and 1940s, social assessment and intervention grew (Olsson, 1999).

After World War II, the number of health care social workers began to increase—from approximately 70 persons in 1944 to 470 in 1962 (Blom, Lalos, Morén, & Olsson, 2014): Social work education in Sweden advanced as social workers sought further education abroad and then returned with inspiring new methods from predominantly English-speaking countries, including approaches to casework. In the 1950s, health care social workers began to be more frequently employed by hospitals or municipalities than by charity organizations. Commonly, they were organized in specific social work departments at hospitals. In the 1960s, the focus of social work shifted from patients' material problems to more social, psychosocial, and existential problems. At the same time, the primary health care system developed, and social workers promoted their inclusion in this context (Blom et al., 2014).

The first professional association for health care social workers was founded in 1944 when an agreement requiring professional education in social work as a criteria for membership was enacted. Other associations followed, focusing on varying medical subspecialties (Isaksson, 2016; Olsson, 1999). Over time, the number of associations fluctuated. Only a few active ones are left today; the most influential of them, Svensk Kuratorsförening, organizes health care social workers from medical subfields such as emergency care, women's health, and rheumatic care (Sjöström, 2013). Throughout the years, the most important tasks for these associations have focused on promoting formal and informal jurisdiction: lobbying for a state licensure for health care social workers; including social services in health care contexts both in legislation and in public regulations or health care procedures; supporting their members in lobbying for specific social work units; and developing a common definition of work tasks for health care social workers.

Social Policy Developments for Social Work in Health Care in Sweden During the Past 30 Years

The Swedish welfare system is often described as an example of the social democratic welfare regime (Esping-Andersen, 1999). This system influences the structure of Swedish health care as well as the interaction between the state and health care professionals, including health care social workers (Sjöström, 2013). One of the specifics of Swedish social policymaking is its focus on preventing social problems through the development of relevant legislation (Pettersson, 2001). In practice, this means that legislation is used as a tool to develop societal structures, including health care, that focus on the development of social justice irrespective of class, status, and other personal attributes. The Swedish health care service is a tax-financed national health service. Services are universally accessible to all legal residents, even those who did not contribute to its funding. The aim is to distribute health care equally and independently from other family members. Sweden implements a collective model of public policy decision-making by politicians, including issues regarding the distribution of health care services. As a result, access to health care services is rather a collective right to more vaguely defined "good quality health care services" than an individual right to a set of specific treatments (Sjöström, 2013).

Even if health care is defined as lying within the competence of counties and social services within that of municipalities, responsibilities of both welfare sectors have been entangled for a long time. During the past 30 years, reforms of health care legislation have aimed predominantly at increasing budgetary efficiency by opening up the health care industry to private health care companies, especially since the financial crisis of the 1990s. Reforms have also aimed at eliminating the overlapping competencies concerning county-financed health care and municipality-financed social welfare. Legal reforms concern predominantly elder care and medical and social care for psychiatric patients. However, the reformed Health and Medical Services Act and Social Service Act remain vague concerning the responsibility to finance and provide health care social work. Several attempts have been made to address this legislative issue by recognizing service providers' responsibility to cooperate so that citizens' biological, psychological, and social needs can be met. However, it remains unclear, for example, whether the provision of social work in primary care is the responsibility of the social or medical services. It is also left to public service providers to decide in which way social welfare, primary care, and specialized health care providers may cooperate. Legislation does not give any clear guidance with regard to social work's jurisdiction in health care because social work remains the only unlicensed profession in the field (Sjöström, 2013).

Responsibility for the management of health care services lies within each county's authority. Currently, counties distribute first-line medical care at primary health care centers, where general practitioners and the most needed specialists cooperate (SOU, 2007). For example, advanced care is given at county-financed inpatient and outpatient hospitals (VGR 2012). Some specific areas of preventive health care, however, are still delivered by municipalities—for example, in elder care and at youth health clinics and schools.

Regarding health care governance, physicians traditionally occupy strategic positions in state and county administration. Apart from politicians, it is mainly these physicians who impact policymaking. The medical profession also exerts a strong influence on the allocation of financial resources, even though this is part of political decision-making. It is likely that the dominant role of physicians in policymaking and public administration has implications for social workers' opportunities to impact policymaking and procedural development in the context of Swedish health care. Likely, this is because physicians' political influence affects health care social workers' options for increasing professional autonomy within the following areas: creation of state licensure, defining formally accepted standards for practice, and effective performance of social work duties within the health care sector. However, research concerning the nature of this interaction is currently lacking (Kuhlmann, 2006; Sjöström, 2013).

Social Work in Health Care

To describe social workers' roles in health care in Sweden is a rather tricky task because health care social work in Sweden is an underdeveloped research area. From 1995 until 2002, only 3% of all senior research in Swedish social work departments concerned social work in health care, as did only

7% of all PhDs earned between 1999 and 2009 (Dellgran & Höjer, 2003, 2011). In addition, none of the newly doctored researchers focused on legal, professional, or organizational aspects of health care social work (Dellggran & Höjer, 2011). The picture is only slightly different when social workers doctored through medical departments are included: Between 1980 and 2007, the majority of these social workers addressed primarily psychosocial phenomena in health care, social conditions relating to ill-health, and experiences of ill-health (Flink, Öjehagen, & Olsson, 2008). In summary, Swedish health care social workers' roles have only rarely been studied, and only recently have such research efforts gained traction (Svärd, 2014). Therefore, this chapter predominantly refers to what social workers publicly claim to be their scope of practice in health care settings instead of research findings concerning their actual roles.

In November 2015, 7,116 graduated social workers were employed in psychiatric and health care social work settings. Unfortunately, exact statistics are not available on precisely where they work. Available data do suggest that approximately 3,000–3,500 work in predominantly health care settings (SKL, 2016a, 2016b).

Social workers in health care work with diverse patient groups: children, youth, adults, elderly, and their private and professional networks. Health care problems vary across these populations and include addiction, reproduction issues, and serious acute and chronic diseases. Swedish health care social workers practice predominantly on teams for acute and chronic conditions, preventive health care, and palliative care (Lalos & Olsson, 2014). Since the 1980s, social workers have increasingly worked on integrated, multidisciplinary teams rather than from autonomous social work units (Sjöström, 2013).

As has happened elsewhere, health care social workers in Sweden have experienced difficulty agreeing on common work task definitions (Sjöström, 2103). In a recent review of research published on this topic, social workers were found to be responsible for professional assessment and were noted as having the professional discretion to draw conclusions concerning suitable social and psychosocial interventions, including crisis, bereavement, and trauma counseling. Patients and their families are also counseled concerning a wide range of other matters—from the use of medical and technical aids to sexuality, reproduction, and issues such as abortion, infertility, funeral preparation, parenting skills, and so on. Swedish health care social workers provide information to patients concerning economic and insurance matters and legal issues. They also provide support in applying for interventions by other social service programs and economic support from various sources (municipal social services, insurances, charity funds, donations, etc.), and they assist family members—especially underaged family members—in adjusting to patient health problems. In Sweden, health care social workers administer psychoeducative programs (for patients with drug abuse problems and those diagnosed with chronic diseases), support individuals in developing relevant coping strategies, provide training for social skills acquisition, and support patients' self-help groups (Gullacksen, 2014; Johnsson, 2014; Kero, 2014; Lalos & Olsson, 2014; Öjehagen, 2014). Discharge management and interprofessional teamwork, especially at the boundaries between health care and social service sectors, are work tasks in decline, but they are still performed in geriatric care (Melin Emilsson, 2014).

According to Forinder (2014), health care social work with pediatric and adolescent patients differs from that with adults. In the former, parents are more often the focus of interventions by health care social workers than the children. Even when social workers have individual consultations with children and youth, they are usually also engaged in counseling parents or entire families because they understand that a child's coping strategies rely very much on the parents' coping capacities and ability to provide support. With this population, counseling often involves providing information on the specific disease and how to handle the provision of information to the child; it also often involves addressing parents' own need for support. Other subjects for intervention often concern the economic consequences of having seriously ill children and supporting parents in legal matters as well as in their contact with the state insurance agency or private insurance companies. Pediatric and adolescent health care social workers in Sweden also support the siblings of sick children. Siblings are provided opportunities to talk about the sister's or brother's disease or death, and they receive assistance in addressing their own feelings and needs. These consultations are held either alone or together with the parents, depending on the age of the children.

Health care social workers in pediatric care contexts also work preventatively. Examples of this work include developing routines to minimize traumatization of children in emergency department settings and providing interventions for children whose quality of life will be affected by their compliance with necessary treatment. They might engage in interprofessional consultations with teachers, employment agencies, and adult health care providers in order to raise awareness concerning short- and long-term consequences (Forinder, 2014).

In addition to the previously mentioned work tasks, health care social workers are also involved in the assessment of children at risk for psychological or physical maltreatment and abuse (Forinder, 2014; Svärd, 2014). Svärd illuminates which roles health care social workers may develop as members of health care teams during the assessment of children at risk: Some of them may take rather passive or reflective roles, but most take active roles. The differences between these roles are in the degree to which health care social workers participate in the assessment process and to what extend they participate in decision-making to report suspicious cases to the social services. In summary, health care social workers have slightly different tasks depending on the medical subfield in which they work. Their jurisdictional claims appear are similar for most medical subspecialties but sometimes overlap with those of other professionals (physicians, nurses, psychologists, work therapists, etc.) in the workplace (Svärd, 2016).

According to Olsson (1999), the work tasks for social workers in health care have shifted from coordinating and distributing resources to assessment, motivational work, informing, and counseling. In the aftermath of the severe economic crisis during the 1990s, health care social workers in Sweden were integrated into medical health care teams instead of social work units. Simultaneously, many health care social workers abandoned discharge management for more therapeutic tasks. It is likely that legal reforms and organizational changes necessitated health care social workers' development of new professional niches within the health care system (Olsson, 1999).

In the 20-year period since the financial crisis, a shift in social work focus has occurred. According to Sjöström (2013), documents written by health care social work associations show that claims concerning health care social workers' work tasks have changed slightly over time. While emphasis on micro-level interventions has grown, work tasks involving mezzo or macro interventions have diminished. Health care social workers also tend to support the value of their contributions to health care by emphasizing their specific therapeutic skills rather than social work-specific diagnostic skills, work tools, or knowledge base. Interestingly, these changes in health care social workers' public jurisdictional claims-making appear to correspond with changes in legislation and new public regulations (Sjöström, 2013).

Sjöström (2013) argues that an increasing tendency to emphasize health care social workers' treatment skills regarding therapeutic intervention and health care-related knowledge is part of a deliberate strategy to blend social work in with other well-established health care professions. In contrast, German health care social workers emphasize training, knowledge, and skills that tend to differentiate them from other health care professionals. Swedish social workers' approach represents a different strategy for maintaining their informal jurisdiction within health care at the same time that legal requirements stipulate the clear separation of social work from health care.

In Sweden, ongoing efforts by health care social workers to achieve state licensure can also be interpreted as a strategy to enhance social work's jurisdiction in health care services: Health care social workers perceive licensure as likely to support the field's increased influence on social policy-making, in the development of public regulations concerning health care procedures, and in multidisciplinary teamwork in the workplace (Sjöström, 2013). These efforts have led to a number of public investigations on the issue. The most recent of these concluded that health care social work should be licensed because it is perceived as a health care profession with specific competencies and skills (Socialstyrelsen, 2014). Preparations for future licensure are underway, but currently health care social work remains the only unlicensed academic profession in health care.

According to Olsson (1999), health care social workers in Sweden have tended to adapt their public jurisdictional claims to reflect government and physician concerns and emphasis. This strategy makes it more difficult for them to ground their arguments for specific work tasks in social work knowledge. This might be one reason why Swedish health care social workers' scope of practice is often perceived as nonspecific by those on other professions who often claim to perform the same tasks (Olsson, 1999). For example, nurses and psychologists have strengthened their role in health care by advocating that their specialized knowledge, perspective, and training best prepare them to address certain patient needs in a manner consistent with the medical model requiring assessment and diagnosis of patient deficits and pathologies. In contrast, health care social workers have often struggled to engender multidisciplinary support from professions oriented to addressing patient symptoms, loss of function, and disease instead of strengths and resources. This has sometimes resulted in a guardedness and dedication to protecting hard fought authority in a context in which all other practitioners are licensed and likely perceived as possessing a higher standing (Gåfvels, 2014).

Framme (2014) shows that social workers in psychiatric care have a paradoxical relation to their knowledge base in social work. Her interviewees claim they have a broader perspective as social workers on the macro-level and with regard to empowerment. At the same time, they state that it is unusual for them to use this knowledge in their work. In addition, social workers in health care perceive their organizations as expecting them to specialize in therapeutic tasks or to gain more knowledge of specific medical diagnosis and treatments relevant in their host units. In Sweden, it is less common that social workers in health care are expected to specialize in specific social advocacy work or macro-level duties (Morén, Blom, Lalos, & Olsson, 2014). Many health care social workers perceive their roles as therapists and believe it is a professional obligation to advocate for client needs. However, few actually include advocacy or macro-level work as a component of their clinic work (Framme, 2014). It may be that this relative dissociation from traditional social work tasks and knowledge base affects popular perception and multidisciplinary opinion of the legitimacy of social workers' claims to their specific jurisdiction in health care.

Several other issues are likely to impact future health care social work's jurisdiction as government strategies, changes in health care policies, patient needs, and society in general evolve. New public management trends and an increasing demand for evidence-based practice will affect social workers' preparation and job duties. Related use of standardized diagnostic instruments and work methods will likely gain in importance. It is also likely that these trends will continue to encourage the medicalization of social problems (Morén et al., 2014). The effect of these changes on health care social work's claims concerning its jurisdiction are difficult to anticipate.

Health care is likely to face continued reorganization efforts in response to changing health care policies and future health care needs. These changes will eventually also call for the revision of the professional jurisdiction in the field and potential reassignment of responsibilities between public primary and specialized health care, social services, and private caregivers. Health care social workers will face continued challenges to adapt their jurisdiction within newly evolving health care contexts in the Swedish health care system, such as more private health care organizations and primary care and e-health services; new diagnostic and therapeutic techniques will impact who will be defined as health care social work patients. A split of health care social workers into specialists and generalists might be one consequence, as is the possible appearance of new professional groups (e.g., genetic counselors) within the professional field of health care social workers (Morén et al., 2014).

According to Morén et al. (2014), other challenges for health care social workers are caused by changes in the composition of patient and staff groups. These create compensatory needs for adjustment and impact social work tasks with regard to considering those with different cultural backgrounds, religious preferences, social situations, and so on.

Health Care Social Work at the Crossroads

The previously described challenges for Swedish health care social workers suggest that the profession has come to a crossroads, where several important decision will impact the future jurisdiction of social work in health care.

Will health care social workers in the future continue the current strategy of blending into the health care environment by promoting their possession of therapeutic and medical competencies—or will they change their strategy and more proactively promote a focus on social work competencies (Sjöström, 2013)? Regardless of how health care social workers choose to proceed, the development of more specific practice theories for health care social work will be an important necessity.

In relation to the basic question of whether to blend in or stand out, future health care social workers will have to make another important determination regarding their purpose. So far, social workers have often defined their work tasks in relation to organizational or private interests (Sjöström, 2013). As Swedish health care changes, social workers will have the opportunity to consider whether they should focus more intently on the profession's larger societal mission and choose to define tasks from a client-based and societal perspective (Morén et al., 2014). This would require health care social workers to be more involved in addressing social policy and organizational demands concerning their work tasks.

Another question concerns when and how social workers will be able to successfully impact policymaking and public administration in order to be able to increase their role in determining their informal and formal jurisdiction according to patient needs and the societal mission of social work. Currently, little is known about health care social workers' potential for impacting social policies and public administration (Sjöström, 2013). Future research in this area could help social workers strengthen future decision-making.

Finally, it is important to note that of all the issues described in this chapter, two potential developments will likely play a particularly significant role in determining which future options health care social workers will or will not be able to choose: the likely future licensure of health care social workers and the extent to which Swedish public administration will further enforce new public management strategies or the use of evidence-based practice methods. It is possible that the introduction of a state licensure for health care social workers will impact the profession's jurisdiction and knowledge base in this area by strengthening the profession's focus on the use of evidence-based therapeutic methods in work with individuals and groups and by normalizing the use of standardized diagnostic methods for the assessment of children at risk (Morén et al., 2014; Svärd, 2016). It is likely that the enforcement of new standards for public management and the related use of evidence-based methods will lead to an increased focus on micro- and meso-level services and continue to diminish the focus on macro-level work tasks (Morén et al., 2014). This is likely to preserve the already existing one-sided interpretation of social workers' tasks in health care.

References

Blom, B., Lalos, A., Morén, S., & Olsson, M. (2014). Hälso- och sjukvården—en central arena för socialt arbete. In B. Blom, A. Lalos, S. Morén, & M. Olsson (Eds.), *Socialt arbete i hälso- och sjukvård: Villkor, innehåll och utmaningar* (pp. 21–27). Stockholm, Sweden: Natur & Kultur.

Brante, Th. (2003). Konsolidering av nya vetenskapliga fält—exemplet forskning i socialt arbete. In Högskoleverket (Ed.), *Socialt arbete: En nationell genomlysning av ämnet* (pp. 133–196). Stockholm, Sweden: Högskoleverkets.

Dellgran, P., & Höjer, S. (2003). Forskning i praktiken: Om den seniora forskningens innehåll och socionomers forskningsorientering. In Högskoleverket (Ed.), *Socialt arbete: En nationell genomlysning av ämnet* (pp. 197–250). Stockholm: Högskoleverkets.

Dellgran, P., & Höjer, S. (2011). Nya Trender och gamla mönster. Doktorsavhandlingar i social arbete 1980-2009. *Socialvetenskaplig tidskrift, 18*(4), 85–106.

Esping-Andersen, G. (1999). *Social foundations of postindustrial economies.* Oxford, UK: Oxford University Press.

Flink, M., Öjehagen, A., & Olsson, M. (2008). Psykosocialt arbete i hälso- och sjukvård—en översikt över avhandlingar inom orådet. *Socionomens forskningssupplement, 2008*(24), 14–20.

Forinder, U. (2014). Socialt arbete med sjuka barn. In B. Blom, A. Lalos, S. Morén, & M. Olsson (Eds.), *Socialt arbete i hälso- och sjukvård. Villkor, innehåll och utmaningar* (pp. 147–164). Stockholm, Sweden: Natur & Kultur.

Framme, G. (2014). Vad gör socionomerna för skillnad i den psykiatriska vården? *Socialvetenskaplig tidskrift, 21*(2), 85–103.

Gåfvels, C. (2014). Socialt arbete i en medicinsk kontext. In B. Blom, A. Lalos, S. Morén, & M. Olsson (Eds.), *Socialt arbete i hälso- och sjukvård: Villkor, innehåll och utmaningar* (pp. 50–68). Stockholm, Sweden: Natur & Kultur.

Gullacksen, A.-Ch. (2014). Socialt arbete och kroniska sjukdomar. In B. Blom, A. Lalos, S. Morén, & M. Olsson (Eds.), *Socialt arbete i hälso- och sjukvård: Villkor, innehåll och utmaningar* (pp. 165–182). Stockholm, Sweden: Natur & Kultur.

Isaksson, C. (2016). *Den kritiska gästen: En professionsstudie om skolkuratorer.* Doctoral dissertation, Institutionen för socialt arbete, Umeå, Sweden.

Johnsson, A. (2014). Socialt arbete och cancersjukdom. In B. Blom, A. Lalos, S. Morén, & M. Olsson (Eds.), *Socialt arbete i hälso- och sjukvård: Villkor, innehåll och utmaningar* (pp. 183–200). Stockholm, Sweden: Natur & Kultur.

Kero, A. (2014). Socialt arbete vid kris och sorg. In B. Blom, A. Lalos, S. Morén, & M. Olsson (Eds.), *Socialt arbete i hälso- och sjukvård: Villkor, innehåll och utmaningar* (pp. 74–90). Stockholm, Sweden: Natur & Kultur.

Kuhlman, E. (2006). *Modernizing health care: Reinventing professions, the state and the public.* Bristol, UK: Policy Press.

Lalos, A., & Olsson, M. (2014). Innehåll i socialt arbete i hälso- och sjukvården. In B. Blom, A. Lalos, S. Morén, & M. Olsson (Eds.), *Socialt arbete i hälso- och sjukvård: Villkor, innehåll och utmaningar* (pp. 71–73). Stockholm, Sweden: Natur & Kultur.

Melin Emilsson, U. (2014). Socialt arbete och sjuka äldre. In B. Blom, A. Lalos, S. Morén, & M. Olsson (Eds.), *Socialt arbete i hälso- och sjukvård: Villkor, innehåll och utmaningar* (pp. 201–215). Stockholm, Sweden: Natur & Kultur.

Morén, S., Blom, B., Lalos, A., & Olsson, M. (2014). Socialt arbete i hälso- och sjukvård—villkor och utmaningar. In B. Blom, A. Lalos, S. Morén, & M. Olsson (Eds.), *Socialt arbete i hälso- och sjukvård: Villkor, innehåll och utmaningar* (pp. 237–254). Stockholm, Sweden: Natur & Kultur.

Öjehagen, A. (2014). Socialt arbete och beroende. In B. Blom, A. Lalos, S. Morén, & M. Olsson (Eds.), *Socialt arbete i hälso- och sjukvård: Villkor, innehåll och utmaningar* (pp. 112–128). Stockholm, Sweden: Natur & Kultur.

Olsson, S. (1999). *Kuratorn förr och nu: Sjukhuskuratorns arbete i ett historisk perspektiv.* Doctoral dissertation, Department of Social Work, University of Gothenburg, Gothenburg, Sweden.

Pettersson, U. (2001). *Socialt arbete, politik och professionalisering: Den historiska utvecklingen i USA och Sverige.* Stockholm, Sweden: Natur & Kultur.

SKL. (2016a). *Kommunal personal 2015.* Retrieved September 21, 2016, from http://skl.se/ekonomijuridikstatistik/statistik/personalstatistik/personalenidiagramochsiffror/tabellerkommunalpersonal2015.8832.html

SKL. (2016b). *Landstingsanställd personal 2015.* Retrieved September 21, 2016, from http://skl.se/ekonomijuridikstatistik/statistik/personalstatistik/personalenidiagramochsiffror/tabellerlandstingsanstalldpersonal2015.8833.html

Sjöström, M. (2013). *To blend in or stand out? Hospital social workers' jurisdictional work in Sweden and Germany.* Doctoral dissertation, Department of Social Work, University of Gothenburg, Gothenburg, Sweden.

Socialstyrelsen. (2014). *Legitimation för kuratorer inom hälso- och sjukvård.* Stockholm, Sweden: Socialstyrelsen.

SOU. (2007). *Hållbar samhällsorganisation med utvecklingskraft.* Stockholm, Sweden: Ansvarskommittén.

SSR. (2016). *Socionom: Var och hur arbetar socionomer?* Retrieved September 21, 2016, from http://www.saco.se/studieval--karriar/studieval/yrken-a-o/socionom

Svärd, V. (2014). Hospital social workers' assessment process for children at risk: Positions in and contributions to inter-professional teams. *European Journal of Social Work, 17*(4), 508–522.

Svärd, V. (2016). *Children at risk? Hospital social workers' and their colleagues' assessment and reporting experiences.* Doctoral dissertation, Department of Social Work, University of Gothenburg, Gothenburg, Sweden.

VGR. (2012). *Regional medicinsk Riktlinje: Ansvarsfördelning och konsultationer mellan primärvård och specialistpsykiatri.* Retrieved September 22, 2016, from http://www.samverkanstorget.se/upload/Samverkanstorget%202014/Strydokument/Psykiatri/Ansvarsfördelning%20och%20konsultationer%20mellan%20primärvård%20och%20specialpsykiatri.pdf

14

Health Care Social Work in Turkey

An Evolving Field of Practice

Tarik Tuncay

Introduction

Social work in health care has been established for more than a century and is one of the largest areas of practice for social workers. Over time, demographic changes, growth in the aging population, increased longevity rates, an explosion in chronic illnesses, and the rapidly increasing cost of health care have created serious challenges for acute hospitals and medical social workers.

In this chapter, the practice and education of health care social work in Turkey are examined within the context of hospital practices, including in-patient and outpatient services and treatment. The development and historical background of the social work profession and medical social work are also examined. In Turkey, health care social work is one of the most effective professional fields in which social work is practiced. It has evolved slowly, based on a biopsychosocial model of service that incorporates interdisciplinary professional teams. Within the cultural context of the country, social work education is developing, as is the role of the social worker in the hospital system. This chapter reviews current hospital social work roles, including the continued role in discharge planning and psychosocial support services. The chapter concludes with a discussion of developing issues and challenges that the health care social work profession must face to ensure that social work remains relevant within this practice context.

Overview of Turkish Social Welfare Services and Social Work

Social welfare services in Turkey have a deep-rooted history, dating back to the early times of the Ottoman Empire. A large number of organizations were engaged in the field of social welfare due to the increasing economic and political power of the Ottoman Empire, which lasted seven centuries until the beginning of the 20th century. In this context, organizations called *vakif* (foundation) were founded by charitable people as foundations focusing on social solidarity and financial aid. *Futuvvet* (also known as *lonca*) were established by the tradesmen and merchants to provide vocational aid and those tasks similar to social security today. Other social welfare organizations that were created then and still exist today include the Himaye'i Etfal Cemiyeti (Child Protection Institution) and Hilal'i Ahmer Cemiyeti (The Red Crescent) (Çavusoglu, 2001). Thus, these organizations performed most of the social welfare functions in the primarily Islamic country, which is also multireligious and multiethnic and secular (Kut, 1983). They served the poor, women, and children, culminating in the present-day social welfare practice that also supports traditions of the Turkish society of Anatolia and Thrace. After the foundation of the Republic of Turkey in 1923, providing social welfare services through the organizations of the state gained renewed importance.

The emergence of organized social services and the social work profession in Turkey can be described as a slow but steady developmental process over several decades. This process is closely related to social changes such as rapid urbanization and industrialization followed by increased demands for scientific and professional standards for all, especially health and welfare services, in the early 1960s. Professional social work education is historically associated with all the developments mentioned previously (Tuncay & Tufan, 2011).

The Early Seeds

Social work has existed in Turkey as an institutional and organized profession for more than 50 years. In the late 1950s, university-level social work education became a major concern of the Turkish state. However, contributing most to the structuring of social work education and to the contemporary design of social welfare services in Turkey were primarily external factors, rather than internal, societal demands. The United Nations (UN) was an active agent in the process of the establishment of a social work school and the development of statewide services, as it was in other developing countries. After the UN's Social Commission of the Economic and

Social Council stressed the need for fostering social welfare staff in its 1947 assembly, a survey about the social service education programs of member countries was prepared and reported in 1949. These UN agencies approved a resolution in 1951 that acknowledged social work as a profession with specific functions and educational requirements (Kosar & Tufan, 1999). The international assemblies concerning social work training that have met since then, the second held in 1954 and the third in 1959, demonstrated the extent to which the institutionalization and professionalization of social work in various countries had been influenced by practices in the United States, the leading country in the UN (Ozdemir, 2001).

According to Göbelez (2003), Turkey played a role in the worldwide phenomena of the diffusion of social work to the Third World through the efforts of Western social advisers provided by the UN. The spread of social work internationally, instigated by Western social work experts, corresponded to the ideals of modernization. The models that these experts utilized to promote modern social work were often based on approaches developed in their own countries, primarily the United States. Turkey received support from a number of US experts commissioned by the UN to develop a national welfare system and to provide solutions for rising social problems. Consultants were assigned to research in the field potential social work areas such as general social welfare, social development, social work education, family welfare, and rehabilitation services. Thus, the emergence and structuring of professional social work education were based on American experience. This is important not only because the institutionalization of social work education in Turkey was influenced by that experience but also because it is emblematic of the processes in other areas of the world, mainly in developed countries.

Establishment of the Social Work Profession

The first significant and policy-based step in the development of the social work profession in Turkey was the enactment of the law for the establishment of the Social Services Institute (Public Law No. 7355). The law was put into practice in 1959 and legally provided a foundation of social work schools in Turkey (Kosar & Tufan, 1999). According to the ninth article of the law, "In order the train social workers and social assistants, the Social Services Academy would carry out theoretical and practical social work teaching at the university or high school level, either directly or via the university."

The law asserted that the curriculum for obtaining a bachelor's degree would be designed in coordination with the Ministries of Health and Social Assistance and Education. Moreover, with the law, the Social Services Institute became responsible for providing coordination between all social welfare, public (statewide and municipal), nongovernmental, and private (voluntary/nonprofit and profit-making) institutions. The second significant step in terms of social work both as a profession and as a scientific discipline was the establishment of the Social Services Academy in 1961, mentioned previously. The academy was founded as part of the Ministry of Health and Social Assistance. It served as a research and higher education institution that taught 4 years of undergraduate education after high school (Kut, 1983).

A Brief History of Medical Social Work in the Turkish Health Care System

The history of health care social work in Turkey runs in parallel with the history of the social work profession. As mentioned previously, the Social Services Academy, the first school of social work in Turkey, was affiliated with the Ministry of Health and Social Assistance. This particular ministry was selected due to its organizational structure, which at the time comprised mainly health, social assistance, and care services. After the foundation of the academy, the UN continued its financial and counseling support. Furthermore, in order to train Turkish faculty members, some people were sent abroad with the support of the UN, the Central Treaty Organization (now defunct), and the Fulbright Commission. Göbelez (2003) indicates that the development of social work was part of a global phenomenon of professionalization of social work. Although the diverse and intensifying needs in Turkey gave impetus to the formation of local demands, the initiation of social work and its continuation would not have been possible without its international component. In addition to financial and educational backing, identification with an international community of social work granted a kind of authenticity and credibility for the emerging profession in the view of the Turkish public.

With the beginning of professional social work education in Turkey in the early 1960s, social problems, public health issues, and, accordingly, social policies diversified. The main components of social change between 1950 and 1980 in Turkey—that is, rapid industrialization, urbanization, and migration—also created social issues such as the disintegration of the traditional family, a rise in crime rates, an increase in the urban–rural population imbalance, and inequality of income. Thus, the Second National Services Conference, held in 1962, opened by asking, "As a country in a changing world, its' ties disconnected with the old [Ottoman Empire], but not exactly in accord with the new world order, how do we handle the country's social problems?" In his opening speech, the Minister of Health and Social Assistance further remarked that "the problems that were invisible like underground waters in the past, surfaced to the ground today. A river is flowing, but we do not know who it will drag along" (cited in Göbelez, 2003). The need to face and cope with the challenge of diverse social problems and health issues was anticipated with the construction of a society that could be planned and controlled. The increased importance of statistics and the establishment of programs and institutions such as population studies, public health institutions, and social services were some of the outcomes of the effort to make society cognizant of more scientific and detailed information and to intervene in its state of affairs at large. As a new process of dealing with social issues, institutionalized and professionalized social work has thus aimed at the social integration of the poor and dependent sections of society by rendering a more harmonious and healthy life with their environment.

By the 1960s, when social work education was introduced in Turkey, substantial progress had already been made in most other developed countries, especially the United States and European countries. For instance, France and the United States had established 41 and 150 social work schools, respectively (Payzin, 1961). Turkey had to go through some important phases to achieve the same level of progress as in other countries. The following view was taken during the first years of social work education: Training of social workers should focus on two bases, namely "theory" and "practice" (which includes hospitals and other health care institutions), and social work should be viewed as both a scientific discipline and a profession. It was also recognized that social work had both the characteristics of science and the quality of the arts (Tuncay & Tufan, 2011).

There was only one school of social work (in Hacettepe University) until 2002. New social work programs in the country were rapidly established between 2002 and 2016. The rapid development of social work schools is strongly related with the general characteristics of the Turkish higher education system. This system has been built on a structural platform that is called the Higher Education Council (YOK in Turkish). YOK has been set up to play a substantive political and technical role in determining operational policies and programs of the country's higher education in accordance with the planned national educational goals and objectives. YOK was responsible for the growth of the social work profession.

Currently, more than 70 departments of social work throughout the country award bachelor's degrees and/or MSWs with medical and psychiatric social work concentration in social work education (and a few award PhDs). They are all affiliated with the various states, foundations, and private universities.

Essential Steps

Medical social work practices began in 1964 at Hacettepe University Hospital. The first graduates of the Social Services Academy became members of a treatment team that would become an integral part in the delivery of health services. The primary roles of the first social work practitioners in hospital settings included providing direct clinical practice through psychosocial work with individual patients on a one-to-one basis (or with families and small groups), discharge planning, facilitating services, and post-hospitalization follow-up. Secondary roles included community work efforts such as program development, fundraising, and budgeting. Tertiary roles included training and teaching, research, and health education.

The person-in-environment focus guided the social work role toward assessment of patients' social situation and interrelationships with others and assisting patients with issues related to chronic disease and disability, drug and alcohol abuse, terminal conditions, and mental health issues. Social workers also took on the roles of educating patients, assisting patients in navigating the health care setting, and providing the link between the hospital and community sectors.

Not surprisingly, the main roles and responsibilities of medical social workers are similar in Europe, Latin America, Canada, and Australia, as well as in various countries of Asia and the Middle East. In the first years of practice, Turkish social workers mainly undertook quite similar tasks and dealt mostly with the problems of the individual and his or her family, like their American counterparts. Because of this functional affinity and also because of a common desire to strengthen the scientific content of social work, educational institutions in Turkey that provide medical social work training have been receptive to theories and ideas formulated and advanced via the United States, such as the biopsychosocial model and human behavior in the social environment perspective.

Administrative and Legal Context

Although social work in Turkey is a developing profession, practicing social work is largely regulated by the Ministry of Health, and the roles of social workers in hospitals and other health care settings are defined. Medical social workers can be employed by both public and private sectors. There is a strong need for social workers in Turkish medical institutions in both of these sectors. The Turkish Ministry of Health is the second largest employer of social workers within the country after the Ministry of Family and Social Policies, providing services in state hospitals throughout the country. These hospitals range from general practice to specialized fields such as oncology and mental health. Social work in the hospital system is one of the most active social work fields practiced in Turkey today. To ensure effective social services, the Departments of Medical Social Work (Tibbi Sosyal Hizmet Birimi) was established within the Ministry of Health, local health directorates, and general hospitals. This department is responsible for supervising practitioners and providing them with infrastructural support.

Currently, the role of the social worker in Turkish health care is related to the fact that many professional practices in the country, including allied health and social work, have been largely adopted from Western countries, especially the United States and other English-speaking countries. The findings from studies in these countries can be used to understand the overall function of medical social workers and to demonstrate the workplace factors that may influence practitioners' ability to effectively execute their duties. Similar to the United States (Gibelman, 2004), the completion of an undergraduate-level degree in social work is the minimum qualification for entry into the occupation of medical social work in Turkey. However, the entry-level requirement in the United States is generally now an MSW (although exceptions to this remain). This reflects the increasing demand for a graduate degree to work in a health care setting.

The Turkish Health Care System

The Turkish state places high expectations on the health care system to provide efficient public health services and immediate access to improved medical treatments and new technologies. Health care in Turkey consists of a mix of public and private health services. Turkey has universal health care under its General Health Insurance (Genel Sağlık Sigortası) system. Under this system, all residents registered with the Social Security Institution (SSI) can receive medical treatment free of charge in hospitals contracted with the SSI. There is also a large private health care sector, which often offers shorter waiting lists and higher quality services.

The Turkish health care system used to be dominated by a centralized state system run by the Ministry of Health. In 2003, the governing Justice and Development Party introduced a sweeping health reform program aimed at increasing the ratio of private to state health provisions and making health care available to a larger share of the population. Today, the costs of health care services for more than 95% of the general population are covered under the umbrella of SSI in the form of insurance payments. The rest of the population is supported with direct payments by social services. As a result of major health care reforms in the early 21st century, universal health insurance coverage for the population has been achieved, and the general quality of health services has improved greatly, with patient satisfaction increasing from 39.5% in 2003 to 75.9% in 2011 (Atun, 2015).

Professional Roles in Hospital Settings

Social work has a long history in hospital settings, including inpatient and outpatient services, and continues to play a pivotal role in addressing psychosocial issues resulting from illness, disability, and hospitalization. Within the cultural context of Turkey, social work education is developing and so too is the role of the practitioner in the hospital system. Turkish social workers are an integral part of the health care system, and they are expected to perform multiple functions in the delivery of health services. These various functions involve patients and other professionals in the hospital and the wider community. In Turkey, the minimum requirement for entering employment as a hospital social worker is a bachelor's degree in a social work discipline. Currently, the vast majority of Turkish medical social workers hold bachelor's degrees in social work, and many of them graduated from Hacettepe University School of Social Work because it was the only higher education institution for social work education between 1961 and 2002. The limited number of postgraduate programs in the country could also explain the limited number of professionals with a higher degree (master's level) qualification.

Medical social workers perform specific roles and responsibilities relating to the nature of Turkish culture. Social workers in hospitals may assume the following responsibilities and functions:

- Planning services (e.g., discharge planning and post-hospitalization follow-up care)
- Information gathering and referral services
- Daily visits to internal wards and outpatient areas and joining physicians' rounds as needed
- Assessments of the psychosocial aspects of health and consultation with other care providers about psychosocial factors and their implications for health
- Counseling and therapeutic services
- Advocacy services
- Community organizing and capacity building (e.g., organizing support groups and liaising with the community for new social services)
- Research services (e.g., collaboration in studies and surveys related to patients' needs)
- Training in psychosocial aspects of illness and intervention strategies
- Preventive services (e.g., contributions to health education activities)
- Administrative duties (e.g., monitoring and reporting patients' or families' complaints about hospital services)

Medical social work departments also deal with domestic violence cases, in which "the battered wife seeking refuge, and physically abused children needing a place of safety can be found" (Stevenson & Unwin, 1990, p. 33). Social workers may play a major role in reassuring and comforting mistreated women (and, in some cases, men) and securing a safe home for them and their children. Abused and neglected children, whether they are abused by other family members or by strangers, are also supported by medical social workers. Turkish medical social workers typically serve as liaisons between medical staff and patients, providing specific mental health referrals or other community resources. This is a common function of medical social work in mainly general state hospitals.

In a cross-sectional research study, Özbesler and Icagasioglu-Coban (2010) investigated the working conditions of Turkish social workers employed at hospitals; the approaches, methods, and techniques they utilize within the scope of professional practice; their postgraduation training needs; and the type of tasks they undertake. Özbesler and Icagasioglu-Coban found that nearly half of social workers (48%) work at general medical social work units in hospitals instead of specialized inpatient clinics; 20.8% work in inpatient clinics such as oncology, hemodialysis, psychiatry, and emergency. Most of the social workers stated a need for postgraduation supervision and specialized training in the field of health care social work. They also found that medical social workers spent most of their time on discharge planning, including connecting and coordinating support services and arranging alternative long-term care for patients. Although there has not been any systematic research on the role and activities of health care social work in Turkey, it is clear that discharge planning has always been a key social work activity, based on a psychosocial assessment of the patient's situation and post-hospital support needs. The study concluded that the majority of clients mainly present problems pertaining to the coverage of hospital costs, lack of instrumental and emotional social support resources, and psychological difficulties faced after diagnosis. The problem-solving approach (76.6%), the psychosocial approach (72.2%), and the empowerment approach (49.4%) were most utilized in professional practice.

In summary, most Turkish medical social workers make visits to wards and outpatient areas and also accompany physicians on their rounds. They conduct assessments in relation to psychosocial aspects of health. The delivery of psychosocial counseling and therapeutic services is regarded as one of the main duties of Turkish practitioners. Medical social workers are also frequently involved with administrative activities in hospitals. They are sometimes asked to perform additional administrative duties that have no relation to social work or are part of the responsibilities of other departments in the hospital. Turkish social workers also frequently undertake information-gathering and referral activities.

Patient Rights

In Turkey, the role played by medical social workers as a patient's advocate is also an important part of medical social work practice. Today, the majority of Turkish social workers who work in state hospitals play the role of "mediator" between medical staff and patients. They are employed not only in medical social work departments but also in "patient communication units" The main purpose of these units is to protect and develop patients' rights by reaffirming fundamental human rights in health care, especially those protecting the dignity and integrity of the patient as a person.

Being a patient can be a disempowering experience that causes fear, anxiety, and suspicion; threatens safety; and renders a person dependent on others. The individual is moved from a familiar social and physical environment to hospitalization and has to obey the rules of health care providers. Social and political developments throughout the world have given rise to a movement toward the reevaluation of patients' rights, with new and more positive concepts of patients' rights being advocated. In Turkey, there is currently a need to recognize this trend, which emphasizes an individual's right to self-determination (Kisa & Tengilimoglu, 2002). Research shows that decisions concerning patients are made by physicians instead of being shared decisions made with patients, who desire to be well as soon as possible. Most patients are not knowledgeable about their disease or the diagnosis and treatment implemented, and due to shyness and fear, the majority of patients do not ask doctors about their health(Tengilimoglu, Kisa, & Dziegielewski, 2000). These findings reflect the need for medical social workers to both advocate for patients and serve as liaisons between medical staff and patients in the hospital system.

Cultural Issues

It is vital to consider some aspects related to religion and culture in Turkey that can further inform social work practice. As an occupation and professional form of charity, social work inspires practitioners to possess a strong dedication to their work, and it promotes high satisfaction from serving the needs of individuals and the society of which they are a part. Religious and cultural issues are important because performing social work in the Turkish context relates to the importance of supporting others, which is a central theme in the Islamic culture. Social work is generally perceived as a spiritually rewarding profession because helping those in need is appreciated by God, irrespective of the amount and the quality of help. This attitude is prevalent in Islamic culture, and it is identified in other cultures as well (Balloch, Pahl, & McLean, 1998). One further issue is that most Turkish people, including social workers, still adhere to traditional cultural practices, particularly in relation to social support, relationships, and unity. This distinguishes them from their counterparts in more developed countries, where modern culture may place a greater emphasis on independence than on collective dimensions of support. Social support issues indicate that Western practitioners deal with more individualistic client problems compared to their counterparts in Turkey.

Another cultural issue is related with the attitudes of clients toward professional help. Due to the lack of public awareness about the focus of medical social work, social workers may encounter a number of problematic issues in cultivating a professional relationship with their clients and also in providing assistance. For instance, obtaining client cooperation and involvement in problem-solving procedures, especially when dealing with behavioral and/or family-related problems, can be a difficult task for the practitioner because many Turkish families regard it as shameful and stigmatizing to engage outsiders in their family's matters and tribulations due to social norms related to a family's social reputation. However, family cooperation during the planned change process is vital for achieving desired practice outcomes.

Looking Forward

Medical social work has been slowly but continuously developing within the Turkish health care system for a half century, and its practice forms part of patient care. Efforts to reposition social work within the organizational environment of the Turkish health system depend on the ability of social workers to describe, measure, and articulate its unique contribution to patient care. Social work research in health settings is limited, and further information about patient demographics, services provided, and the effectiveness of those services is needed. Future social work research in Turkey needs to focus on the health care field of the profession. Research findings have the potential to contribute to the profession's knowledge base in health care. The shift in the focus on care from acute to ambulatory care and the increased emphasis on primary and preventive care could lead to a major role for hospital social workers if they can demonstrate that their interventions are effective.

Turkish medical social workers' primary job responsibilities are working directly with patients and families while they are in the hospital and performing administrative work. Social work departments in hospitals must develop clearer job descriptions that reflect an inventory of new tasks that staff will be expected to perform and the new knowledge and skills they will require. Departments must also devise screening instruments for high-risk patients that include improved assessment, treatment, and outcome measures. In addition, they must create new treatment protocols and outcome measures that link psychosocial and medical approaches to patient care.

Social workers are vital in the delivery of effective health care not only because they are trained to empower patients and their families to deal with psychosocial and economic issues related to the illness process but also because they have the capacity to support health care professionals in successfully dealing with issues concerning patients and the social environment. They also have the necessary skills to assist hospitals in the provision of effective health care services at minimal cost. The potential of social workers, however, may be minimized and their attitudes toward their employing organizations can be negatively affected if they perceive they are receiving insufficient support for effective practice or if they experience personal pressures in the workplace. Social workers, like all professionals, need to feel valued and appreciated in their place of work.

Emerging Trends and Potential Future Issues

After more than a half century of development and response to system changes, the major functions of medical social work in Turkey today have evolved to include crisis intervention and bereavement, psychosocial assessment and intervention, brief counseling and group work, documentation and record-keeping, discharge planning and case management, post-discharge follow-up and outreach, emergency services, and interprofessional collaboration and patient advocacy services.

Turkish social workers in the hospital settings need to recognize the importance of an evidence-based practice strategy and how this can lead to the documentation that supports program effectiveness (Dziegielewski, 2013). From this perspective, social workers must continually update their knowledge base by clearly outlining the goals and objectives to be accomplished that show the greatest benefit for clients. The adoption of this evidence-based practice linked directly to individual and program success creates the need for lifelong learning. In turn, an evidence-based practice strategy can indirectly benefit the client's immediate needs as well as have a tangible positive effect on organizational maintenance and building the profession (Gossett & Weinman, 2007).

More in-service training opportunities, especially in relation to communication and practical skills, should be offered to Turkish social workers. This can promote the development of effective partnerships between practitioners and other members of health care teams in the workplace, especially hospital management, and effectively strengthen their roles in hospital settings.

References

Atun, R. (2015). Transforming Turkey's health system: Lessons for universal coverage. *New England Journal of Medicine, 373*(14), 1285–1289.

Balloch, S., Pahl, J., & McLean, J. (1998). Working in the social services: Job satisfaction, stress and violence. *British Journal of Social Work, 28*(3), 329–350.

Çavusoglu, T. (2001). *Türkiye Çocuk Esirgeme Kurumu: Himaye-i Etfal Cemiyeti 30 Haziran 1921–5 Mayis 1981* [*Turkish Child Protection Agency: Himaye-i Etfal Society 30 June 1921–5 May 1981*]. Istanbul, Turkey: Turkish Association of Social Workers.

Dziegielewski, S. F. (2013). *The changing face of health care practice: Opportunities and challenges for professional practice*. New York, NY: Springer.

Gibelman, M. (2004). *What social workers do*. Washington, DC: NASW Press.

Göbelez, S. (2003). *The history of social services in Turkey: Social change, professionalism and politics*. Unpublished manuscript, Bogaziçi University, Istanbul, Turkey.

Gossett, M., & Weinman, M. (2007). Evidence-based practice and social work: An illustration of the steps involved. *Health and Social Work, 32*(2), 147–150.

Kisa, A., & Tengilimoglu, D. (2002). Patients' rights in Turkey. *Clinical Research & Regulatory Affairs, 19*(1), 55–62.

Kosar, N., & Tufan, B. (1999). Sosyal hizmetler yüksekokulu tarihçesine genel bir bakis [A general look at the brief history of the school of social work]. In N. Kosar & V. Duyan (Eds.), *Prof. Dr. Sema Kut'a armagan: Yasam boyu sosyal hizmet* (pp. 1–20). Ankara, Turkey: Hacettepe Universitesi Sosyal Hizmetler Yuksekokulu.

Kut, S. (1983). Sosyal hizmet egitiminde 22 Yil [22 years in social work education]. *Hacettepe Üniversitesi Sosyal Hizmetler Yüksekokulu Dergisi, 1*(1), 1–13.

Özbesler, C., & Icagasioglu-Coban, A. (2010). Social work practice in the hospital setting: The case of Ankara. *Society and Social Work, 21*(2), 31–46.

Ozdemir, U. (2001). Sosyal hizmet egitimi [Social work education]. In K. Karatas (Ed.), *Sosyal hizmet sempozyumu: Toplumsal gelisme ve degisme sürecinde sosyal hizmet (16–18 Ekim 1996)* (pp. 85–97). Ankara, Turkey: Hacettepe Üniversitesi Sosyal Hizmetler Yüksekokulu.

Payzin, S. (1961). Sosyal hizmetler yüksekokulu amaclari [The goals of the school of social work]. *Sosyal Hizmet, 1*(2), 21–22.

Stevenson, S., & Unwin, J. (1990). The nature of medical social work. In M. Badawi & B. Biamonti (Eds.), *Social work practice in health care* (pp. 127–148). Cambridge, UK: Woodhead-Faulkner.

Tengilimoglu, D., Kisa, D., & Dziegielewski, S. F. (2000). What patients know about their rights in Turkey. *Journal of Health and Social Policy, 12*(1), 69.

Tuncay, T., & Tufan, B. (2011). Social work education and training in republican Turkey. In S. Stanley (Ed.), *Social work education in countries of the east: Issues and challenges* (pp. 543–562). New York, NY: Nova.

15

Health Care Social Work in Ukraine

Tetyana Semigina

Introduction

This chapter presents the limited experience of Ukraine in introducing social work in health care facilities and discusses its development. For purposes of this chapter, social work is the professional activity of specially trained persons based on social work theory and indigenous knowledge as well as the broader social sciences as defined by the global definition of social work (International Federation of Social Workers & International Association of Schools of Social Work, 2014).

The chapter is based on the author's observations and reflections from participation in a number of international projects, direct communications with social workers from health care facilities, data from the author's research conducted throughout the years, as well as a review of documents undertaken for preparation of this chapter.

The Development of Social Work in Ukraine

Social work is a relatively new profession and academic discipline in Ukraine. In April 1991, the State Register of Professions (the official list of employee positions) was completed. It included a few newly added professions—"social work specialist," "social pedagogue," and "social worker." They have become equivalents of a universally accepted term "social worker." In 1997, social work was approved as an educational specialty by presidential decree and by the Order of the Ministry of Education and Science of Ukraine. In 2004, social work was first included in the Ukrainian Occupations Classification; since then, it has been an officially accredited profession in Ukraine.

A precursor to social work existed in Ukraine prior to the profession's emergence. Ukraine, as well as other countries (e.g., Georgia, Latvia,

Lithuania, and Moldova), inherited from the Union of Soviet Socialist Republics (USSR) a network of social institutions in which no social workers were employed. These institutions operated on the ideological perspective of social pathology (Ramon, 2000) and the medical model of disability (Bridge, 2005). The current prevailing strategy to addressing social issues was also inherited by Ukraine. Historically, social issues were viewed as requiring responses informed by the concept of social control and focused on "helping relations" (i.e., interventions employed when a client is perceived to be a victim of social circumstance).

Despite innovative social services being developed early in this century, mainly by nongovernmental organizations (NGOs), the existing public social services system requires further organizational, legal, and personnel development. The current system is characterized by fragmented structures, predominantly residential arrangements with little continuity in providing services to specific groups of clients at the community level. Ukraine still needs to adopt deinstitutionalization as a goal and introduce community-based models of care (Semigina, Gryga, & Volgina, 2005). Such reforms have been declared but not yet introduced. The development of NGO activities offering social services and self-help groups (clubs and day centers for disabled children and their parents, people with mental health problems, drug users and their families, people living with HIV/AIDS, etc.) suggest models for possible future changes.

Social work, as a relatively new profession and academic discipline in Ukraine, has a marginal status (Semigina, Kabachenko, & Boyko, 2017), and many paraprofessionals or people with education other than in the field of social work, if any education at all, are working in social services. Those services—developed during implementation of international projects—do not usually require specialists with social work education. The important feature of social work as a profession in Ukraine is that a title of "social worker" may be granted to anyone working in social services; people without training may call themselves social workers. In addition, no registration or licensing system exists, nor do operational professional standards.

There is a gap in Ukraine between the social work practice and education, and the impact of the professional community with regard to setting standards or rules is limited. Therefore, although social work as a profession and as a discipline was introduced in the country, it does not possess the whole range of specific features of "a professional project" (as described by Weiss-Gal & Welbourne, 2008). It is characterized by contradictory tendencies of preserving old paternalistic welfare traditions, strengthening of neoliberal societal conditions, and employing a postmodernistic multi-faceted paradigm of "new" social work practice (Semigina & Boyko, 2014).

History of Health Care Social Work in Ukraine

It is worth starting this historical review of social work in health care settings in Ukraine from the Soviet times because its legacy is still shaping the model of service provision.

The only social services that operated in the USSR were large (having the capacity to serve 200–300 patients simultaneously) public nursing homes (residential homes for the lonely elderly and disabled persons), children's homes, and boarding schools for orphans and disabled children. Medical-labor centers were engaged in mandatory medical treatment of people with addictions to alcohol. Psychiatric and neuropsychiatric hospitals were serving people with mental health problems. Militia offices supervised teenagers who had criminal records. All these units were predominantly focused on offering medical services and had no staff trained as social workers. Instead of being based on academic research, the social care system was guided by governmental decrees and resolutions adopted by the Communist party that stipulated the spectrum of persons in need of support as well as the ways of caregiving (Semigina et al., 2005).

With the exception of mandatory medical treatment for people suffering from addictions, all services established in Soviet times are still operating. The health care settings (hospitals, including psychiatric hospitals, AIDS centers, etc.) are subordinate to the Ministry of Health, whereas social services (including residential homes for the lonely elderly and disabled persons; day care centers; centers for children, family, and youth, rehabilitation centers for disabled people; and boarding schools for children with severe disabilities) are under the supervision of the Ministry of Social Policy. Medical and social services rarely overlap; they have very strong vertical ties, not the horizontal ties on the level of communities (with some minor exceptions).

Distinctions between "medical" and "social" were blurred in Soviet times, and this tendency has continued during the post-Soviet period. A vivid example of this is the so-called home of infants. These homes existed in

Soviet times and continue to operate in the Ukrainian health care system to help abandoned newborn children. Children who are left at maternity hospitals by their mothers are accommodated at homes of infants for up to 3 years. With the aim of playing a social role in raising young children, these institutions in fact were and still are staffed only with medical doctors, nurses, and auxiliary personnel, thus providing at most only physical care. Other cases of this blurred distinction are so-called neuropsychiatric pansionats or geriatric pansionats—large boarding homes in which people with mental health problems or lonely elderly people with severe health problem reside for years. These homes are part of the Ministry of Social Policy (in Soviet times, the Ministry of Welfare Provision). Despite their names and subordination, these residential homes provide medical help and physical care, with no social work interventions.

Since the turn of the millennium, the situation in Ukraine has been gradually changing. Ukrainian NGOs with the support of international donors (the European Union, US Agency for International Development [USAID], UNISEF, etc.) started to provide social services and implement different interventions on the basis of health care facilities, especially in those targeted at marginalized populations—people living with HIV (PLWH), intravenous drug users, people with mental health problems, people who need palliative care, and so on.

Shifts in professional (not administrative) boundaries between medical and social services emerging in post-Soviet times have not yet resulted in the introduction of full-scale social work in health care settings (Semigina, 2015b). Only a few health care services officially have social workers on their staff. This is due to the Ministry of Health's Order No. 33 issued in 2000 and operational until 2016. The order regulated staffing of all types of health care facilities in Ukraine, from primary care to all tertiary medical services. The document had the following impact on social work in health care development: (1) It prescribed the introduction of the social worker position only in hospices, of which only a relatively small number exist in Ukraine; (2) it recommended that chief doctors of narcological clinics introduce social workers as auxiliary personnel in day centers for people with drug addiction; (3) it suggested that social workers as auxiliary personnel could work for some specialized settings, such as AIDS centers and mental hospitals, if a chief doctor found resources to finance these positions; and (4) no social workers were supposed to be introduced in other types of health care settings.

In 2003, the Law of Ukraine "On Social Services" was adopted. It provides classification of social services. According to this legislation, medical social work belongs to one of the social services. Nevertheless, the legislation states that such types of services that include health promotion and social support of people with health problems are provided through social care facilities, not in health care settings. Thus, this law is reinforcing the bureaucratic, formal departmental distinction between health and social care.

Political and Social Context of Health Care Social Work in Ukraine

Since 1991, Ukraine has undergone a transition from a centrally planned economy to a market-oriented one. In the 1990s, the country faced a system crisis: Numerous political, economic, social, and cultural problems suddenly became urgent. The breakup of the Soviet Union and the following collapse of the state economy triggered such social problems as unemployment, emigration, homelessness, and poverty. Major political and social changes were accompanied in Ukraine, as well as other post-socialist countries, by dramatic growth in juvenile delinquency, drug and alcohol misuse, mental health issues, an HIV/AIDS epidemics, and so on (Semigina et al., 2005).

In 25 years of independence for Ukraine, political, economic, and social circumstances have had a significant impact on social work, including social work in health care services. So far, the political context has been characterized by the dominance of rich elite groups. They intend to preserve their own power and are not interested in societal development. Meanwhile, public discourse is based on socialist political rhetoric—populist proclamations of helping the poor and the provision of social guarantees and social equality. It has resulted in the ambivalent combination of state paternalism (with the intention of the state to regulate all areas of society) and neoliberalization. The constitution adopted in 1997 proclaims Ukraine a welfare state; however, standards of living are very low, and the socialist-style system of privileges for elite groups has been preserved (Semigina & Gusak, 2015).

International norms and actors have had ambivalent and limited influence. Major international conventions, such as the Convention on the Rights of the Child and the United Nation's Convention on the Rights of

Persons with Disabilities, have been adopted in Ukraine, but they have not been implemented. International organizations provide huge financial support to the Ukrainian government, but they have minimal impact on political traditions in the country, in which there is deeply rooted corruption.

Two more features of the Ukrainian context are incoherence of political changes and social policy reforms. Since independence in 1991, Ukraine has been claiming that it is implementing health care system reforms. However, this system formally remains unchanged from Soviet times. Health care challenges include inequitable access, an underdeveloped primary care system, high nonprescription use among the prescribed medicines, and inefficient financing. Out-of-pocket expenditures are 42.8% of total health expenditures, which is one of the largest shares in Europe (Stepurko, Pavlova, Gryga, Murauskiene, & Groot, 2015; Lekhan, Rudiy, & Richardson, 2015). This practice contradicts the Ukraine's official "free-of-charge" health policy. The absence of health care reforms is quite convenient for medical doctors and health care managers who serve in this isomorphic system that is still (post)socialist but in reality is market-driven and nontransparent. Social workers are not considered desirable in this system because they might serve as "gatekeepers" between service providers and medical personal receiving "out of pocket" payments (Semigina, 2013).

A depopulated, aging society with a high level of migration, extreme social stratification and overall culture of intolerance, and socially accepted informal practices in many areas of life constitute the current social context of Ukraine. Currently, with a population of 45.5 million people, Ukraine is at the bottom of a threshold of middle-income jurisdictions. Noncommunicable diseases are a leading cause of death (70%), and the prevalence of HIV, hepatitis C virus, and tuberculosis is higher than in Western Europe (Lekhan et al., 2015).

For example, Ukraine has one of the highest rates of HIV infection in Europe. Ukraine declared combating the HIV/AIDS epidemic as one of its political priorities. The Law on the Prevention of the Spread of AIDS and Social Protection of Population was adopted by the Parliament of Ukraine in December 1991 and substantially revised in 2011. This legislation is quite progressive by international standards, and it defines how the rights of PLWH to health care, social welfare, and against discrimination can be protected. However, reality has not matched rhetoric because there is an evident gap between adopted HIV policy and its implementation. Although a system of specialized medical centers for diagnosis and treatment of HIV/

AIDS is operating in Ukraine, it focuses on limited medical services. The social services for PLWH are mainly provided by NGOs (branches of the All-Ukrainian Network of People Living with HIV/AIDS) and subsidized through different short-term international projects. The state proclaims a right of PLWH to social services, but municipal social organizations do not serve this category of clients (Semigina, 2015a).

The "hybrid war" in that started in 2014 in eastern Ukraine and the emergence of a new vulnerable group—internally displaced persons (in mid-2016, approximately 1.8 million such people were registered by the Ukrainian authorities)—as well as lack of public funds have further deteriorated the situation in Ukraine.

Thus, although major social problems in Ukraine demand the development of social work in health care, the societal and political context has been challenging its progress.

Social Work Practice in the Context of the Health Care Setting in Ukraine

In Ukraine, social work in health care institutions is more developed for combating HIV, narcology, oncology, mental health, and family planning. An overview of health care facilities and social work is presented in Table 15.1. These facilities may subordinate to different ministries or authorities, and they may or may not have officially introduced the position of social worker (depending mostly on the chief doctor or executive officer of each facility).

Defining the roles of social workers in Ukrainian health care facilities is not an easy task because the system is not transparent, and many formal or informal public–private partnerships have been established. Thus, it is more productive to analyze some vivid cases than to describe the whole fragmented network of facilities.

First, social work within Ukrainian AIDS centers is discussed. Ukraine inherited the systems at these centers from Soviet times. These centers were considerably broadened in post-Soviet times: Now such centers operate in all regional capital cities and in some cities with a high prevalence of HIV. AIDS centers are responsible for HIV testing and counseling (free of charge and voluntary for all population groups but mandatory for pregnant women

Table 15.1 Key Facilities Providing Different Types of Health Care

Type of Health Care Facility	Key Services	Social Work Within Facility				
		Positions of Social Workers Introduced	Official Cooperation with Workers from State Social Services	Official Cooperation with Social Workers from NGOs	Ad Hoc Activities of Social Workers from NGOs	No Social Work Interventions
Ministry of Health						
Policlinics, ambulatories	Primary health care					•
"Youth clinics"	Primary health care for young people (aged <35 years), family planning services		•			
Hospitals	Secondary inpatient health care					•
Maternity hospitals	Health care for pregnant women				•	
Specialized hospitals and centers	Tertiary health care					•
AIDS centers	Testing for HIV and provision of antiretroviral treatment	•		•		

(*continued*)

Table 15.1 Continued

Type of Health Care Facility	Key Services	Social Work Within Facility
Narcological clinics and dispensaries	Treatment of drug addictions	•
Tuberculosis dispensaries	Treatment of Tuberculosis	•
Sexually transmitted diseases clinics	Testing and treatment of sexually transmitted diseases	•
Homes for infants	Care after abandonment, children younger than age 3 years	•
Hospices	Health care of terminally ill persons, mainly oncological patients	•
Mental health hospitals and dispensaries	Health care for people with mental health problems	•
Ministry of Social Policy		
Neuropsychiatric pansionats	Residential home with health care for people with mental health problems	•

Geriatric pansionats	Residential home with health care for lonely elderly people				•
State Penitentiary Service					
Prison hospitals	Health care for people in prisons				•
Regional and Local Authorities					
Rehabilitation centers for disabled people	Day or residential care centers with programs for early interventions, health care services	•	•	•	
NGOs					
Rehabilitation centers for drug addicts	Treatment of drug addictions	•			

NGOs, nongovernmental organizations.

in most areas), registration of PLWH (voluntary for such people), providing antiretroviral treatment (ART) to PLWH, and other activities.

For a long period of time, no social work positions were introduced in these health care facilities. The drug procurement for them was initially supported by international organizations and only then was managed by the government. Because the issue of adherence to ART was rather acute among patients of such centers, the chief doctors allowed social workers from NGOs to provide psychosocial support to their patients. Later, in some regions, the AIDS centers signed formal agreements with NGOs, set up referral and counter-referral systems, and provided social workers from NGOs with space in the facilities to perform consultative work.

For some facilities, this model of public–private partnership worked well; for others, it did not work at all. Interviewed in 2012, chief doctors of the AIDS centers acknowledged the limitations of only providing medical services to PLWH and viewed the NGOs as helping them provide more comprehensive care to their patients. At the same time, in a few regions, NGO representatives described a deep divide between the public and private sectors (Bongiovanni, Sergeyev, & Semigina, 2013). The need for better integration of services within Ukrainian medical and health care was expressed by many international organizations (World Health Organization [WHO] et al., 2012).

International donors (mostly the Global Fund to Fight AIDS, Tuberculosis and Malaria) and their local recipients (including the All-Ukrainian Network of People Living with HIV/AIDS and the International HIV/AIDS Alliance in Ukraine) have pushed AIDS centers to introduce social worker positions within the facilities. However, the number of such workers is insufficient. For example, in the Poltava regional AIDS center, there are three social workers for nearly 4,000 registered HIV-positive patients.

It is defined that social workers within AIDS centers should provide counseling support and referrals to other services. The expectation was that a multidisciplinary team involving nurses, social workers, psychologists, doctors specializing in communicable diseases, and other medical specialists as required will provide HIV treatment and care. In reality, social work centers are often used by doctors and health care facilities for the processing of paperwork rather than to undertake social interventions with patients. Often, social workers at state-run health care facilities work for the governmental organization for part of the day and for the NGO-supported services for the remainder of the day. Alternatively, they work several days of the week for the state facility and the remaining days of the week for the NGO (salaries at NGOs are higher because of funding by international donors).

A disturbing issue is the increasing number of patients who are "dropping out" of the HIV/AIDS continuum of care. Thus, it is not surprising that international donors launched a set of new projects to support social work for PLWH. As a result, since early 2013, 27 NGO partners of the International HIV/AIDS Alliance in Ukraine in 11 regions of Ukraine have been involved in supporting the provision of ART for PLWH case management due to the apparent poor performance of other agencies to support treatment and care services for the targeted group (WHO, 2014).

In 2014, a 2-year USAID-funded project, Improving HIV/AIDS Services for Key Populations in Ukraine, was initiated in four regions—Dnipropetrovsk, Cherkasy, Chernihiv, and Poltava. Among its activities is integrated intervention. The first part of the intervention (called "Patient School") is aimed at supporting PLWH who have just started taking antiretroviral drugs or who experience severe problems with adherence to treatment. Social workers from NGOs in collaboration with medical doctors from AIDS centers enroll clients into the intervention. Then they arrange for six individual sessions to be held at the AIDS centers; sessions last 45–65 minutes, with intervals of 2 or 3 weeks between sessions. The sessions are structured and focus on topics such as HIV/AIDS, ART and adherence to it, disclosure of status to partners, other health issues and services, and health behavior and aftercare health. Between sessions and 6 months after they are completed, a social worker contacts clients, mainly via phone (RESPOND, 2015).

The second part of the intervention, "Studio of Opportunities," works with women living with HIV who have children younger than age 6 years and have completed Patient School. It is aimed at strengthening economic opportunities. Based on the approach of sustainable livelihoods, bringing attention to a women's potential in terms of skills, social networking, and access to physical and financial resources, this innovative intervention builds up—through training, case management, and direct advocacy—the dignity and self-esteem of its clients and runs contrary to Ukraine's deeply rooted self-stigmatization related to HIV status.

This intervention is grounded in the following conceptual frameworks that build on each other: (1) the sustainable livelihoods framework, which places people at the center of their livelihoods strategies and examines the various assets they use and have access to as well as the structures, processes, and contexts of vulnerability that affect the extent of their access to those assets; (2) the theory of self-efficacy and, based on it, "90 days motivating training" (with its weekly goal cards and scores, daily actions to develop skills and new behavioral patterns, committed partners, affirmations and mediations, etc.)—it emphasizes what people have and what they lack; and (3) the social ecological model, which helps strengthen and diversify people's resources by empowering them to influence and access the various aspects that make up their enabling environment (Semigina & Tymoshenko, 2016). All these concepts represent a departure from the Soviet-style paternalistic perspective and welfarism-based models still present in Ukrainian social work. They represent an opportunity for social workers in the Ukraine—a chance to facilitate a profession's evolution and positively impact clients' lives.

A very similar situation is found in the narcological facilities. In 2005, opiate substitution therapy (OST) was introduced in these facilities as a free-of-charge service to patients/clients through a public–private partnership and by the demands of international organizations. WHO (2014) notes that the drug treatment doctors were very reluctant to accept OST as a treatment option for opiate-dependent people, and social workers from NGOs advocated for this new service and then provided social and psychological support for patients/clients taking OST. All this was done in the context of a lack of state ownership of the OST program until very recently. Social worker positions have been introduced at narcological centers. In some cases, social workers at NGOs have transferred from their positions at the NGOs to positions with state-run facilities and have continued to do the same job of supervising patients on OST. Social support is aimed at helping the person receiving OST apply for the necessary government documentation, such as an identification card, in order to access a broad range of services, including ART; helping the individual restore family relations; helping the person stabilize mental and/or emotional conditions; and helping with the recovery and the formation of safe behavior of the individual through psychological intervention. Social support and assistance are also given to the OST patient/client with regard to accessing education, finding employment opportunities, and the development of resocialization and reintegration skills to help the individual become part of mainstream society again. No multidisciplinary teams operate within narcological facilities.

In some narcological facilities, social workers support drug-addicted teenagers. For example, in the city of Dnipro, the special unit for inpatient medical and social rehabilitation of young people operates within the regional narcological dispensary. The unit is staffed by two medical doctors specializing in drug treatment, a pediatric doctor, two psychologists, three social workers, and four educators. In addition to medical treatment and educational classes, role games and cognitive therapy methods are used, along with individual counseling.

The previously discussed cases provide evidence that social work in health care settings in Ukraine is gradually developing. However, it is a novelty and needs to be scaled up based on local examples and best practices along with the support of medical social work from other countries. The extensive support that is required of international projects to maintain social services within health care settings raises questions about the sustainability of these services.

Prospects for Development of Social Work in Health Care Facilities in Ukraine

Further development of social work in Ukraine will require overcoming a number of structural barriers. First, social worker positions should be introduced in all Ukrainian health care facilities, including those under the authority of the Ministry of Social Policy and local authorities. In addition, the existing public–private partnerships between health care facilities and NGOs as social service providers should be formally recognized through legal means. This might be done through the "social contract" approach based on subsidies from local budgets to the nongovernmental social service providers.

Second, the functions and responsibilities of social workers within Ukrainian health care facilities must be clearly defined according to the type of facility to avoid improper utilization of social workers for primarily administrative tasks. Such responsibilities may include the following: for inpatient care—counseling and work with emotional components (anxiety, confusion and memory problems, stigma, and self-devaluation), financial and legal assistance, assessment of patient needs, discharge preparation, and ensuring that the services a patient will require are in place before the patient is discharged; and for outpatient care—work with the patient's family and other service provider agencies to develop a plan for care of the patient in his or her home or other living arrangement.

Third, multidisciplinary approaches and multidisciplinary (multiprofessional) teams must be formally introduced in Ukrainian health care settings so that social workers may not only assess a patient's social, emotional, environmental, financial, and support needs but also inform other members of the health care team about these factors, which may affect the patient's health and well-being. Medical doctors should be trained to work within the multidisciplinary teams and understand the roles of social workers and cooperate with them.

Fourth, the curricula of social work education must be revised and include more courses to prepare students for medical social work. Currently, the standard programs for bachelor's and master's degree students offer a limited variety of courses to equip future specialists for work within health care settings. The development of NGOs serving people living with HIV stimulated the preparation of courses on social work in HIV services, but many other health care areas have been neglected. The introduction in select universities of this new educational concentration on medical social work might be a prospective and fruitful step for further professionalization.

Of course, all these new approaches can be implemented only within the broader transformations of the post-socialist health and social care system that is still based on ideas of welfarism and social pathology. Such broader transformations have to take into account the experience of other post-socialist countries in which social health insurance, decentralization, and a certain level of dehospitalization and community health programs have been introduced (Saltman, Bankauskaite, & Vrangbæk, 2007).

Conclusion

Professional social work emerged in Ukraine with the collapse of the Soviet regime and the proclamation of Ukraine's independence. At that time, the network of health care and so-called social services already existed. During 25 years of independence, there has been a slow and incoherent development of new social work interventions, contrasting with the continued preservation of the old-fashioned welfaristic model of thinking and provision of social resources and services to entitled groups while the needs of other populations are disregarded. Health and social care reforms have not been effectively implemented in Ukraine. As a result, both formal and informal public–private partnerships have emerged to fill the void.

The main driver for change and development of elements of social work within the health care system has been cooperation with international organizations. As a result of this cooperation, social worker interventions have been introduced in AIDS centers, narcological facilities, palliative care, "youth clinics," and other settings. However, a number of structural barriers must be overcome in order for continued change in Ukrainian health care and health care social work to occur.

References

Bongiovanni, A., Sergeyev, B., & Semigina, T. (2013). *End-of-project performance evaluation of the HIV/AIDS Service Capacity Project (USCP) in Ukraine: Final report.* Bethesda, MD: Mendez England & Associates.

Bridge, G. (2005). Disabled children and their families in Ukraine: Health and mental health issues for families caring for their disabled child at home. *Social Work in Health Care, 39*(1–2), 89–105. doi:10.1300/J010v39n01_07

International Federation of Social Workers & International Association of Schools of Social Work. (2014). *Global definition of social work.* Retrieved from http://www.ifsw.org

Lekhan, V., Rudiy, V., & Richardson, E. (2015). Ukraine: Health system review. *Health Systems in Transition, 12*(8), 1–183. Copenhagen, Denmark: World Health Organization.

Ramon, S. (2000). *Creating social work and social policy education in Kiev, Ukraine: An experiment in social innovation.* Cambridge, UK: Anglia Polytechnic University.

RESPOND. (2015). *Patient school: Intervention for PLWH on ART adherence and receiving medical services: Draft implementation manual.*

Saltman, R. B., Bankauskaite, V., & Vrangbæk, K. (2007). *Decentralization in health care.* New York, NY: Open University Press.

Semigina, T. (2013). *Politychny aspecty ohorohy zdorovya: Na peretyni globalnogo I localnogo* [*Political issues of healthcare: On the crossroads of global and local*]. Kiev, Ukraine: Kyiv- Mohyla Academy.

Semigina, T. (2015a). HIV-activism in a post-socialist state: The case of Ukraine. *Kyiv- Mohyla Law and Politics Journal, 1,* 113–133.

Semigina, T. (2015b). Sotsialna robota u modeli paliatyvnoui dopomogy: Functsii ta vyckluky [Social work in the palliative care model: Functions and challenges]. *Reabilitatsya ta paliatyvna meditsyna*, 2(2), 54–58. doi:10.15574/IJRPM.2015.2.54

Semigina, T., & Boyko, O. (2014). Social work education in post-socialist and postmodern era: Case of Ukraine. In C. Noble, H. Strauss, & B. Littlechild (Eds.), *Global social work education: Crossing borders blurring boundaries* (pp. 257–269). Sydney, Australia: Sydney University Press.

Semigina, T., Gryga, I., & Volgina, O. (2005). Social work education in Ukraine. In F. Hamburger, S, Hirschler, G. Sander, & M. Wobcke (Eds.), *Ausbildungforsoziale Berufe in Europa. Band 3: Mit Beitragenuber Finnland, Russland, Belgien (Flandern), Frankreich, Luxemburg, Tschechien, Ukraine, Ungarn, Rumanien, Moldawien, Liechtenstein* (pp. 152–170). Frankfurt, Germany: Institut fur Sozialarbeit und Sozialpadagogik.

Semigina, T., & Gusak, N. (2015). Armed Conflict in Ukraine and Social Work Response to It. *Social, Health, and Communication Studies Journal*, 2(1), 1–24.

Semigina, T., Kabachenko, N., & Boyko, O. (2017). Piloting a social work doctoral programme: Ukraine's vignette. *European Social Work Journal*, 20(2), 265–276.

Semigina, T., & Tymoshenko, N. (2016). I feel alive! Developing an empowering intervention for HIV-positive women in Ukraine. *Social Dialogue, 14*, 28–31.

Stepurko, T., Pavlova, M., Gryga, I., Murauskiene, L., & Groot, W. (2015). Informal payments for healthcare services in Lithuania and Ukraine. In J. Morris & A. Polese (Eds.), *Informal economies in post-socialist space: Practices, institution and networks* (pp. 195–224). London, UK: Palgrave Macmillan.

Weiss-Gal, I., & Welbourne, P. (2008). The professionalization of social work: A cross-national exploration. *International Journal of Social Welfare, 17*, 281–290. doi:10.1111/j.1468-2397.2008.00574.x

World Health Organization. (2014). *Good practices in Europe: HIV prevention for people who inject drugs implemented by the International HIV/AIDS Alliance in Ukraine.* Copenhagen, Denmark: Author.

World Health Organization, International HIV/AIDS Alliance in Ukraine, US Agency for International Development, & Clinton Health Access Initiative. (2012). *Providing integrated services at health care facilities for people who use drugs in Ukraine: Guidelines.* Copenhagen, Denmark: Author.

Index